Dark Futures:

A VOYA Guide to Apocalyptic, Post-Apocalyptic, and Dystopian Books and Media

Brandy Danner

VOYA Press

an imprint of E L Kurdyla Publishing, LLC

Bowie, Maryland

ISBN 978-1-61751-005-2

Copyright © 2012 by Brandy Danner

Published by VOYA Press, an imprint of E L Kurdyla Publishing LLC

LCCN: 2012935475

The paper used in this publication meets the minimum requirements of the American National Standard for Information Sciences-Permanence of Paper for Printed Materials, ANSI Z39.48-1992.

Printed in the United States of America

Table of Contents

Introduction

When George Orwell published his landmark *1984* more than a half-century ago, could he have predicted the number of dystopian novels and films that would be published after it, or the appeal they would have for teens? When Aldous Huxley penned *Brave New World* in 1932, did he imagine the science of in-vitro fertilization that did not become mainstream for nearly fifty years?

The future has always captured our imaginations. Plato's *Republic* and even the biblical Garden of Eden are early examples of utopias; the Bible also includes the Book of Revelations, a story of the apocalypse if ever there was one. Stories of travelers discovering utopian worlds were particularly popular through the late 1500s, the stories being fantastic ways of showing how much better society could be if run according to philosophical, religious, or other ideals, but the lack of conflict made for somewhat flat, dull tales. Around 1600, Joseph Hall wrote *Mundus Alter et Idem*, a satire of both the popular utopian fiction of his day and his current society featuring a traveler who encounters strange lands populated with thieves, fools, and gluttons. His skewering of Catholic and philosophical traditions and the similarities in plot structure to the utopias published around the same time earn Hall's parody the distinction of being the first *dys*topia.

With the recent explosion in the genre, *dystopia* is being used as a catch-all term for any kind of future world, frequently being misapplied to apocalyptic and post-apocalyptic plots. There is definitely some cross-over potential, so the term isn't always a complete misnomer, but it is worth taking some time to evaluate the differences among them, especially when recommending materials to teens who have distinct preferences.

Besides being a reaction to utopias, what does the term *dystopia* mean, anyway? Officially, it's an anti-utopia, a world that is decidedly *not* perfect. It's more than just an imperfect future, though, and this is the element missing from many of the books being considered dystopian in the current publishing landscape. A utopia is a society built on perfection; a dystopia—an anti-utopia—is a world ostensibly built on perfection but deeply flawed. At least for the purposes of this book, a dystopia is a society that has attempted to eradicate all societal ills through strict rules or conditioning, or to improve upon everyday life though technological innovation, but has instead created new problems through its rigid control.

Apocalyptic and post-apocalyptic materials are exactly what they sound like: works that deal with the end of the world and its aftermath. Even here, there are subtle distinctions, though both tend to be rolled together under a post-apocalypse label. The difference between the two is mostly a matter of its temporal setting: apocalyptic stories take place as the world ends; post-apocalyptic stories feature people moving on in the changed world. The time periods can be fudged a bit in either direction; apocalypse tales frequently deal with not just the immediate time period of the event, but the lead-up to and aftermath of said event. Regardless, the focus of the story is on the event: the approach of a comet; a series of superstorms; a virus decimating a population (and sometimes changing the population into zombies). Post-apocalypses pick up after these stories, as people have dealt with the immediate dangers and built new lives and routines in the irreparably changed world.

Reading any news source reveals that, in a lot of ways, the world is already in chaos: global population is swelling; every year brings a new flu epidemic; warring countries are discovered to have stockpiles of catastrophic weapons. With these sorts of things in our reality, what is the appeal of reading these end-of-the-world scenarios? And why *now?* 2011 Printz Award winner Paolo Bacigalupi speculates that it is exactly *because* of these real-life fears that dystopian and post-apocalyptic works have caught on with teens: "I suppose that to the extent that it has something relevant to say, it always will have a place. [R]elevance doesn't get played out. If dystopian literature has something worthwhile to say, it will survive; if it's a shtick, it will die in favor of some new shtick."[1] Certainly enough trends in teen literature have come and gone, but dystopias (as previously discussed) have survived for hundreds of years; clearly the wonder about the future has remained relevant all that time, and now teens are becoming more aware of—and interested in—what the future may hold for them.

Andrew Clements agrees with the sentiment that the recent popularity of these bleak futures is due to their parallels in current events. "A study of world history shows that truly awful things have always happened. In our current media-saturated lives, however, every single awful thing that happens anywhere is pressed upon us in full-color, live-action images, both instantaneously and repetitively," he points out.[2] He adds that scary stories have always found popularity with readers of all ages, allowing us to keep perspective with regard to our own lives. Seeing brutal images of countries devastated by tsunamis is scary, but what if it happened to us? Apocalyptic literature and movies are a safe way of exploring those very ideas: how would we react? We see on television what happens to the population, but what happens to the *individual* in a crisis like that?

Current events could explain the teen appeal of apocalyptic and post-apocalyptic stories; after all, it's best to be prepared. But as yet, we have not seen much evidence of our world turning into a dystopia—though in most cases, the characters didn't see the dystopia coming, either. With the world falling apart and attempts to save it going horribly wrong, what is there to save us from the cloud of pessimism? Lisa Rowe Fraustino suggests that even the bleakest of dystopian worlds "makes us feel hope for humankind, even if . . . it turns out that the society is beyond repair. All the protagonist can do in that failed world is begin to understand and care about where we went wrong — which is exactly what the reader needs to do now to prevent a dystopian future."[3] In other words, part of the appeal of dystopia is the same as for apocalyptic scenarios: we read them in order to feel prepared to face these potential futures, to feel in control of an ever-changing—or *never*-changing—world. Teens may feel uncertain and powerless in their lives, but seeing a character not too different from themselves able to lead a revolution and change the world can be empowering, inspiring teens to contribute to the world in a way that might help avoid the very dystopia we may be headed toward.

The recent explosion in dystopian, apocalyptic, and post-apocalyptic publishing for teens is what drove this book. Its primary role is as a readers' advisory tool for librarians, a guide to both recent and backlist titles on the theme. Its content goes beyond a basic bibliographic catalog. A list of titles and brief plot synopses has its use and this book will provide that, but each entry will also provide a booktalk hook that can be delivered in approximately thirty seconds, notes on the item's recommended audience, readalike suggestions, and some discussion of the work's dystopian, apocalyptic, or post-apocalyptic characteristics.

Librarians, booksellers, and others who recommend books to teens will find the thirty-second booktalk particularly helpful. Shorter than the standard jacket copy, this seventy-five- to one hundred-word plug takes about the same amount of time to deliver as the average television commercial,

---

[1] Paolo Bacigalupi, Author Interview and Giveaway: "Paolo Bacigalupi Discusses" *Ship Breaker*
http://presentinglenore.blogspot.com/2010/08/author-interview-and-giveaway-paolo.html

[2] Andrew Clements, "What Poe's Publishers Could Not Imagine"
http://www.nytimes.com/roomfordebate/2010/12/26/the-dark-side-of-young-adult-fiction/what-poes-could-publishers-not-imagine

[3] Lisa Rowe Fraustino, "The Comfort of Darkness"
http://www.nytimes.com/roomfordebate/2010/12/26/the-dark-side-of-young-adult-fiction/the-comfort-of-darkness

with a similar goal of hooking potential readers or viewers. Who those potential consumers of the material are is identified in the sections on potential audience, which includes not just age or grade levels (ranging from upper-elementary age through college students and beyond) but also, as applicable, recommendations for male or female readers and consumers, avid or reluctant readers, and other characteristics. Suggestions for similar materials provide the rationale for recommending a particular title in relation to the one being discussed. Lastly, this book is different from more typical bibliographic guides in its discussion of thematic elements. In some cases, this section highlights the elements that mark a particular work as dystopian, apocalyptic, or post-apocalyptic; in other cases, it provides historical or scientific context for major plot points.

Primarily this is a reference guide for librarians looking to better serve their teens, but it can easily be used by anyone seeking a better idea of what this subgenre of science-fiction is about. Teens can use this guide to direct their own reading; to get recommendations based on their interests, curiosities, or previous reading (or viewing) discoveries; or to cultivate a deeper understanding of this popular category in teen collections. Parents and teachers are welcome to explore what their teens are reading, both to stay current and to gain a better understanding of the concerns teens may currently be facing.

The titles included are largely contemporary, but no collection of this type would be complete without some classics and overlooked gems. The majority of the titles are books, though movies and television shows are not without representation. Within the confines of science fiction, most of the titles are realistic, though it is difficult to discuss the current apocalyptic and post-apocalyptic movement without at least glancing at a few vampires or alien invasions.

The book is broken into four parts: dystopias, apocalypses, post-apocalypses, and non-fiction. The first section, dystopias, subdivides these future societies according to their dominant themes or concerns: population control, technology, games, and social issues. The second section is limited to apocalyptic works, with a nearly even division between books and visual media. The third section deals with the post-apocalyptic period, and is grouped according to the likely cause: wars, viruses, and natural disasters or environmental ruin. The final section explores speculative non-fiction, the titles that use either science or humor to consider ways the world could end—and what could happen afterward.

Our futures—individually and as a planet—are uncertain, despite them growing closer each day. Those futures may be smooth and trouble-free—but there is also every possibility that there are some dark futures ahead of us. Preparation may be our only hope.

Part 1: Dystopias

The optimist proclaims that we live in the best of all possible worlds; and the pessimist fears this is true. —James Branch Cabell, *The Silver Stallion*

As vampires and paranormal romances begin to cool on the teen shelves, dystopias are ramping up to take their places. This subgenre of science fiction has been steadily growing in teen collections, at least since Scott Westerfeld's *Uglies* was released in 2005, but the number—and volume, and breadth, and diversity—of titles has exploded since Suzanne Collins' 2008 offering, *The Hunger Games*. Dystopias have clearly captured teens' imaginations, as have dystopia's cousins, apocalypses and post-apocalypses. But what are these alternate worlds that have sucked in so many teens, and what makes them so popular?

At the most basic level, dystopias are simply utopias gone wrong: a seemingly-perfect society that hides dark secrets, or perfection on the surface that turns out to be considerably less perfect on closer examination. Usually these societies are repressive and tightly controlled, stripping citizens of choices and emotions in the name of making the ideal choices for the society, instead of the individual. These dystopian governments frequently rise out of bad situations: lack of food, water, or employment; too much individualism compromising the overall strength of society.

Overthrowing these totalitarian regimes will not necessarily lead to an immediate, rosy future, though. Writer and blogger Sommer Leigh points out that "you can't bring down the big bad government [...] and tomorrow everything will be good again.... At the end of the day, the characters still have this messed up world with no water, not enough food, and thugs, cannibals, zombies, and robots on every corner. [...] There's still the tedium of tomorrow to face."[1] *New Yorker* columnist Laura Miller disagrees with this bleak perspective, at least within the titles aimed at young readers.

---

[1] Sommer Leigh, "The State of the Genre in 5-4-3-2-1". *http://sommerleigh.com/archives/4034*

1

"[O]ur errors and delusions may lead to catastrophe, but if—as usually happens in dystopian novels for children—a new, better way of life can be assembled from the ruins, would the apocalypse really be such a bad thing?"[2] In either case, an overthrown government will provide a chance to get things right, thus setting the stage for another dystopia taking the place of the recently-overthrown one.

The ideas behind many recent dystopian fiction titles are rooted within current social issues, extrapolated to—and past—logical conclusions. This process could create perfect societies, but the lack of conflict in utopias does not make for interesting reading. "Utopian fiction looks at current social problems and imagines how they could be fixed," asserts author Robinson Wells in his blog post *The History of Dystopia*. "Dystopian fiction looks at current social problems (and social 'successes') and imagines how they could get horribly worse."[3] Philip Reeve makes a similar point in his article for *School Library Journal*, "The Worst Is Yet to Come": "It's as if optimism has become so hopelessly quaint that we can no longer allow ourselves even to imagine a better future."[4] Is this pessimism really what the world has become for teens, though, or do they read dystopias as cautionary tales, taking lessons from the novels and movies about how *not* to enact social change? If the stories truly are as bleak as Reeve believes, what is the draw for teens?

The teenage years are a period of great change and growing awareness about the world and its problems. Teens get news from social networking feeds, from friends and family, from television, from humor broadcasts like Comedy Central's *The Daily Show*; as a result, they are likely to be better informed about current events than teens of even a decade ago. Teens are at least passingly aware of the realities of life in other countries, places where everyday life more closely resembles the oppression in their dystopias than their own lives.

Teens are also becoming aware of their own choices as they grow into adulthood: they understand that they will soon be choosing career paths, romantic partners, and reproductive options, and the plethora of choices before them can be, at some level, terrifying. Seeing all those choices stripped away in the pages of a dystopian novel or movie can provide a certain wish-fulfillment: "If I lived in *this* society I wouldn't have to pick a major/decide who to date/feel disappointment," they may think—but they'll also get a glimpse of the perils of abdicating their choices. Eric Norton, writing for *School Library Journal*'s "Focus On" column in August 2011, confirms that dystopias "serve a bibliotherapeutic purpose, allowing teens to face their fears of the future, whether outlandish or all too possible."[5]

Despite all the negativity, teens are gravitating toward dystopias. Whether the main ideas in the story focus on surveillance, control, relationships, or anything else, many teens will find parallels to their own situations and lives. There are moments of levity in the dystopian landscape, though, particularly in the case of author Erin Bowman's "Is It Dystopia?" flowchart.

---

[2] Laura Miller, "Fresh Hell: What's behind the boom in dystopian fiction for young readers?"
http://www.newyorker.com/arts/critics/atlarge/2010/06/14/100614crat_atlargc_millcr

[3] Robinson Wells, *Dystopia Blog Series, Day Two: The History of Dystopia*
http://www.robisonwells.com/2011/05/dystopia-blog-series-day-two-the-history-of-dystopia/

[4] Philip Reeve, "The Worst Is Yet to Come: Dystopias are grim, humorless, and hopeless—and incredibly appealing to today's teens".
http://www.slj.com/slj/printissue/currentissue/891276-427/the_worst_is_yet_to.html.csp

[5] Eric Norton, "'Focus On' Dystopia: Turn on the Dark"
http://www.schoollibraryjournal.com/slj/home/891162-312/focus_on_dystopia_turn_on.html.csp

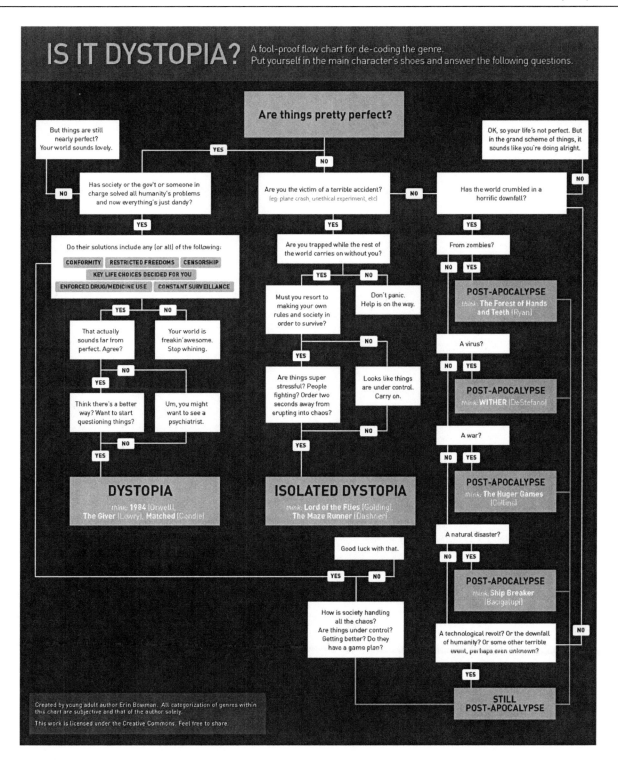

The dystopias featured in this book are broken down into categories: Population Control, which deals with reproductive rights, eugenics, and global overcrowding; Technology, featuring surveillance devices, androids, and cloning; Games, in which the population is controlled by a variety of sports that feed the governmental propaganda engines; and Social Issues, where we'll look at gender, relationships, employment opportunities, free choice, and more. Some titles fit into more than one category; others all but defy any attempts to categorize. Regardless of where they fit, there are more than fifty titles by nearly forty creators with appeal to a wide variety of teen readers.

Chapter 1

Population Control

The world is a crowded place. Current estimates put the earth's population near seven billion people; the United Nations projects that the earth could house approximately 10.1 billion by the year 2100.[1] That projection is based solely on birth and mortality rates; it does not adjust for potential crises—and attempting to feed 10.1 billion people with resources already being stretched for seven billion certainly qualifies as a crisis point.

So what can be done about this rapid population growth? Opinions vary, but the most obvious solution is to lower the birth rate. Many countries are already finding their growth rates slowing with access to voluntary birth control; China's one-child policy is estimated to have prevented 400 million births between 1979 and 2011[2]. While China in particular has had good results with their program, the costs of such results are indeed the stuff of dystopias: strict population control there has led to skewed ratios of male to female births, an increase in the percentage of elderly citizens, and an avoidance of medical care among pregnant women.[3]

China's one-child policy is something of a harbinger of dystopian ideas regarding population control. Margaret Peterson Haddix's *Shadow Children* series focuses on a society in which third children are so illegal that the children are taken from their homes and eliminated, lest they disrupt the carefully-balanced resource allocation. The penalties of being born illegally are less harsh in Gemma Malley's *The Declaration*, in which "surplus" children are forced into domestic work to atone for their sins of taking up valuable space on earth; the scrubs of Maria Snyder's *Inside Out* are raised similarly, many second children and taken from their aristocratic families at birth.

Slowing the birth rate is only one way of limiting the number of people on earth, and global overpopulation is only one reason to place limits on who can be born into the world. Neal Shusterman's *Unwind* uses a retroactive abortion, the result of a facetiously-proposed compromise between the pro-life and pro-choice camps, to make unwanted teens into organ donors in a network of Harvest Camps across the United States. *Epitaph Road* shows David Patneaude's idea of a highly-selective birth rate by means of a deadly virus that targets only men, clearing the way for women to gain political, military, and social power. Lastly, the 1997 movie *Gattaca* tests babies at birth for potential mental and physical flaws, though this step is largely unnecessary when so many babies are conceived with the assistance of geneticists who select only the strongest traits to pass on to the fetus.

One of the things that makes dystopias so chilling is their extrapolation from current events and familiar cultural ideals. In this section, we will explore six creators' ideas on how a population can be controlled, from its size to the more unique properties of its citizens. With even relatively minor changes to a population, the entire social system can be disrupted—only sometimes for the better.

---

[1] http://www.nytimes.com/2011/05/04/world/04population.html
[2] http://english.cntv.cn/20111028/108440.shtml
[3] http://www.nejm.org/doi/full/10.1056/NEJMhpr051833

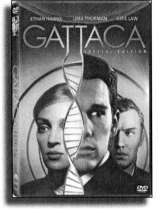

Gattaca

DVD. Color. 106m. Produced and dist. by Columbia/TriStar, 2008. $14.99. 978-1-4248-9847-3.

- Originally released 1997
- Written and directed by Andrew Niccol

Plot Summary:

Vincent was conceived in love by parents who believed in nature's ability to create a perfect child. At birth, Vincent's blood sample is quickly analyzed: he has a strong chance of developing mental disorders and attention-deficit disorder, of being nearsighted, of having a heart defect, of dying shortly after his thirtieth birthday. Faced with Vincent's limitations, his parents conceive a second child in what has become the "usual" way, using genetic modification to make their second child, Anton, the absolute best he could be.

As the boys grow up, Vincent is constantly reminded of Anton's genetic superiority, from their growth to athletic stamina. Vincent dreams of joining the space program at Gattaca, but people with genes like his—Invalids—are screened out of all but the most menial positions. Vincent is not dissuaded from his dream, though, and takes a custodial job in the prestigious building.

There is a way—only one way—for Vincent to bypass the screenings that keep him from achieving his dreams of space travel, and that is to become a "borrowed ladder"—to adopt the identity of a "Valid," a person with a more ideal genetic makeup. Through an unscrupulous broker, Vincent is connected with Jerome Morrow, a genetically-ideal man who was paralyzed in a car accident. Each day, Jerome provides blood, urine, and hair samples, along with exfoliated skin cells and other every-day DNA detritus; Vincent vigorously scrubs any loose DNA off himself and cleans his work areas before planting Jerome's material instead. Vincent, living as Jerome, is admitted to Gattaca and quickly rises to the rank of chief navigator before being selected for a mission to one of Saturn's moons.

On the day of the launch, Jerome shows Vincent all the biological samples he has prepared for Vincent's return. Jerome claims he has plans to travel, but as soon as Vincent departs, Jerome pulls himself inside the incinerator and commits suicide; Vincent arrives at Gattaca and is subject to a new screening routine for which he is unprepared; the doctor performing the security check clears Vincent's results and waves him through, revealing that he has known about Vincent's borrowed identity for some time. Vincent joins the rest of the crew in the rocket and lifts off into space, having overcome all his supposed genetic flaws.

Dystopian Elements:

Gattaca is set in "the not-too-distant future," a time by which genetic engineering has become standard procedure in the conception of children. Parents are able to select only the best traits for their children, eliminating everything from inheritable diseases to nearsightedness. As Vincent and his parents discover, the widespread acceptance of this engineering puts children conceived without the aid of a geneticist at severe social disadvantages, rejected from school programs and all but unemployable without a "Valid" gene structure.

The movie is structured around an idea of liberal eugenics—that is, genetic selection of embryos based on the parents' wishes for the child, not out of any public health or potentially genocidal governmental demands. While genetic discrimination is technically illegal, that does not stop potential schools, employers, or other agencies from testing legally-obtained substance screening samples for validity. Through his determination, Vincent is able to prove that it is possible to overcome his genetic profile and fulfill his dreams, in spite of the government's sanctioning of eugenics and inequality in violation of current civil rights.

30-Second Booktalk:

Vincent is an Invalid, a person conceived without the aid of genetic modification for optimal DNA. His inferior status blocks him from all but the most menial positions, effectively killing his dream of space travel. A borrowed identity gets Vincent through the doors at Gattaca and his skills—and supposed genes—put him on the team for a mission to Saturn, but one stray eyelash could reveal everything.

Readalikes:

Machine of Death (Ryan North, Matthew Bennardo, and David Malki, eds.) for longevity and cause-of-death predictions

Shadow Children series (Margaret Peterson Haddix) for living under an assumed identity

The Prestige (Christopher Priest) for the mystery of one person's identity

Potential Audience:

With its PG-13 rating, *Gattaca* is perfectly suitable for the high school and adult audiences who will most enjoy it. Many teens will identify with the inferiority complex Vincent has when compared to his genetically-flawless brother Anton, and will root for Vincent to fulfill his dream without being caught in his fraudulent identity.

Haddix, Margaret Peterson

Among the Hidden
Simon & Schuster, 2000. 153p. $6.99 pb. 978-0-689-82475-3.
$6.99 ebook. 978-0-689-84807-0.

Among the Impostors
Simon & Schuster, 2002. 172p. $6.99 pb. 978-0-613-61844-1.
$6.99 ebook. 978-0-689-84808-7.

Among the Betrayed
Simon & Schuster, 2003. 156p. $6.99 pb. 978-0-689-83909-2.
$6.99 ebook. 978-1-4424-4306-8.

Among the Barons
Simon & Schuster, 2004. 182p. $6.99 pb. 978-0-689-83910-8.
$6.99 ebook. 978-1-4424-4305-1.

Among the Brave
Simon & Schuster, 2005. 229p. $6.99
pb. 978-0-689-85795-9.
$6.99 ebook. 978-1-4391-0670-9.

Among the Enemy
Simon & Schuster, 2006. 214p. $6.99
pb. 978-0-689-85797-3.
$6.99 ebook. 978-1-4391-0672-3.

Among the Free
Simon & Schuster, 2007. 194p.
$6.99 pb. 978-0-689-85799-7.

- Shadow Children series
- Originally published 1998-2006

Plot Summary:

Luke has two brothers. This is unusual, and the fact that his two brothers are both older makes Luke illegal: due to the overpopulation that led to the Famine, families are allowed no more than two children. Population Police make raids on houses suspected of harboring illegal Third Children, killing the illegal Third Child and inflicting harsh penalties on the parents who disobeyed the order.

Luke has managed to stay reasonably happy, though he does wish he could go to school with his brothers. He still has the run of the house, plus the space outside on the farm behind the house, but that limited freedom is curtailed when a new housing development is built on the adjacent land. To avoid being seen, Luke is confined to the house, his only contact with the outside world the news his family brings back and whatever he can glimpse through an attic window.

The view from the window surprises him: peeking through the curtains of one of those new houses is a girl, in a house that has two other, known children. Risking everything, Luke runs to the house and meets Jen Talbot. Jen objects to the ban on Third Children even more than Luke does, and attempts to convince him to join her at a rally she's organized in support of Thirds. Luke refuses, afraid of the consequences, and is troubled when she doesn't return.

When Luke finally musters the courage to go back to Jen's house, he meets her father for the first time. He learns that Jen's rally turned into a slaughter, with all the protesters shot and killed. Mr. Talbot is an official with the Population Police, and he objects to the laws as strenuously as his daughter did. He offers Luke a fake ID and a cover story: a chance for Luke to become a legal child, taking on the identity of a boy who had been killed in an accident the day before, at the cost of having to leave his own family forever. Luke takes the opportunity, and sets off on his new life.

After being given his new identity, Luke—now Lee—is going to school in *Among the Imposters*. He's paranoid that someone will find out that he is an illegal, that he has assumed someone else's identity, that he will soon be arrested for his crimes—but that moment doesn't come. In time, Luke discovers several other Third Children at the Hendricks School for Boys. When Luke hears one of them, Jason, on the phone one night with the Population Police, ferreting out the actual Third Children, he knocks Jason unconscious and calls Mr. Talbot. When Mr. Talbot arrives, he tells the other Population Police officer that Jason was lying about the presence of illegals at the school. Jason is arrested, as is Nina (his accomplice at an equivalent school for girls). Luke is given the option to leave the school, but chooses to stay and help his friends.

Among the Betrayed tells Nina's story after her arrest: she had not been actively working for the Population Police, but rather is a Third Child herself. She loved Jason and did his bidding, assuming she was working for the Third Children instead of against them. Following her arrest, she is in jail, facing death unless she can convince three children to admit that they are illegals. She chooses to help the three children instead of betraying them; together the four escape into the grounds of the Hendricks School for Boys. Here she learns that Jason was working for the Population Police; after some thought, Nina agrees to join the fight against them.

In book 4, *Among the Barons*, Luke meets his new family. The Grants are prominent Barons, wealthy and powerful. Luke's "brother," Smits, burns the school down on a visit; in the remains, Luke finds two fake IDs, one for Smits and another with no picture attached. At a party at the Grants' home, the Grant parents are killed by a falling chandelier, and Luke and Smits escape and return to Luke's real parents.

Among the Brave again shifts the character focus away from Luke, this time following Trey, a Third Child friend of Luke's from school. Trey gets left behind after a raid, and in sneaking into a house to hide, he meets Mrs. Talbot. A news report informs them both that the official government has been overthrown and the Population Police have taken its place. Mrs. Talbot and Trey leave separately, Trey in search of Luke and their friends. When they are ultimately reunited, Trey presents some important-looking papers he's taken, and Mr. Talbot explains that they identify all the Third Children under false identities. Rather than allowing the papers to be burned, Trey takes them, vowing to bring down the Population Police from the inside.

The three children Nina spared earlier are back in *Among the Enemy*, where they've just escaped a work truck. Matthias leaves to find help, and the younger two disappear by the time he returns. Matthias saves a Population Police official in a shootout, ending up in the commander's favor. He soon finds Nina also working undercover in the Population Police, and the two escape together. They are caught by a double agent and taken to a warehouse filled with food and fake IDs. They distribute the food to the local population and destroy the ID cards, to prevent the Population Police from enacting their plan to lure illegal Third Children out of hiding. After a few days in hiding themselves, Matthias and Nina find their way back to Mr. Talbot and the rest of their friends.

The series concludes in *Among the Free*, in which the Population Police have been overthrown, but the new officials are spreading propaganda blaming Third Children for all of the crimes committed by the

Population Police. Desperate for his voice to be heard, Luke takes the stage at a news conference and tells his story, and his friends' stories, making sure the people understand that the government was at fault. After his speech, Luke rejoins his friends, and recognizes all the possibilities his life now holds.

Dystopian Elements:

The primary issue in the *Shadow Children* series is overpopulation: sometime in the country's past, the population became too large to be sustained by the country's resources. A drought has crippled the agriculture industry, so food is now carefully rationed, and families with more than two children will disrupt the careful allocation of those precious resources. Limiting family size will create a zero-population-growth system, and if any families have *fewer* than two children, can even create a negative growth system. The government has an overwhelming amount of power, delegating the enforcement of the strict two-children-per-family rules to Population Police, an entire government branch devoted to exterminating the children believed to be stealing resources from the already-strapped country.

But buried beneath this obvious issue is one of classism: as Jen is pressuring Luke to join her rally, he reminds her that "It's people like you who change history. People like me – we just let things happen to us."[4] Jen is the daughter of Barons, wealthy, upper-class families with power and influence. Luke, from a middle-class family of no political influence, is used to the government setting rules and forcing his family to abide by them. The disparity between them is palpable in the relative descriptions of Luke's and Jen's homes, and in their assumptions about the sort of things they can accomplish. This is also evident through the series, where Third Children are reliant on donated identities, usually from wealthy families, and on well-positioned (but duplicitous) agents among the Population Police.

30-Second Booktalk:

Luke is jealous of his two brothers. They get to go to school, go out in public, and they don't have to worry about being seen. But Luke is a Third Child, and the Population Police are there to make sure no family has more than two children. Luke has to obey the rules and remain hidden—until he meets Jen, another Third Child who lives in the house behind his. Jen has plans, though, that will change everything—if Luke is brave enough to join her movement.

Readalikes:

Shadow Children series (Margaret Peterson Haddix) for the remainder of Luke's story

The Declaration (Gemma Malley) for population control themes

The Diary of a Young Girl (Anne Frank) for hiding and isolation

The Secret Under My Skin (Janet McNaughton) for assumed identity

The Limit (Kristen Landon) for government taking children from parents who violated social norms

Potential Audience:

Middle schoolers, particularly boys, have been enjoying this series for over a decade. The mix of action sequences and friendship themes appeal to a wide range of teens, and the brisk, well-paced plot pulls readers straight through to the novel's conclusion.

---

[4] p117 (paperback)

Malley, Gemma

The Declaration

Bloomsbury USA, 2007. 300p. $16.95. 978-1-59990-119-0.
$8.99 pb. 978-1-59990-295-1.
$2.99 ebook. 978-1-59990-415-3.

Plot Summary:

By 2030, scientists had finally found the cure for aging: a simple pill called Longevity will keep people from aging, and thus provide immortality. By 2080, the world is a crowded place, the birth rate climbing while the death rate plummets. People are forced to sign the Declaration, agreeing to forgo having children if they take Longevity. There are some holdouts, people who sign and still have children. These children are considered Surplus, and are taken away from their parents at young ages to live in Surplus Halls, where they will be trained in domestic chores and other tasks to become Valuable Assets.

Anna is nearly 15, and is not far off from becoming a Valuable Asset. She has been living in Grange Hall since she was a toddler, being taught that she is an abomination who takes up valuable space, and as a result she has learned to hate the parents who broke their Declarations to have her. Still, she works hard, attempting to justify her place in the world and help the people who signed—and obeyed—the Declaration.

All is going as well as it can when Peter moves into Grange Hall. There is nothing about Peter that doesn't rankle: he constantly badgers Anna, insisting on calling her Anna Covey, insisting that he knows her parents and that they love her. She attempts to ignore him, but her curiosity eventually overwhelms her and she accepts his offer to help them both escape from Grange Hall and seek answers.

The pair manages to evade capture as they flee toward Anna's parents, where she is reunited with the people she's been taught to hate for most of her life. Here she learns not only why her parents broke their Declarations, but also that she has a brother, Ben. Their parents commit suicide in order to make both their children legal.

Dystopian Elements:

The advances in medical technology to prevent aging have seemingly unforeseen consequences: preventing aging prevents deaths from old age, and with the finite resources the Earth has, that sort of overpopulation is completely untenable. Present-day, the worldwide annual birth rate exceeds the death rate by nearly 400,000 people per year, meaning we are already heading toward a dangerously overpopulated planet. Projections from the United Nations suggest that the planet will house between 7.5 and 10.5 million people by the year 2050—and that's assuming nearly 300,000 people will die annually.[5]

---

[5] http://esa.un.org/unpd/wpp/index.htm

Malley's inspiration came from a number of articles she'd read on science's efforts to find a cure for aging, and she questions what life would be like when new people are no longer born into the world: "There would be no progress," she says[6]. She suggests that scientific and artistic achievements would cease with the lack of new perspectives, and that threat of intellectual stagnation is a theme throughout the book. Young people are almost universally despised, as most of them are illegal Surplus children, taught that their lives are valueless and selfish. It is no surprise, then, when we see the beginnings of a revolution, organized by Surplus teens and the parents who broke their Declarations.

30-Second Booktalk:

With the advent of longevity drugs, few people die—which means that without population control, the world will become a crowded place. Anna is a Surplus, a child born to parents who signed the Declaration (longevity drugs in exchange for a promise not to have children). But then she meets Peter, a new boy brought to Surplus Hall—a boy who claims to know her parents, and who suggests Anna's life could be much, much more than it is…

Readalikes:

Among the Hidden (Margaret Peterson Haddix) or *The Handmaid's Tale* (Margaret Atwood) for population control

Turnabout (Margaret Peterson Haddix) for medication to halt aging

The Secret under My Skin (Janet McNaughton) for identity and parentage

Tuck Everlasting (Natalie Babbit) for immortality

Potential Audience:

Ninth grade and up will be intrigued by the ideas presented here, many of which could easily sustain a book discussion group: overpopulation, medical advancements, global resources. The stereotypical characters might dissuade more advanced readers, but the politics and plot may pull them through.

---

[6] http://www.youtube.com/watch?v=vQI39dAejYA

Patnaude, David

Epitaph Road

Egmont USA, 2010. 266p. $16.99. 978-1-60684-055-9.
$8.99 pb. 978-1-60684-189-1.
$8.99 ebook. 978-1-60684-294-2.

Plot Summary:

A generation ago, Elisha's Bear wiped out 97 percent of American males. No one knows what caused the virus, and since then, smaller Bears have attacked outlying settlements and male-heavy communities, keeping the population of men down. Since that first Bear, women have taken over all positions of power, and as a result, wars and other conflicts have been nearly eradicated. Tight birth control and hormone treatments keep the male-to-female ratio at 1:13.

Kellen is that one in thirteen. Now 14 years old, he's been prepping for the exams that will dictate his future options—even though he has fewer options than the girls in his class do. After the exams, he's planning to visit his dad, a loner fisherman off the Seattle coast. Kellen's mom has been waffling about letting him go, though, and when her boss—a major political figure—comes by the house, Kellen suspects there's something up. What he overhears chills him: there's another outbreak coming on, and it's going to center on his dad's fishing community. With no one else able—or willing—to send a warning up there, Kellen and two female friends grab their bikes to head up.

Getting to the isolated community and locating his dad turns out to be the easy part. After finding relative safety, Kellen's friend Tia starts putting her research together, and finds that outbreaks of Elisha's Bear aren't as random as they've been made out to be—and that there isn't just one bear. Conspiracies abound through research and political channels, and in the end, nobody will be safe from the Bear.

Dystopian Elements:

Despite the emphasis on the new matriarchal political system, the dystopia is more about the social structure than political. With 97% of the men dead, women by necessity took over power, and soon after wars, poverty, and crime were nearly eradicated. Men and boys are no longer trusted to make good decisions politically, militarily, or socially, limiting the kinds of positions they can hold. Men are a minority, expected to be subservient, and they recognize how much better things are now: the emptied prisons repurposed as schools and libraries, the lack of political unrest.

At a glance, it would seem that this is a reversal of everyday sexism against women, only taken to an extreme. We as a society have made big strides in gender equality, but the sorts of limitations Kellen finds himself under are the same ones women lived under throughout American history. It is only relatively recently that women were allowed to vote and hold political office. Jobs for women outside the home were uncommon until the 19th century, and even then women were subject to employment laws that limited their working hours and all but prohibited them from holding upper-level positions.[7]

Patneaude created a video showing his inspirations for *Epitaph Road* (available at http://www.youtube.com/watch?v=EzIpmLOWXXk), explaining that he chose to look at not what the future could be, but what it currently is. His video focuses primarily on environmental damage, wars, and public health, but there is one shot of an Islamic woman, suggesting that Kellen's status as a male in his society—his limited career choices, his need to be escorted everywhere by women—was inspired by the treatment of women in traditional Islamic cultures.

30-Second Booktalk:

Thirty years ago, the Elisha's Bear virus struck, wiping out 97% of the male population. The female-to-male ratio now stands at about 13 to 1, and Kellen is that one. Now there's another Bear on the way, and it's targeting Kellen's dad's isolated fishing community. Kellan has to go to the community to warn his dad about the virus, but what he finds when he gets there could mean he'll never get home again.

Readalikes:

Herland (Charlotte Perkins Gilman), *Nomansland* (Lesley Hauge), and *Gate to Women's Country* (Sherri S. Tepper) for gender-divided societies

Wither (Lauren DeStefano) for reproduction impacted by illness

Restoring Harmony (Joélle Anthony) for Seattle setting

Y: The Last Man (Brian K. Vaughan) for limited male population

Potential Audience:

Girls, particularly those who recognize the social and historical constraints put on their gender, may appreciate seeing a female-focused society; both boys and girls will enjoy the action-heavy second half. Short chapters keep the plot moving briskly (though the first half moves more slowly). and discussions of schoolwork keep the plot at least semi-relatable for reluctant readers. 7th-10th grade readers will get the most out of this thought-provoking novel.

Discussion Guide:

Book trailer is available at: http://www.youtube.com/watch?v=D2HYgm4y9Z0

---

[7] http://www.wic.org/misc/history.htm

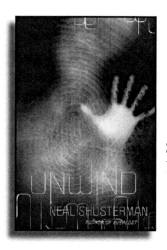

Shusterman, Neal

Unwind

Simon and Schuster, 2007. 335p. $8.99 pb. 978-1-4169-1205-7.
Brilliance Audio, 2009. $24.99 mp3-CD. 978-1-4233-7309-4.

Plot Summary:

The Second Civil War was waged over reproductive rights, pro-lifers against pro-choicers. In the end, the debate was settled with a compromise move: unwinding. Unwanted pregnancies can no longer be aborted, but unwanted children—once they are over 13—can be unwound, a process in which each part of the body is harvested and transplanted into other people. Unwinding doesn't kill; the unwound continue to live on in a separated state.

Connor isn't quite a bad boy, but he'll be the first to admit that he acts before he thinks, which gets him into fights and other trouble pretty frequently. Still, it's a shock to him when he finds the paperwork, signed by his parents, for his unwinding. With his usual impulsiveness, he makes a daring escape at the first opportunity, ending with a bus accident behind him, an accomplice, Risa (scheduled for unwinding due to budget cuts in the state home she was living in), and a hostage, Lev (a tithe of his religious parents).

Evading capture isn't easy—not with Lev along, determined to tithe himself. After attempting to turn all three of them into the authorities, Lev gets separated from Connor and Risa and befriends a boy named Cyrus. While the pair travels together, Lev begins to understand that tithing meant more to his parents than Lev himself did, and his anger fuels his change in outlook.

Connor and Risa travel through a series of safe houses until finally arriving at The Graveyard, an expanse of land in the Arizona desert filled with decommissioned and broken-down airplanes. A hardened Lev arrives shortly after and quickly falls in with a group of revolutionaries. When the Admiral, the no-nonsense man who runs the Graveyard, has a heart attack and needs to be flown by helicopter to a hospital, the pilot (Roland, a rival of Connor's from the safe house network) turns them into authorities, getting Connor, Risa, and Roland sent directly to a Harvest Camp.

Roland is the first of the three scheduled for Unwinding, a process that is detailed and horrifying without being gruesome. Connor is due to be unwound immediately after, but as he is being marched into the building, Lev and his group launch a suicide attack, using themselves as human bombs to take down the camp. At the last minute, Lev chooses not to blow himself up, and instead digs through the rubble to find both Connor and Risa.

At the book's conclusion, Connor has taken over running the Graveyard for runaway Unwinds. Connor tells them that they will not be silenced and will become a threat to any who champion unwinding, setting up a sequel (tentatively scheduled for publication in 2012).

Dystopian Elements:

More than any political system or the new reaches of technology, *Unwind* presents a sociological dystopia in which parents can retroactively abort their teenagers out of frustration, economic necessity, religious tithing, or virtually any other reason. Unwinding had been proposed as a joke, a moment of levity at the bargaining table between both sides of the Reproductive Rights war, but the bluff was called and now it's a horrible reality.

Unwind raises questions about when life has value, and for whom. The argument for unwinding (as compared to abortion) is still about the sanctity of life, but in the case of unwinding, life is preserved. Unwound teens are not killed, but they live on in a separated state. The body parts retain a sort of muscle memory (i.e., a man receiving an Unwound's hand can suddenly do card tricks; a donated chunk of brain tissue compels an otherwise-honest boy to shoplift), making some Unwind's parts more desirable than others and commanding a higher price. The value a teen's life has is measured in the sum of his individual parts and talents that can be transplanted into other people. The teens who are going to be unwound are minors and therefore do not have the legal right to refuse an unwind order; they are subject to their parents' or guardians' decisions, raising other questions about teens' rights and decision-making capabilities.

30-Second Booktalk:

Connor finds the paperwork his parents signed: he's scheduled for unwinding, having all his parts harvested and redistributed into other people. Sure, he'll live on in a separated state, but he has no plans to let it happen to him. If he can survive until his 18th birthday, he'll be free—but that's a long time to survive with so many people willing to turn him in.

Readalikes:

Shadow Children series (Margaret Peterson Haddix) for illegal teens on the run

The Adoration of Jenna Fox (Mary E. Pearson) for rebuilding of a physical life

Uglies (Scott Westerfeld) for transplants and grafts to enhance a person's abilities

Potential Audience:

Short chapters and varied viewpoints keep the pace moving briskly, engaging both reluctant readers and avid sci-fi devotees. The light romance between Connor and Risa doesn't overshadow the plot. Great for 8th grade and up, particularly boys, and the premise provides plenty of material for book discussions.

Discussion Guide:

Book trailer is available at: http://www.youtube.com/watch?v=_DAYyvcUMIM

Snyder, Maria V.

Inside Out

(*Inside Out*, Book 1). Harlequin Teen, 2010. 315p. $9.99 Trade pb. 978-0-373-21006-0.
$9.00 ebook. 978-1-4268-5178-0.

Plot Summary:

Trella is a scrub, responsible for keeping the air ducts clean. Trella is also a bit of an explorer, able to travel through the levels and observe in places she has no business being. Cog, her best friend, introduces her to a new prophet, Broken Man, who has heard of her reputation as Queen of the Pipes and enlists her help in retrieving information discs he'd left in a vent—discs that prove the existence of a gateway to Outside.

Trella is skeptical, but curiosity gets the better of her and she searches out the discs. In her surprise at finding them, she accidentally trips an alarm, triggering a manhunt for the prophet and a sharp increase in security on the lower levels. Trella and Cog find a place to hide Broken Man, but that relative safety is threatened when Trella falls through a vent into an Upper's hiding place. Even knowing the boy she fell on could turn her in at any minute, Trella cautiously trusts Riley, and the two work together with Broken Man, a handful of scrubs, and even some highly-placed uppers to topple the ruling family and fight their way to Outside.

Dystopian Elements:

Mostly this title hits the notes of standard science-fiction: an isolated world, untrustworthy hints of a better future, a hero rising out of the lower class to lead a revolution. It takes a little bit for *Inside Out* to find its dystopian footing, most of which isn't revealed until the last third of the novel. Prior to that point, the world is one where the lower classes—Trella and her fellow scrubs—are taken from their mothers at birth and raised in care groups until they are old enough to do jobs of their own. The only people concerned about mixing bloodlines and family groups are the Uppers, those legitimately part of the nine Upper families or the Pop Cops—the population control officials who track every person Inside.

What sends this into dystopian territory is Trella's discoveries about the world Inside. While the Scrubs are raised in their care groups, the Uppers are allowed families—but there is a strict enforcement of One Child Per Family, and any subsequent children are taken away and sent to the lower levels to be raised as scrubs. Trella herself was one of those children, her eyes artificially darkened to help her better blend in with the lower class. The Pop Cops and the one ruling family, the Travas, have spent generations cultivating distrust and isolation between the Uppers and Lowers, partly to ensure their secret is never revealed, and partly to punish those who would threaten the social balance.

30-Second Booktalk:

Trella is the Queen of the Pipes, able to get nearly anywhere in the Cube via the air ducts. She finds herself knee-deep in conspiracy when she agrees to retrieve information discs for a new prophet claiming to know about the Gateway to Outside. While searching for more information, Trella falls through a vent into a storage room currently being used as a hideout for an Upper-level boy her own age. With little choice but to trust him, she's launched into an adventure she never could have anticipated.

Readalikes:

Incarceron (Catherine Fisher) for escape from a closed system

Ender's Game (Orson Scott Card) for social structures in closed systems

Across the Universe (Beth Revis) for conspiracy, colonization, and forbidden romance

Shadow Children series (Margaret Peterson Haddix) for population control

The Declaration (Gemma Malley) for moving illegally-born children into servitude

Potential Audience:

Upper-middle school and junior high students will appreciate this briskly-plotted adventure as they try, along with Trella, to find the location of the Gateway and discover its purpose. High school students will enjoy these elements, too, but will also appreciate the subtle commentary on classism and population control.

Chapter 2:

Technology

Human advancement has always been driven by technological breakthroughs, from the discovery of fire to modern innovations in nanotechnology. In our current lives, technology provides us with many things unheard of in previous years: video conferencing, bionic limbs[1], electronic paper. Technology will continue to progress as long as people are free to dream up new ideas and find ways to implement those ideas.

The number of things that humans have invented in service to making our lives better is astonishing, as is the variety of technological innovations. Philip Reeve, in his essay "The Worst Is Yet to Come," suggests that "Some of today's technologies are far more impressive than flying cars. Some of this may have come about precisely because the children of earlier generations were excited by fictional visions of a brighter future and ended up as the scientists and social reformers, innovative engineers and hi-tech entrepreneurs who helped to make it happen."[2] With that in mind, what sorts of innovations will come a generation or two from now, when today's teens become the scientists and engineers? The technologies that are currently used for social benefit—safety, unified record-keeping and access, surveillance—can rapidly be turned to less benign purposes.

This nefarious purpose is most obvious in Cory Doctorow's *Little Brother*, a dystopia lacking in science-fictional elements and set against a present-day backdrop of surveillance technologies used by the Department of Homeland Security. Doctorow's ideas are grounded in news reports and current policies, but are also clearly influenced by the wealth of dystopian literature focusing on surveillance issues. Orwell's *1984*, from which Doctorow's title borrows, shows one man's rebellion against his totalitarian government while his every action is observed. *Minority Report*, both the novel by Philip K. Dick and the movie adaptation, deal with the observations of everyday lives in the efforts to prevent crimes. Each prisoner in Incarceron (*Incarceron*, by Catherine Fisher) is carefully watched, with their every movement logged. The world that Kristin Landon creates in *The Limit* monitors families' budgetary practices; the Japan of Project Itoh's *Harmony* monitors every citizen's health and wellness through devices implanted in peoples' brains.

Implants are also common in *Feed*, by M.T. Anderson, in which children are implanted with feeds at young ages to provide them with advertising opportunities and other information. The stream of filtered information and entertainment informs much of the classic Ray Bradbury novel *Fahrenheit 451*. The idea of corporate sponsorship and advertising is present in debut-author Rae Mariz's *The Unidentified*, and corporations are at the heart of both *The Lab* (Jack Heath) and *The Surrogates* (Robert Venditti). This last also features the technological marvel of nearly-perfected android technology, which also drives the stories of Bernard Beckett's *Genesis* and the movie *Blade Runner*.

As we'll see in these sixteen titles, technology can make lives better—but at a price. How much are we willing to give up for ease and convenience?

---

[1] http://news.discovery.com/tech/bionic-arm-moved-by-thought.html

[2] http://www.schoollibraryjournal.com/slj/home/891276-312/the_worst_is_yet_to.html.csp

19

Anderson, M.T.

Feed

Candlewick, 2004. 299p. $7.99 Trade pb. 978-0-7636-2259-6.
Listening Library, 2008. $30. CD. 978-0-7393-5620-3.

- Originally published 2002

Plot Summary:

The Internet has evolved, reduced to a tiny transmitter implanted into a person's brain, giving them a constant "feed" of television, commercials, instant communications, and more. Almost three-quarters of Americans have them, a boon for marketers who like to target potential consumers. With the feeds installed from early ages, not only can corporations effectively data-mine the public, but the feeds will take over certain brain functions, tying people into the corporate culture.

Titus's feed, installed when he was very young, has always been a way of life to him, not something worth questioning. He and his friends are on a quick vacation to the moon when their feeds get hacked, causing them to spout anti-feed sentiments before falling unconscious. On waking in the hospital, Titus finds Violet, the girl he'd been talking to while partying on the moon, and she encourages him to think beyond his feed, to examine what the feed is actually doing. She has a feed herself, but it wasn't implanted the same way as everyone else's—which makes it all the more worrisome when the hack causes it to malfunction.

Dystopian Elements:

The world of *Feed* still has a political structure to it, but the politicians are fully in the grips of the corporations. School is now School™, where the corporations have stepped up when no money was available to fund public schools anymore. In Titus's words, "It's good because that way we know that the big corps are made up of real human beings, not just jerks out for money, because taking care of children, they care about America's future. It's an investment in tomorrow." Investment is right—School™'s focus is on teaching students how best to use their feeds, find bargains, and work technology. Automated customer service is available when feeds go wrong, but even this is subject to the whims of the corporations: as Violet petitions for her feed to be repaired, FeedTech Corp turns down her request due to her lack of consumer history; corporations are not interested in helping someone whose continued health would not lead to future profits for them.

In Anderson's words, "It's impossible for us to think of our life without conceiving of it in images that are taken from movies, from songs, from ads, all of which are images that are challenging us to be better consumers rather than better people."[3] *Feed* takes this idea to the extreme: it is more important to buy the right products and establish oneself as a consumer than it is to think for oneself and draw conclusions about the world at large.

---

[3] Taken from "A Readers Guide," 2004 paperback edition of *Feed*

30-Second Booktalk:

The feed tracks your shopping habits and recommends similar products; it advertises things you're walking past—its television shows and news and IM and maps—and it's all right there in your head. But what happens when your feed gets hacked? Titus and Violet are about to find out, because a malfunctioning feed is one thing—but a malfunctioning feed that was installed atypically besides is a much bigger problem.

Readalikes:

Be More Chill (Ned Vizzini) for brain implants

The Unidentified (Rae Mariz) for corporation-run schools and corporate invasion into everyday life

Teen, Inc. (Stefan Petrucha) for corporate invasion into everyday life

When It Happens (Susane Colasanti) for romance between a smart girl and a slacker boy

Little Brother (Cory Doctorow) for computer hacking and constant surveillance

Brave New World (Aldous Huxley) for consumer culture

Minority Report (film) for corporate tracking

Potential Audience:

High school students will enjoy this novel, with upper-grade students getting more out of the political subplots and discussions. Short chapters will appeal to reluctant readers; the balance between the science-fiction and romance plots will hold the interest of a variety of readers.

Bachorz, Pam

Candor

EgmontUSA, 2009. 256p. $16.99. 978-1-60684-012-2.
$8.99 pb. 978-1-60684-135-8.
$8.99 ebook. 978-1-60684-116-7.

Plot Summary:

Parents move to Candor, Florida, when they can't control their teenagers anymore. That's because Candor is a very special town, one with a message for each resident, a town founded—or *created*, more accurately—by Oscar's dad. The town's messages are actually subliminal messages, played directly to the teens and out in the common areas of town to keep everyone in line.

Oscar knows that his dad is controlling Candor's teens, and he's established a profitable side business helping rich teens escape Candor's grasp. Then he falls for Nia, the new girl, whom he *knows* he should smuggle out of town for her own sake—even though he wants to keep her around for his own. He'll have to risk everything, including himself, if he truly plans to sabotage his father's entire system.

Dystopian Elements:

Subliminal stimuli was first introduced in 1897; marketers latched onto the concept in 1957, at which point subliminal messages became controversial in their abilities to control thought and decisions. Scientific experiments have since failed to prove long-term efficacy of subliminal advertising, but have found that it can influence short-term goal-focused decisions (e.g., decisions to try specific soft drinks if, and only if, the subject of the experiment is already thirsty).[4] Despite these at-best-inconclusive findings, the idea of using subliminal messages to control a population is an intriguing one.

What parents wouldn't love a chance to "reprogram" their unruly teens to make them polite, diligent workers, and overall more compliant with parental directives—even if it means, effectively, brainwashing them? The town of Candor makes this a permanent solution, including the original subliminal tapes and following it with "upkeep" tapes, to ensure that the teens don't go without the subliminal messages for any length of time. The messages become a kind of aural addiction, and the withdrawal for those who leave town without the upkeep music is deadly. While the larger world outside Candor is our standard, everyday world, the inability to easily leave the town's borders, coupled with Oscar's father's control over every detail of people and place, pushes this title into dystopian territory.

---

[4] Strahan, Erin J., Steven J. Spencer, and Mark P. Zanna. "Subliminal priming and persuasion: Striking while the iron is hot." *Journal of Experimental Social Psychology* 38.6 (November 2002): 556-568. http://dx.doi.org/10.1016%2FS0022-1031%2802%2900502-4

30-Second Booktalk:

Oscar Banks is a straight-A student and Student Council President. All the teens want to be like him. They don't know what Oscar knows: the teens of Candor are controlled by subliminal messages. Lucky for them, Oscar has a plan to sabotage the system.

Readalikes:

A Clockwork Orange (Anthony Burgess), for subliminal messages

Stargirl (Jerry Spinelli), for romance between a conventional(-seeming) boy and an outcast girl

Brave New World (Aldous Huxley) for subliminal messages

Potential Audience:

Upper-middle and lower-high school students will find a lot here to relate to: parental pressure to be perfect, the need to conform, and the need to break away from that conformity when they risk losing themselves. Teens who are not fans of science fiction may still be sucked in by Oscar's growing romance with Nia, or by his shrewd sense of business opportunities.

Beckett, Bernard

Genesis

Mariner Books, 2010. 150p. $10.95. 978-0-547-33592-6.
Brilliance Audio, 2009. $24.99 CD. 978-1-4233-8150-1.
$10.95 ebook. 978-0-547-39438-1.

- Originally published 2006

Plot Summary:

Anaximander is standing before the committee, answering each part of her grueling 4-hour entrance exam. If she passes, she will be a member of the Academy, one of the elite rulers of the island Republic. Anax has prepared thoroughly, choosing as her topic Adam Forde, a long-dead hero: a man who broke through the Republic's extensive security measures to reconnect with the outside world. For his actions, Forde is thrown in prison and forced to participate in an artificial intelligence experiment, teaching an android to develop personhood.

Anax provides the examiners with her interpretation and understanding of Forde's life and actions, a thorough history of their modern culture without any discussion of their world as it currently stands. Anax's logic is sound and her speculations are well-grounded, but the examiners have a final question for her: what does she make of this never-released video file, showing the android killing Forde? Anax is faced with a radical change in her worldview, trying to fit this new information alongside the conclusions at which she has meticulously arrived.

While she tries to process these new facts, the examiners present her with more: the novel reveals that the panel, and Anax herself, are all replications of that original android, and Anax's interest in the life of Adam Forde mark her as carrying a particular virus. The virus infects those who can understand the free will and power of the androids, and those carrying the virus must be exterminated before they can spread their seeds of dissent around the Republic.

Dystopian Elements:

By 2075, the world has already been permanently changed by the plague. The island Republic has been completely locked down, with barricades and guards to ensure the safety of the island. Technology is advancing rapidly, though, with experiments in artificial intelligence and robotics.

The elements that mark this as a true dystopia, with a government ensuring that its society remains perfect at all costs, remain hidden until the end of this novella, when the examiners reveal that no one is ever granted access to the Academy. The examination only gauges each scholar's interest in Adam Forde, the man who is both a hero and a rebel to the Republic. For someone to be interested enough in Forde's life to study it closely, they must be infected with the virus, the one that gives ideas and speculations about free will, human consciousness, and the existence of a soul. Any of those ideas would make that person difficult to control—and therefore make the society very difficult to control, especially a society that has been replicated from an AI unit.

30-Second Booktalk:

Anax is standing before a panel of examiners, the three people who will decide her fate: will she be admitted to the Academy? Is her knowledge and understanding of her topic—Adam Forde, the historical figure whose actions may have changed the course of their utopian Republic—enough to prove herself worthy?

Readalikes:

I, Robot (Issac Asimov) for the rise of robots and androids

The Republic (Plato) for similar themes and structure

Planet of the Apes (1968 or 2001 films or Pierre Boulle's novel) for a society run by apes

Chaos Walking trilogy (Patrick Ness) for colonization and the elimination of dissidents

Potential Audience:

The academic nature of this novella will make it difficult to match to a general audience. However, upper-high school intellectuals will appreciate the deep themes in this rigorous science fiction story.

Blade Runner

4-Disc Collector's Edition DVD. Color. 117m. Produced and dist. by Warner Home Video, 2007. $34.99. 978-6-3114-6375-8.

- Written by Hampton Fancher and David Peoples
- Based on the novel *Do Androids Dream of Electric Sheep?* by Philip K. Dick
- Directed by Ridley Scott
- Originally released 1982

Plot Summary:

On a rainy November night in 2019, former police officer Richard Deckard is pulled out of retirement to track down four replicants—bioengineered robots—who have illegally come to Earth. The replicants are late models, the Nexus-6, designed with a four-year lifespan to avoid their AI developing emotions, and are suspected of coming to Earth to demand their lives be extended.

Before starting his search, Deckard visits the Tyrell Corporation to ensure that the test to identify replicants works properly. He administers the test to a young assistant, Rachel, and after many questions he identifies her as a replicant. Rachel is an advanced model, implanted with someone else's memories; she believes herself to be fully human. When, in a later meeting, Deckard explains to her that she is a replicant and that her memories are false, she is devastated and runs away. Deckard soon gets a call: Rachel is to be found and retired, along with the original four replicants, due to her disappearance from the Tyrell Corporation.

Deckard finds and kills the first replicant, but a second, Leon, sees him do it. Leon attacks Deckard, but Rachel intervenes and shoots Leon. Deckard promises not to kill Rachel, despite his orders. Meanwhile, Roy, one of the remaining two replicants, pays a visit to eponymous corporation head Tyrell, demanding more than four years. When Tyrell confesses that the designers have not found a way to extend replicants' lives, Roy kills him.

Deckard tracks Roy back to the building where the last two replicants have been hiding. He quickly dispatches the first, but Roy proves more challenging. Roy breaks two of Deckard's fingers and then allows him a head-start to escape before ultimately forcing him up toward the building's roof. Deckard attempts to leap to another building, but his jump falls short and he clings to a girder wet with rain. Roy makes the jump easily, though his four-year lifespan is just about up, and hauls Deckard up to safety. Roy speaks about his life, then dies. Deckard manages to get himself home, where he finds Rachel sleeping; the film ends with Deckard and Rachel leaving the building together.

Dystopian Elements:

Replicants are androids, produced by mega-corporations for the purpose of doing menial and/ or dangerous jobs. The corporations who create the replicants have control over this workforce, even ensuring that none of the androids live longer than four years, so as to avoid allowing their artificial intelligence to develop human emotions. The corporations also have power over the environment: "real" animals are all but extinct, replaced with artificial equivalents that are indistinguishable at a quick look from the real thing. Citizens are bombarded with a constant stream of advertising, a background element in the movie that does not affect the plot but helps to create the world this has become.

There is an implication that those who could afford to have moved to off-Earth colonies, where they keep replicant workers as a slave labor workforce. This leaves the less well-off citizens back on Earth, populating cities with only the poor and the few powerful corporation heads who have remained. The resulting cities are ethnically diverse and physically chaotic, with a wide income disparity, allowing the executives at the top to view the rest of the dangerous and unstable city.

The illegality of replicants on Earth makes it easy to view these androids as "others," as threats to the relative peace and smooth functioning of the city as it is. As a viewer, it is difficult to see the replicants as pure villains, though, when their only objective is to be granted more than four years of life. For them, their brief lifespan is what makes the film dystopian; that they are created to be slaves for a finite time until their deaths make life barely worth living for these not-quite-human creatures.

30-Second Booktalk:

Deckard is one of the best blade runners there's been—which is why he's tasked with hunting down and "retiring" the group of four replicants who have come back to Earth illegally. The androids are used for manual labor in off-Earth colonies and have a four-year lifespan to keep their artificial intelligence from developing emotions—but as Deckard tracks them down for elimination, he finds their will to live is all too human.

Readalikes:

Do Androids Dream of Electric Sheep? (Philip K. Dick) for novel on which the movie is based

A.I. (film) for androids developing human-like characteristics

Robocop (film) for corporations filling jobs with cyborgs/androids

The Surrogates (Robert Venditti) for robotic stand-ins for people

Minority Report (film) for ad saturation

Potential Audience:

The slow pace of the movie may turn off viewers more accustomed to action-heavy films, but many more will be drawn in by the twisting plot. Its R rating (for violence and nudity) makes it more appropriate for upper-high school and college students, than younger viewers.

Bradbury, Ray

Fahrenheit 451

Ballantine Books, 1996. 192p. $15. 978-0-345-41001-6.
Simon & Schuster, 2012. $11.99 pb. 978-1-4516-7331-9.
Tantor Media, 2010. $24.99 CD. 978-1-4001-1818-2.
$19.99 mp3-CD. 978-1-4001-6818-7.
$9.99 ebook. 978-1-4391-4267-7.

- Originally published 1953

Plot summary:

Guy Montag has been a fireman for ten years: a decade spent rounding up and burning books people had hidden away. He's never questioned the way things work, but everything changes when his wife overdoses on sleeping pills and a young neighbor, Clarisse, asks him if he's happy in his life. Montag is still considering this question when he witnesses a woman burn herself alive with her books rather than give them up. He begins to see the value of the books he's been burning, the time men and women of previous eras spent thinking of things and committing them to paper, and knows that something must change. Montag seeks out an old friend who may be able to help him, becoming a fugitive along the way, and encounters a band of men and women preserving the books orally until such time as they can be printed on paper again. Back in the city, war has broken out, destroying nearly everything, ultimately paving the way for civilization to rise back up and rebuild itself.

Dystopian Elements:

Bradbury's classic novel is generally considered one of the stand-out anti-censorship novels of all time, a cautionary tale against governmental control over media streams and content. Bradbury himself disputed this idea in a 2007 interview[5], in which he stated that it was never about censorship at all, but rather society's reliance on television over printed literature for news, interaction, or entertainment. "I wasn't worried about freedom; I was worried about people being turned into morons by TV," he said in a 2001 interview in his home.[6] "*Fahrenheit*'s not about censorship, it's about the moronic influence of popular culture through TV news."

The dystopia created in *Fahrenheit 451* is not one based on a government swooping in and assuming control, but one in which the citizens have willingly given up all control in favor of being entertained by their "walls" (large, flat-screened, wall-mounted televisions) and "families" (the actors on the various shows). Though more than half a century has passed since Bradbury first published his cautionary tale, his messages regarding the soporific effects of television are even more relevant today than they were when he first voiced them.

---

[5] http://www.laweekly.com/2007-05-31/news/ray-bradbury-fahrenheit-451-misinterpreted/
[6] http://www.raybradbury.com/images/video/about_freeDOM.html

30-Second Booktalk:

Fireman Guy Montag understands his job: he's responsible for burning books that people hide, because books—and knowledge, and intellectual thought—really just make people unhappy. But then Montag meets Clarisse, a young neighbor who is interested in the world around her and wants to share it with him. When Clarisse disappears suddenly, Montag starts hoarding books of his own, even making plans to print new copies of old classics. Can he get away with it? Is there anyone who can help him?

Readalikes:

A Canticle for Leibowitz (Walter M. Miller Jr.) for preservation of society materials

Equilibrium (film) for criminalization of artistic/literary materials

Potential Audience:

Fahrenheit 451 is a modern classic; most teens who encounter it will likely do so in a classroom. While the writing is accessible to middle-school students, high schoolers will get more out of this title when looking at it in context of current popular culture and through the historical lens of the Cold War era United States.

Dick, Philip K.

Minority Report

Available in:

- *Minority Report and Other Classic Stories.* Citadel, 2002. 380p. $14.95. 978-0-8065-2379-8.
- *Selected Stories of Philip K. Dick.* Pantheon, 2002. 496p. $29.95. 978-0-375-42151-8.
- Originally published in *Minority Report and Other Stories*, 1956

Plot Summary:

Thanks to John Anderton's development of precrime predictions, violent crime has been almost completely eradicated. A team of three precognitives has their visions analyzed and translated into reports of upcoming crimes, so that the would-be perpetrators can be arrested before they have a chance to kill. Anderton is showing his new assistant around the Precrime division when he picks up a new batch of cards—and is shocked to find his name at the top. Convinced it's part of a conspiracy to get him out of the way and allow his new assistant to take over, Anderton flees, but it's not enough for him to escape: he needs to find out why he's accused of killing a man he's never heard of. The answer may lie in the safeguard to the precog system: the cards are generated when two of the three precogs reach the same conclusion. Anderton's eventual crime, however, hides in the spaces between the predictions. If Anderton is to prove his innocence, he has to prove the existence of the Minority Report—and figure out what information it's based on.

Dystopian Elements:

While Dick does not show much of the societal or governmental structure in the world he's created, he nonetheless sets up a dystopian structure in its embrace of the precrime system. Violent crime is not the only thing the precogs are looking for: they also generate reports for other felonies as well, giving a sense that the government is watching every move of each citizen under the guise of making the world safer. (In fact, Anderton states in the early pages of the novella that "precrime has cut down felonies by ninety-nine and decimal point eight percent.") The idea that crime can be eradicated does suggest a positive change in society, but the cost of such peace is the incarceration of potential criminals before they've done anything wrong.

As Anderton discovers, the very knowledge of his potential crime can change his trajectory, and starts him questioning the very system he created. Everyone detained under the Precrime system is technically innocent, having been apprehended before any crimes could take place, but how many would have actually gone on to commit crimes? Would any of them have been dissuaded had they been told about it in advance?

The main implications in the story's conclusion are less about its dystopian structures than in divergent timelines and the observer effect[7] (in which the act of observing, or knowing about, an event influences the outcome); the novella is too brief to fully explore any of its ideas about governmental monitoring of private citizens or about free will. The ideas present plenty of material for discussion of governments examining the private lives of citizens under the guise of increased safety, a concept common in dystopian science fiction and echoed in reality through (for example) the USA PATRIOT Act of 2001.

30-Second Booktalk:

John Anderton created the Precrime system: three people with precognitive abilities are connected to machines that analyze their every thought and translate it into reports about upcoming crimes. Anderton is shocked when his name appears on a card, accusing him of killing a man he's never heard of. He's certain it's a conspiracy, set to force him out so his new assistant can take over, but the more he uncovers, the less likely conspiracy seems. If Anderton is to prove his innocence, he has to prove the existence of the Minority Report—and figure out what information it's based on.

Readalikes:

Rash (Pete Hautman) for incarceration for minor crimes

1984 (George Orwell) for governmental observation

Meanwhile (Jason Shiga) for divergent timelines

A Crack in the Line (Michael Lawrence) for alternate paths (Many Worlds theory)

The Predicteds (Christine Seifert) for prediction of future crimes

Potential Audience:

Minority Report is an adult book, though it has definite appeal for upper-high-school students, particularly those who enjoy a smarter, more thought-based science fiction.

---

[7] "Quantum Theory Demonstrated: Observation Affects Reality," *ScienceDaily* (Feb. 27, 1998), http://www.sciencedaily.com/releases/1998/02/980227055013.htm

Minority Report.

DVD. Color. 146m. Produced and dist. by Dreamworks Pictures, 2007. $9.99. 978-0-7832-9258-8. Blu-Ray. Produced and dist. by Paramount, 2011. $22.99. 978-6-3134-9950-2

- Written by Scott Frank and Jon Cohen
- Directed by Steven Spielberg

Plot Summary

John Anderton joined the precrime police force nearly six years ago, shortly after the disappearance of his young son. He still grieves the boy, and when not working he buries himself in home movies and psychotropic drugs. The precrime system he's devoted his life to is about to go national, but before that can happen, the Department of Justice demands an audit: they want to see exactly how the system works and uncover any hidden flaws.

While the DoJ auditor is inspecting the system, the precogs send out a brown ball: a premeditated murder, nearly unheard of in the years since the precrime division went live. The victim will be a Leo Crow, but it's the perpetrator's name Anderton recognizes: in 36 hours, *he* will kill a man he's never heard of.

Certain there's a mistake, Anderton seeks out the doctor responsible for creating Precrime science. She assures him that the precogs occasionally disagree, and tells him that the "minority report"—the dissenting opinion—would be deleted from the official records, but would still be recorded inside the precog who saw it. With this in mind, Anderton breaks into his old lab and kidnaps Agatha, the precog who would have his minority report.

Agatha's memories of her visions unfortunately match the original report: there was no outlier opinion, no minority report; Anderton will kill Leo Crow. However, Agatha also provides her minority report on a thwarted murder, evidence that will incriminate Precrime director Lamar Burgess. After Anderton outs Burgess, Burgess hunts him down, culminating in a confrontation and a choice: if Burgess kills Anderton, as the precogs have predicted, he proves the Precrime system works at the cost of his own freedom. If he does not kill Anderton, it will show fallibility in the Precrime system, just as it is about to be launched nationally.

Dystopian Elements

The movie adaptation of Philip K. Dick's classic novella begins with the same idea, but places the Precrime division against a more political backdrop: this time, the story takes place in and around Washington, DC, just as the system is undergoing a Department of Justice audit to probe for any faults with the system.

John Anderton's world is one in which every citizen is constantly monitored by retinal scanners placed in subway stations, shopping malls, and seemingly anywhere else, providing tracking data and shopping histories to any organization trying to collect it. This is evident in early chase scenes, when Anderton is fleeing his coworkers via subway, and later when he takes Agatha for new clothing at the Gap, where the store inquires about some tank tops that were purchased on the same retinal ID.

Similar to the original novella, the government's willingness to intrude on civilian lives in the guise of safety calls up comparisons to the USA PATRIOT Act of 2001. The intrusions are far more overt in the movie version, particularly in the scene in which Anderton is hiding in a residential building: the agents searching for him release robotic spiders to scan the retinas of every resident, heedless of the terrified children left in their wake and unconcerned with the disruption they've caused to any other neighbors.

30-Second Booktalk

Precrime officer John Anderton recognizes only one of the two names that come from the precogs, and it's not the victim's name—it's his own, on the ball designating the murderer-to-be. Anderton is certain of his innocence, but proving it is impossible. There's no trace of a minority report on his crime, and even if he knew where to find it, there's no guarantee he'd make the right choices.

Readalikes

Feed (M.T. Anderson) for corporate tracking

1984 (George Orwell) for governmental observation

Minority Report (Philip K. Dick) for comparison

Potential Audience

A smart action-thriller of a movie, this will find its audience among adults and high-school sci-fi and/or conspiracy fans. The lack of explosions may take this option off the radar of die-hard action movie buffs, but those invested in its concepts will be well rewarded.

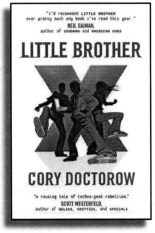

Doctorow, Cory

Little Brother

Tor Teen, 2008. 384p. 17.95 978-0-7653-1985-2. $9.99 Trade pb. 978-0-7653-2311-8. ebook free from http://craphound.com/littlebrother/download/.

- *Little Brother*, Cory Doctorow
- Originally published in 2008

Plot Summary

Marcus and his friends are participating in a half-online, half-real-world scavenger hunt when the Bay Bridge blows up. As people are directed toward fallout shelters, one of Marcus's friends, Darryl, is stabbed, and the other three teens take him back up to the surface streets to find help. The Department of Homeland Security (DHS) finds them and, deciding they are suspicious for not being in the shelter, takes them into custody. Individually, the four are questioned, then interrogated. None are given information about any of the others, including about their injured friend. After five days, Marcus is forced to sign papers claiming he was held voluntarily and strongly cautioned not to say any differently, then released.

Returning home a different teen, Marcus swears revenge, and launches a campaign to take down the DHS. He finds a small piece of hardware clumsily inserted in his laptop and knows he's under strict surveillance, so he utilizes a small hack for XBox system, loading on a new operating system (Paranoid Linux) and setting up an enormous amount of security. He distributes discs and instructions to teens all over the Bay area, building up what becomes known as the Xnet, and the movement is born. DHS is tracking citizens via RFID in transit passes and other cards: the Xnetters clone the cards and swap data, making every person's movements look suspicious. DHS calls nearly any youth gathering a riot: the Xnetters stage huge concerts and get press coverage.

On learning that Darryl is still alive and being held in a separate prison, Marcus reveals everything: he confesses to his parents and Darryl's father what really happened while they were gone immediately after the bridge bombing. He turns all his information over to a friend of the family, an investigative journalist. This results in Marcus being again taken into DHS custody and tortured this time, waterboarded for information that he does not actually have. His reporter-friend's article is published, forcing California's governor to act on the information, and Marcus is rescued from the prison by the California Highway State Patrol.

The DHS loses a lot of its power, though the people responsible for his torture are never actually punished. Marcus is as happy as he can be with his return to a normal life, though he spends much of his time campaigning against the political party that allowed Homeland Security to have so much power over US citizens on US soil.

Dystopian Elements

Calling *Little Brother* a dystopia is a little disingenuous, given its contemporary setting and grounding in current events, but it is clear that that is exactly the author's point: the intrusiveness of surveillance on private citizens, in particular, is very common in dystopias but easily overlooked in daily life. Those who believe that surveillance is perfectly fine because they have nothing to hide overlook the costs of such monitoring, both at an individual level (what it costs them personally to be detained without reason) and at an organizational level (the "return on investment," i.e., the time and energy spent following everyone versus how many potential crimes are actually discovered through such wide-spread surveillance).

So much of *Little Brother* echoes Orwell's *1984* that it is almost impossible to talk about the former without referencing the latter, right down to surveillance cameras monitoring citizens in the streets and the coerced confessions of anti-governmental thoughts and plans under torture. The methods used to extract information from *1984*'s Winston Smith are not radically different from those DHS uses to interrogate Marcus (whose online handle at the novel's start is *w1n5t0n*, echoing *1984* once again), and the methods result in similar failures of useable information.

While it is easy to read *Little Brother* as a vision of a not-too-distant future, it is even more troubling to see it through the lens of current Homeland Security measures and the USA PATRIOT Act of 2001, especially since several parts of the PATRIOT Act (among them, wiretaps and surveillance of individuals) were granted extensions by President Obama in 2011. Marcus's exact story is fiction, and to those not well-versed in computer and online technologies, science-fiction, but there is no reason to believe that the security measures the DHS enacts could not happen, as they are already legal—and, in some cases, they have already been enacted.

30-Second Booktalk

Marcus and his friends are in the wrong place at the wrong time when the Bay Bridge blows up, and they're quickly taken into custody by the Department of Homeland Security. When he's released after days of interrogation, Marcus swears revenge. He develops the Xnet, a hidden network accessed through a hack in the XBox console, and uses it to organize protests and sabotage against the DHS. Marcus knows it's only a matter of time until the DHS catches up to him. Marcus values his safety, but he values freedom even more.

Readalikes

1984 (George Orwell) for surveillance

The Trial (Franz Kafka) for unexplained imprisonment

Homeland Security (Current Controversies series, Debra A. Miller) for explanation of Homeland Security

Pattern Recognition (William Gibson) for online tracking, security, and encryption methods

Potential Audience

Budding (and adept) hackers and online technologists will have no trouble understanding Doctorow's novel, but non-techies may have some difficulty following all of the plot twists and action. Upper-high school and college students will most identify with the idealistic youth movement and be able to discuss the ideas at great length in the book groups that this title lends itself to.

For further reading, Doctorow provides an extensive bibliography of websites and books that he used in his research and that would further the knowledge of readers. The bibliography is reproduced, with hyperlinks to the books and websites mentioned, at http://bc.tech.coop/blog/080821.html.

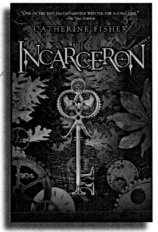

Fisher, Catherine

Incarceron

Dial Books, 2010. 442p. $17.99. 978-0-8037-3396-1.
Firebird, 2011. $9.99 Trade pb. 978-0-14-241852-9.
Listening Library, 2010. CD. $48. 978-0-307-70707-9.
$9.99 ebook. 978-1-101-53714-5.

Plot Summary:

Incarceron is a completely sealed prison: its inhabitants are the descendants of the original prisoners, and legend has it only one man has ever escaped. Finn clings to this legend, certain that there must be a way out, because there's obviously a way *in*: after all, he came from the outside, didn't he? His fellow inmates don't believe him—nobody has gone in or out of the closed system since its creation—but Finn's faith in the world outside is unwavering.

There is an outside, though: Claudia, the warden's daughter, lives there, in Era, her futuristic world impeccably mimicking a past she didn't live through. Anachronistic items and technology are outlawed. She dreads her arranged marriage (a dynastic pairing rather than a romantic one) and longs for the boy to whom she was betrothed as a child, the kind Giles who was killed in an accident before they were teens.

Claudia's and Finn's paths intersect when they find identical crystal keys through which they can communicate with each other, and together they begin plotting Finn's escape. But in order to get Finn out, Claudia needs to find Incarceron. The prison itself—sprawling, massive, sentient—should be impossible to hide, and yet there is no hint where the city-like structure could be.

Dystopian Elements:

There are two distinct dystopian-like words present in *Incarceron*: the closed prison and the open Realm of the Warden.

Incarceron was created to house and rehabilitate prisoners to form a perfect world, helped by the prison's own artificial intelligence and all-seeing eyes. This was an experiment, and to control for all potential variables, the prison was sealed off from the outside world. The one exception is the Warden, who oversees the prison's functioning. However, the formation of this flawless society is dependent on the inhabitants' buy-in to the world, their acceptance of Incarceron as both inescapable and all there is. Finn's insistence on finding a world outside the system unsettles the status quo among his fellow prisoners, among the Sapienti who created Incarceron and are locked within it, and with the sentient AI that the living prison has become.

The Warden lives out in the Realm, a world in which the King has decreed time be stopped in the 1800s, so that humanity could live without fear of changes. The Protocol of living in this make-believe past forbids using or pursuing any technological possibilities. Foregoing any technological advancement or study may keep the Realm's inhabitants from being needlessly troubled by change, but it also allows the residents to stagnate—or encourages them to subvert the regime. In either case, the insulation from change also requires the compliance and cooperation of the Realm's residents, but the Warden's hidden technologies subvert the King's intentions.

In both cases, the necessary belief in the worlds creates an environment in which compliance is valued above all else. On the one hand, an unchanging environment remains at the same level of perfection it attained at its cutoff; on the other, the inability to progress discourages citizens from considering ways to improve current conditions. Assuming a closed system like Incarceron will become perfection is counting on unpredictable elements of human behavior from people who are not reliably driven to achieve or maintain that perfection.

30-Second Booktalk:

Finn is a prisoner in Incarceron, the sprawling, living prison from which only one person has ever escaped. Claudia, the warden's daughter, is in another kind of prison: her father has arranged a marriage for her based on his own political aspirations. Claudia's and Finn's paths intersect when they find identical crystal keys through which they can communicate with each other. Together they plot Finn's escape, but getting him out will require finding the prison—which *should* be impossible to hide.

Readalikes:

Sapphique (Catherine Fisher) for more of Finn's story

Inside Out (Maria V. Snyder) for inescapable imprisonment

Ender's Game (Orson Scott Card) for political maneuverings juxtaposed with technological setting

The Maze Runner (James Dashner) for mysteries of enclosed spaces

House of Stairs (William Sleator) for psychological effects of unending enclosures

Potential Audience:

Dark, technological futures butt up against non-specific historical past in this blend of science fiction, fantasy, and romance. The primary audience will be high-school girls, but boys may also be intrigued by the living prison.

Book Trailer is available at: http://www.youtube.com/watch?v=gjbY2PtGqlQ&feature=player_embedded

Heath, Jack

The Lab (*The Lab*, Book 1)

Scholastic, 2008. 311p. $17.99. 978-0-545-06860-4.
$7.99 Trade pb. 978-0-545-07595-4.
$7.99 ebook. 978-0-545-28162-1.

• Originally published 2006

Plot Summary:

Special agent Six of Hearts is the best agent the Deck has. He can run faster, jump higher, and fight harder than any other agent, and his skills at escaping detection—and danger—are second to none. Or so he thought, until the day he broke into (and back out of) the ChaoSonic research facility and met his match—his *literal* match: someone with his same DNA, cloned in the same illegal experiment that made Six what he is. Kyntak claims to be a double agent, both working for and spying on the Lab, but his very presence threatens to expose Six's secret origins. The Lab is just as eager to protect that secret. Time is running out for Six to gather all the information he can and shut down the Lab—and the Lab is every bit as eager as he is to protect his secret.

Dystopian Elements:

By this unspecified future time, the ice caps have melted, flooding the earth and drowning all but one continent. That remaining continent survived only because of the seawall ChaoSonic built, sealing the City and its nine billion people into a space approximately the size of Australia. ChaoSonic controls everything, and also destroys it: thanks to the fog of pollution hanging over the city, life expectancy has been sharply curtailed, and it's unusual to see anyone older than sixty anymore.

Six isn't entirely human: he was created in a genetic experiment in the ChaoSonic-subsidiary Lab, splicing DNA from cheetahs, sharks, falcons, bloodhounds, and more into humans to create super-soldiers. The Lab's experiments haven't stopped at altering genetic code, though: ChaoSonic has also been working on cloning and aging. After cloning new potential super-soldiers, they can now rapidly age the cloned babies to adulthood almost overnight. Clones can also be used as "replacement parts" for these super-soldiers (a technology that saves Six's life).

ChaoSonic's control over the City is absolute; there are no other official entities functioning as any sort of government. The corporation has taken over the entire City, and under the guise of making things "equal," has forced all citizens to register for their Triple C's: ChaoSonic Citizen Card. The cards make sure that every registered citizen gets enough to eat, for example, but conversely this means that unregistered citizens will starve, unable to acquire food or other basic supplies. Periodic checkpoints at which citizens must have their Triple C's verified scrupulously log their whereabouts throughout the day. The corporate Takeover of the city and its subsequent security do not factor heavily into the plot, but may be relevant in the sequel.

30-Second Booktalk:

Car chases, hostages, robotic fighting machines—it's all in a day's work for Special Agent Six of Hearts. Six is the best agent the Deck has, and he's the Deck's best hope for bringing down ChaoSonic, the company that has taken over what's left of the world. But Six has a secret to protect about what makes him the Deck's best agent, and it's a secret that ChaoSonic is equally driven to protect—except they're less concerned about his survival.

Readalikes:

The House of the Scorpion (Nancy Farmer) for cloning elements

The Gardener (S.A. Bodeen) for cloning elements

Alex Rider (Anthony Horowitz) for espionage and secret agent tactics

Maximum Ride (James Patterson) for genetic enhancements and action-heavy plot

Remote Control (Jack Heath) for more of Agent Six's adventures

Potential Audience:

Avid readers may find issue with plot contrivances and stilted explanations, but teens more comfortable with action movies than books will enjoy the breakneck pace and episodic missions.

Itoh, Project

Harmony

Haikasoru, 2010. 252p. $14.99 pb. 978-1-4215-3643-9.

Plot Summary:

After the nuclear bombs and the diseases of the Maelstrom destroyed so much of the world's population, society has been rebuilt in such a way as to prevent it from happening again. Adults are implanted with "medicules," nanotech implants that monitor a person's physical and emotional well-being and summon assistance when necessary. Miach can see all the ways in which the technology that keeps them safe can be modified to cause destruction, and she plots a way she and her two best friends, Cian and Tuan, can destroy some of society's most valuable resources: themselves. Miach finds a way to override her technology, disallowing her body to absorb any nutrients from food, effectively starving herself to death. Cian and Tuan make similar attempts, but fail in their efforts.

Thirteen years have passed since her suicide effort, and Tuan is now working for the World Health Organization, investigating a recent wave of suicides: over 6,000 people attempted to end their own lives simultaneously and nearly half that number succeeded, including her old friend Cian. Tuan is the only one left from that original suicide pact—except in her research, she finds evidence to suggest that Miach may have survived.

To learn what Miach has been up to, however, Tuan has to go to the last person who officially saw her: Tuan's own father, a researcher with the Next-Gen Human Behavior Monitoring Group. In particular, the group sought ways to control a person's will to keep them from becoming a danger to themselves—a way to prevent suicides. The Harmony project unintentionally went beyond such benign motivations, though, ultimately finding a way to kill (or at the very least, shut down) consciousness and allow another's will to be exerted. As a child, Miach was one of the first subjects in the Harmony project, and now she's finding ways to exploit those early findings.

Dystopian Elements:

Following the Maelstrom, the survivors have an understandable fear of war and disease, the twin problems that decimated the world's population. In an effort to avoid disease in the future, scientists have developed nanotechnology to monitor and treat health, nutrition, and well-being. The WatchMe and the medicules send information back to servers, where it is used to track epidemics, immunizations, and individuals.

The medical standardization in Japan makes for a uniformity among its people: everyone maintains a healthy weight range and has a particular body type, with only slight standard deviations for variety. Poor skin or dark circles under the eyes are symptoms of poor self-care, and will result in a lowering of one's Social Assessment score. An individual's physical body is a public resource, and not taking care of oneself is reason enough to be carefully monitored as a potential threat to the well-ordered society.

Augmented Reality, or AR, lenses are in common usage, providing information about whatever the user looks at. The lenses also record what the wearer sees, storing the movies on a global server to be accessed by WHO staff. The conveniences of the Augmented Reality lenses outweigh the negatives, at least in the general public, though there are resistors to this and other technologies.

It is not the technology, however, that makes *Harmony* a dystopia, but rather humanity's willing embrace of it in the spirit of avoiding conflicts and discomforts. The widespread acceptance of the WatchMe makes it easier for the Next-Gen Human Behavior Monitoring Group to shut down human consciousness and free will in order to ensure sameness and equalize all members of society, creating a unified whole.

30-Second Booktalk:

As teenagers, Tuan, Cian, and Miach tried to starve themselves to death to prove they could override the health-monitoring nanotechnology implants. Only Miach succeeded. Thirteen years later, Tuan is researching a recent suicide epidemic with the World Health Organization, and learns some troubling things: first, that Miach may have survived after all, and second, that she might be behind the coordinated suicides of nearly 3000 people.

Readalikes:

Rash (Pete Hautman) for monitoring of health and safety

Little Brother (Cory Doctorow) and *1984* (George Orwell) for government surveillance

Uglies trilogy (Scott Westerfeld) for physical improvement and uniformity though medical technology

Feed (M.T. Anderson) for Augmented Reality's similarity to the feed

Potential Audience:

Targeting young 20-something sci-fi fans, *Harmony* has definite crossover appeal for mature high school readers. The bulk of the book is science-fiction dystopia, but the last third brings in elements of noir fiction, as Tuan searches for answers from wily, covert organizations.

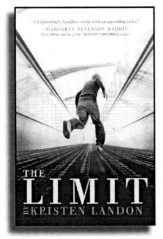

Landon, Kristen

The Limit

Aladdin, 2010. 288p. $15.99. 978-1-4424-0271-3.
$6.99 pb. 978-1-4424-0272-0. Simon & Schuster, 2012.
$34.99 CD. 978-1-4423-3416-8.
$12.99 ebook. 978-1-4424-0273-7.

Plot Summary:

A routine trip to the store for some groceries and other minor goods shouldn't have ended with Matt's mom being informed she was over her Limit. By the time they get home, an agent from the Federal Debt Rehabilitation Agency is waiting for them, ready to take Matt to the workhouse to work off some of his family's debt, bringing them back under their government-mandated limit.

Matt's first full day in the workhouse is one of testing: math, logic, computer animation, software manipulation. Matt scores well enough on the logic and technical parts that he qualifies for the Top Floor, where only the smartest teens go, doing the most interesting work. At first glance, the Top Floor is pretty swank: big rooms, state-of-the-art computers, a pool, a gym with all the best sports equipment. Matt's enjoying himself and his work, but he's still desperate to go home to his family, though he hasn't been able to get a message through to—or from—them.

Determined to find answers that the FDRA agent won't give him, Matt hacks into the computer system and searches the files. He's shocked to find a record of his sister, living and working a few floors beneath him, and he makes an attempt to find her. What he learns on that trip piques his curiosity, and now he's certain that there's more to this workhouse than it seems. With the help of some of his Top Floor friends, they can try to expose the exploitation in the workhouse system and the abuses that are specific to their facility.

Dystopian Elements:

Inspired by the realization that a parent's personal debt will get passed on to their children[8], *The Limit* takes that idea further, sending children to workhouses to pay down their parents' debts. The dystopian aspects here are twofold: first, that the government keeps close enough tabs on individuals' bank balances to know when a family is overdrawn, and second, that that government can take away children to settle the debts without giving families a choice of other debt-reduction processes.

In the first aspect, each family has a Limit, the amount of money they can safely spend, a sort of enforced budget. The Federal Debt Reduction Agency monitors families and enforces the limits, offering offenders different plans based on circumstances. Matt's family was not given a choice when they exceeded their limit, skipping ahead to Choice D: sending Matt to the workhouse.

---

[8] Author's website; http://www.kristenlandon.com/my-books/the-limit/behind-the-scenes-of-the-limit/

As Matt asks more questions of both the FDRA and his family, he uncovers some answers that change everything: after Matt went to the workhouse, the FDRA raised his family's limit to account for the money he was earning, and when his parents again exceeded it, the FDRA took his sister as well. But this is hardly the worst of it: Matt also uncovers the true costs of his stay in the workhouse, and how little of his money earned will actually help his family after room, board, and incidentals are deducted. The workhouse system has incentive to keep the teens they've taken from going back home; the teens do a variety of jobs (from menial tasks to highly-sophisticated computer programming) for relatively little pay.

There is little discussion in the novel about the work Matt is doing, for whom, or even any knowledge of what the other workhouses are like. The reader is left with a vague sense that the shadowy, all-seeing, all-monitoring government clearly has a purpose in mind for the workhouse kids and a reason for keeping their families in debt, but there is no indication of what that larger purpose might be.

30-Second Booktalk:

Matt is flipping through a magazine near the check-outs when his mom gets the news: their family is over their limit. Humiliations aside, this is Bad News. By the time they've gotten home from the store, there's already a black limo outside, waiting to take thirteen-year-old Matt to the workhouse to earn the money his family needs to get them back under their government-mandated limit. Matt's smart enough to know there's something fishy going on about the work that they're doing, and he is just the computer hacker to find out what.

Readalikes:

Carbon Diaries: 2015 and *Carbon Diaries: 2017* (Saci Lloyd) for government monitoring of commodity usage

Rash (Pete Hautman) for enforced employment to pay economic or societal debts

For the Win (Cory Doctorow) for children's/teen computer time as a business

The Sky Inside (Claire Dunkle) for similarities in tone of main character

Margaret Peterson Haddix for similarities in writing style

Potential Audience:

With a thirteen-year-old boy at its center, this novel will appeal to 7th-10th grade teens. The athleticism and computer hacking elements will draw in boys without alienating girls. Teens thinking about the current economy in the US will be interested in seeing one possible solution to individual economic crises.

http://www.youtube.com/watch?v=yasug1AB0t0&feature=player_embedded

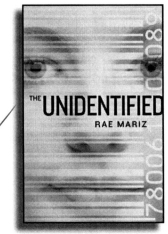

Mariz, Rae

The Unidentified

Balzer & Bray, 2010. 304p. $16.99. 978-0-06-180208-9. Harper Collins, 2010. $9.99 ebook. 978-0-06-201278-4.

Plot Summary:

As budgets shrink, educational quality shrinks, too. That is, until the corporations volunteer to take over, turning abandoned shopping malls into Game Centers that feed students educational content through video games and challenges. Social networking is a fact of life, and getting branded (a game sponsor taking an interest in you personally, using your every move as PR for their company) is the best thing that can happen to a student.

Katey—Kid—is vaguely uncomfortable with the surveillance, but it's the way things are. The students in her Game Center have pretty free reign to pursue whatever interests them, and one morning she witnesses that freedom taking the form of an anti-corporate prank. Who are the Unidentified who committed it? What kind of marketing are they trying to accomplish? Kid's questions get her noticed by the high-tech security firm Protecht, and their branding of her gives her far more social capital than she could have expected. But it also gives her more incentive to uncover the Unidentified—and not in the way her sponsors hope.

Dystopian Elements:

Nationwide, public schools contract with companies to bring funds to their cash-strapped district. A 1999 contract with Coca-Cola, for example, brought Washington, D.C., schools over $50,000 a month in extra funds, in exchange for selling exclusively the company's beverages.[9] *The Unidentified* takes this concept to the extreme: once local governments can no longer finance public schools, corporations step in to take over. Education becomes a matter of making good investments in students; that is, doing the most for the students who can and will provide the most profit to the company sponsoring those students. Individual corporations choose students to sponsor, branding the ones who are the most popular or influential, reinforcing their social status while encouraging students to distinguish themselves academically, athletically, or socially.

On the surface, this encouragement does not sound like a bad idea; anything that pushes students to excel is good. Creative budget-solving aside, what pushes this into dystopian territory is the control the corporations have exerted over society. Securing a good sponsorship is a ticket to a better life, and those sponsorships can be dropped (and with it all benefits, social and financial, afforded to the

---

[9] Kaufman, Marc. "Fighting the Cola Wars in Schools." *The Washington Post* March 23, 1999: Z12. http://www.washingtonpost.com/wp-srv/national/colawars032399.htm

branded individual) for any perceived infraction. Unbranded students, while not afforded the same opportunities as the branded, are still useful to the corporations for market research purposes.

Schools have become Game Centers, where learning is self-directed and students are encouraged to follow their own interests provided they complete regular "Challenges"—questions requiring research and learning that are sent to them via social network. The Facebook-like InTouch is a way of both bringing the student body together, following each other's actions and thoughts, and isolating them, making the online world more real than offline. One's social worth is announced by the number of followers, and the more followers, the better investment a company is making by branding that particular student.

Government has all but abandoned the world of *The Unidentified*, leaving behind corporations to be the new political structure. Surveillance is a fact of life. In Kid's words, "the world is a giant squinty eye, peeking in through the skylight, spying. Does that creep us out? No. We like the attention."[10]

30-Second Booktalk:

Kid goes to school in the Game Center, what corporations turned public schools into when they took over. The students are free to pursue their own interests, and Kid is shocked one morning to find that freedom taking the shape of an anti-corporate prank. High-tech security firm Protecht takes notice when Kid starts asking questions about the group who committed the prank, and their branding of her gives her far more social capital than she could have expected. But it also gives her more incentive to uncover the Unidentified—and not in the way her sponsors hope.

Readalikes:

So Yesterday (Scott Westerfeld) for cool-hunting and corporate power

Pattern Recognition (William Gibson) for cool-hunting and conspiracy

Feed (M.T. Anderson) and *Teen, Inc.* (Stefan Petrucha) for corporate invasion into everyday life

Little Brother (Cory Doctorow) for surveillance through internet channels

Scored (Lauren McLaughlin) for clear hierarchical rankings assigned by corporations

Potential Audience:

High school students, particularly those who are already questioning authority and social codes, will be drawn to this novel of educational decay and rebellion. The mystery into the Unidentified's mission will pull readers along into a well-developed future that can seem all too likely.

---

[10] *The Unidentified*, Rae Mariz, pg 2

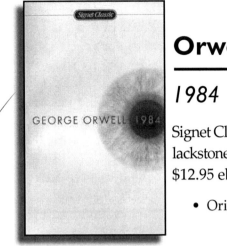

Orwell, George

1984

Signet Classics, 1990. 328p. $9.99 pb. 978-0-451-52493-5. B
lackstone Audio, 2007. $29.99 mp3-CD. 978-1-4332-0247-6.
$12.95 ebook. 978-0-547-24964-3.

- Originally published 1949

Plot Summary:

Winston Smith is an excellent member of the Outer Party: he's a dutiful civil servant, able to rewrite news releases and revise older reports to match the current political climate. He is skilled with Newspeak, but he has a secret: he is a rebel, engaging in Thoughtcrime regularly. Winston writes the revisionist histories but he does not *believe* them; he remembers evidence of the earlier truths and cannot bring himself to accept the Party's reinventions.

He is not alone: a young woman who works in the Ministry of Truth's fiction department slips him a note professing her love for him, and from their first clandestine meeting, finding Julia gives him an outlet. The knowledge that he's not alone in his thoughtcrime, in his distrust of Big Brother and the Party and Newspeak and everything else that goes along with their world, bolsters him, allowing him to take more risks toward rebelling against the Party.

Winston and Julia have plans for joining the Brotherhood, an organization dedicated to overthrowing the Party and Big Brother. Together they meet with Inner Party member O'Brien, Winson's boss at the ministry, believing him to be a member of the Brotherhood. O'Brien indeed provides Winston with a copy of a forbidden book on which the Brotherhood is founded, but also cautions him that he is not going to protect Winston, should Winston be found out.

Winston and Julia are eventually caught and arrested for Thoughtcrime, revealed by Thought Police officers posing as friends and shopkeepers. Through beatings and interrogation, O'Brien forces Winston to accept what the Party says as truth, in spite of any evidence to the contrary. Winston remains unwavering in his beliefs, though he attempts to tell O'Brien the things he assumes the Thought Police are waiting to hear from him. It is not until he is taken to Room 101 and faced with his deepest fears that he breaks and betrays Julia, relinquishing his love for her and accepting Big Brother in her place.

Dystopian Elements:

1984 is the bar by which all other dystopias are judged, not only because it is a classic, but because it features so many now-classic dystopian elements: totalitarianism, nationalism, thought control, censorship, surveillance.

As Winston learns in his interrogation, the point of the Party has never been about the good of the people, but rather about power. The Ministry of Truth, or the minitrue, has gone so far as to create Newspeak to prevent rebellious ideas from forming, removing select meanings and nuances from words to make it impossible to express ideas that would run counter to the party's ideals. The impossibility of expressing "bad" in any terms other than "ungood" is but one shade of meaning that Newspeak controls.

Winston's job is to rewrite history to agree with what the Inner Party has decided the new truth is, destroying evidence of the way events happened. Winston excises people from historical records, destroys photographs that would prove innocence of convicted criminals, transports wars from country to country, all on the whims of Inner Party officials. Occasionally the revisions involve not only removing material, but creating whole, fictional people and events in their place to cover the newly-jettisoned history.

Cameras and speakers are virtually everywhere, recording facial expressions and vocal intonations as well as overt conversations, and the recording devices are hardly the most insidious surveillance tools. Family members, particularly children, are encouraged to spy on each other and report the smallest signs of discontent with the Party or Big Brother. Thought Police are everywhere, frequently undercover as friends, shopkeepers, passersby.

Thought criminals are re-educated with a variety of torture techniques, from beating and questioning straight through Room 101, in which criminals are confronted with their worst fears (drowning, rats, fire, etc.) until they recant their beliefs. In Winston's case, the variety of techniques used against him eventually wears him down until he confesses to everything, even to things he hasn't done, and implicates everyone he's met regardless of their involvement in his supposed crimes. The torture leaves him not demoralized and unwilling to hold back information, but genuinely confused over what the truths are. The information Winston provides is unreliable at best, consistent with current research about the effectiveness of torture as an interrogation tool.[11]

It is no surprise that *"Orwellian"* has become the word of choice for discussing nightmarish, dystopian worlds, given the popularity of Orwell's novel and its unsettling, richly developed world.

30-Second Booktalk:

Winston is a dutiful civil servant, writing the revisions to history for the Party. He doesn't really *believe* them, though, and Thoughtcrime like that will eventually be his downfall. Winston knows that the price for not loving Big Brother is death, and his goal is to avoid it for as long as possible. Little does he know that his time is running out, his clandestine love affair is not as secret as he thinks, and the people he trusts are not to be trusted.

Readalikes:

Fahrenheit 451 (Ray Bradbury) for hoarding of old-world artifacts

Candor (Pam Bachorz) for brainwashing

Brave New World (Aldous Huxley) and *Delirium* (Lauren Oliver) for forbidden romances and emotionless, government-mandated pairings

Little Brother (Cory Doctorow) for surveillance and governmental abuse of power

Potential Audience:

Most teens will first read *1984* in a classroom, and the assignment of the classic may cause some resistance to its quality. However, they are likely to be drawn in by the richly-developed world and the book's cultural significance. Grades 10 and higher, into adulthood, will get the most out of this title.

---

[11] "Torture Debate: Is the U.S. War on Terror Legitimizing Torture?"

http://www.irct.org/Files/Filer/publications/CQGlobal_ResearcherTortureDebate.pdf

Venditti, Robert and Brett Weldele

The Surrogates

Top Shelf, 2006. $19.95. 978-1-891830-87-7.

The Surrogates: Flesh and Bone

Top Shelf, 2009. $14.95. 978-1-60309-018-6.

Plot Summary:

By 2054, Virtual Reality has advanced enough that people no longer have to physically leave their homes in order to go to work, socialize, or interact with the world in any meaningful way. With a simple helmet link-up, users can remotely direct their Surrogates through conversations and experiences and have all the data and sensations ferried back to the user. The Surrogates are androids, custom-made to fit each user's specifications for physical appearance, allowing users to choose how they will be perceived in the world.

Lt. Harvey Greer with the Central Georgia Metropolis is investigating a rare violent crime that has left two surrogates permanently disabled. Initially, he and his partner assume the androids were victims of a lightning strike, but when a third surrogate is disabled the same way—only indoors—they know they are dealing with something more than a simple storm. Greer catches up to the assailant near the second crime scene and learns his motive: to set the world back the way it was before surrogates were commonplace, and force people to live their lives in the flesh instead of through a helmet and a virtual-reality link. Then the assailant—nicknamed Steeplejack—tosses Greer's surrogate off the roof of the 15-floor building.

A break-in at a nearby lab results in another battle between police and Steeplejack, and this time, a piece of Steeplejack's robotic arm is left behind. Each part of a Surrogate is supposed to be engraved with serial numbers, but close examination reveals none. Following this lack of evidence leads Greer to Lionel Canter, inventor of the original surrogate. Canter had invented surrogates as a tool to assist the disabled interact in society, but their widespread adoption for purely superficial reasons has angered him into action. Steeplejack is revealed to be an early prototype Surrogate, controlled by Canter, but he is not neutralized in time to avoid the detonation of an electromagnetic pulse (EMP) over the city, disabling every Surrogate.

The prequel, *Flesh and Bone*, focuses on the investigation of a homeless man's murder by three teens who were operating their fathers' surrogates. Surrogates are only just becoming common among the upper classes, and the defense is building a lot of their case on reasonable expectations of privileged teens surrounded by these life-size avatars. A key witness is killed before the boys' trial, making conviction unlikely. Virtual Self, the company that created the Surrogates, is preparing to launch youth surrogates within the year. However, in the wake of the murder trial and the public outcry, the company scraps the project. These plot points are all referenced in the first book; this prequel fleshes out the back stories.

Dystopian Elements:

In a 2009 interview with *The Graphic Novel Reporter*, author Robert Venditti remarked that "we have a tendency to welcome technology into our lives without considering the impact it will have on us in the long run. Technology is a very seductive thing, and because of that, we don't often look before we leap."[12] Indeed, the applications of technological innovation to everyday life are almost always embraced, particularly when they can make everyday lives easier and safer. A technology that allows police officers to maintain order without risking their own lives in the process, or that allows people to socialize and interact with strangers without fear of rape or other violent crime, is hard to argue with. When a simple matter of a Surrogate's physical appearance can land jobs or seal contracts, it is no surprise how rapidly the technology is embraced.

The availability of the technology to overcome discrimination and all but guarantee personal safety should be the makings of a near-perfect society—but there will always be the potential for those worthy uses to be eclipsed by more superficial ones. Changing one's appearance to be more attractive is nothing new; the American Society of Plastic Surgeons reports a 77% increase in cosmetic surgery procedures performed in 2010 over 2000's data[13], including a 584% increase in anti-aging treatment Botox. Being able to experiment with one's physical appearance can give all people the same advantages, creating a meritocracy rather than relying on first physical impressions colored by racism, sexism, or other forms of discrimination.

The Surrogate system also keeps people safe from accidents and violence as well as health concerns. The VR link between Surrogate and user will ferry sensations from one to the other, allowing users to continue enjoying harmful habits (e.g., smoking, alcohol, and drug use) with the attendant lung, liver, and other bodily damage being absorbed by the surrogate rather than the user. Users can even send their Surrogates as stand-ins for sexual activity, again with the sensations being relayed back to the user without fear of disease.

But these things come at a price: what happens to one's identity when it is so easily transferred into an external persona? What happens when the Surrogate is replaced? While certain social binaries (male/female, young/old, black/white) are removed, does this sort of physical anonymity help or hinder social connections? *The Surrogates* raises many questions about identity and also about how far science can advance, before more is lost than gained.

---

[12] http://graphicnovelreporter.com/content/surrogate-father-interview
[13] http://www.plasticsurgery.org/Documents/news-resources/statistics/2010-statisticss/Overall-Trends/2010-cosmetic-plastic-surgery-minimally-invasive-statistics.pdf

30-Second Booktalk:

Nearly everyone has a Surrogate, an android with a virtual reality link-up to ferry physical input back to the user. Violent crime has been almost completely eradicated. Personally leaving the house is completely unnecessary. All in all, it's a perfectly safe society, allowing interactions without any of the dangers—Except for the techno-terrorist bent on destroying surrogates and forcing people to live their own lives—rather than experiencing them via a helmet.

Readalikes:

Uglies (Scott Westerfeld) for desire to change physical appearances to conventional beauty

Rash (Pete Hautman) for societal changes to improve personal safety

A.I. (film) for design of human-like androids

Surrogates (film) for the adaptation to the big screen

Powers (Brian Michael Bendis) for police team investigating crimes involving super powers

Blade Runner (film) for use of androids to perform tasks remotely

Potential Audience:

With its fairly straightforward layout and prose-based supplemental material, this graphic novel could be a good entry point to crime drama enthusiasts new to reading comics. While the characters are all middle-aged adults, the potential applications of robotics and virtual reality will interest older teens looking for a science-fiction story with substance.

Audio interview is available at: http://hw.libsyn.com/p/c/c/f/ccf5e25cc9583238/Comic_Book_Outsiders_ Episode49.mp3

Chapter 3:

Games

When times are good, officials encourage citizens to have fun, to relax, to engage in sports and recreation. When times are bad, it is even more pressing that people find ways to connect with each other and play games. This was evident even in America in World War II: by the fall of 1942, many minor-league baseball teams had disbanded due to the drafting of their players; with the need for entertainment, the All-American Girls Professional Ball League was formed by spring of 1943[1].

Games can provide a much-needed morale-boost—or distraction—in times of national crisis. They can highlight people with particular strategic or athletic abilities. They can also become a form of propaganda, and, as we'll see below, they can be a form of punishment and retribution in the name of entertainment and control.

Pete Hautman's *Rash* is a good example of many of these elements coming together: set in the United Safer States of America approximately 50 years from now, dangerous sports like football are outlawed, while sports like track & field have been modified to include far more safety equipment. In a world where harsh words toward another are grounds for imprisonment, a football team, however illegal, can be a great outlet for teens who need to vent rage and develop a focus and sense of teamwork that may be lacking in their regular lives.

The need for a physical outlet could be what drives teens to volunteer in *The Long Walk*, by Stephen King, in which 100 teens are chosen for a competition of endurance to see who can keep a steady walking pace the longest, all competing for the prize of having their every material wish fulfilled. The competition is the invention of the totalitarian Major, and the crowds of onlookers suggest that the walk is solely for the entertainment of the people.

This sort of last-man-standing battle is also seen in Suzanne Collins' *Hunger Games* trilogy and Koushun Takami's *Battle Royale*. In both these cases, the games are aired in mandatory broadcasts, ensuring that the citizens are aware of what is happening in the arenas at virtually any time. In this way, the government reminds its people what it is capable of and what can become of dissenters. Making participation in these games into an honor is a success of propaganda, distracting people from the government's harsh rules and totalitarian regimes.

Sports can help to identify the physically strong members of a society, but what about the mentally agile? Virtual games can highlight these skills: In *The Roar* (Emma Clayton), Mika Smiths is found to have a number with several special skills are discovered through a video-game tournament designed to identify those teens with mutant powers for the benefit of the government that can use them in a coming war. Conor Kostick's *Epic* features a teen with an unconventional approach to the problems presented in the virtual world on which their whole government is based.

Sports and games should be an easy way to foster teamwork and encourage relaxation—but there is nothing relaxing about a fight to the death, or a "game" that is more of a grueling, repetitive task than an enjoyable pastime. The six authors featured below show us the dark side of popular entertainments.

---

[1] http://www.aagpbl.org/index.cfm/pages/league/12/league-history

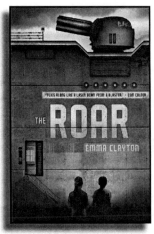

Clayton, Emma

The Roar

Chicken House, 2009. 496p. $17.99. 978-0-439-92593-8.
$8.99 Trade pb. 978-0-439-92785-7.

Plot Summary:

Mika Smith is one of the oldest teens inside the wall, among the first children born after a thirty-year moratorium on pregnancy. His twin sister Ellie would also be among the oldest, if not for her kidnapping and death a year before. Mika has never gotten past his sister's death, though, because he's certain it didn't really happen: he can *feel* Ellie out there, and he's certain her death was a cover-up.

Deeply suspicious of authority, Mika begins getting into trouble at school, refusing to drink the vitamin supplements the new Youth Development Foundation has provided to all students. His small rebellion earns him a week-long suspension, during which time his classmates have been obsessively playing the new arcade game Pod Fighter. Mika soon discovers he is a natural pilot, and intuitively knows that playing the game will bring him closer to finding Ellie. With his new friend Audrey in the gunner seat, Mika passes through the qualifying round into a Pod Fighter competition, and the pair begin advancing through the rankings until the final championship. Most of the teens are playing for coveted apartments in the Golden Turrets, a chance for their families to move out of the slums and into unthinkable luxury, but Mika 's win affords him a bigger prize: a reunion with Ellie.

Before he can see his sister, though, the Golden Turrets are shaken by rioters from the Shadows beneath them, parents whose children have been taken to fight a war. Mika and Audrey escape in a stolen pod fighter, flying over the wall to freedom. They are shocked to discover that the world beyond the wall is not the poisoned, desolate landscape they'd been taught about, but rather a lush, green world full of uninfected animals and people. The knowledge that the plague was a hoax and that the wall was built, so that the rich and powerful could save the planet for themselves is enough for Mika to understand why the children are being drafted into a war effort, and who the war will be waged against. He is finally reunited with his sister, and the siblings are allowed to go home to their parents.

A sequel, *The Whisper*, was published in early 2012.

Dystopian Elements:

Forty-three years ago, some plague-ridden animals escaped from a laboratory and infected the other animals. Televised news clips showing the insane, murderous animals told citizens of the dangers of the world outside the wall. Now there is a test of the plague sirens every Sunday, to make sure people still know what to do if an animal should happen to get inside the wall.

Against this post-apocalyptic backdrop is dystopia built on propaganda. The hoax of the plague, accomplished through faked televised reports instead of any real, firsthand accounts, was kept going by the weekly plague siren tests and the government's rules about plague preparedness. The immediacy of television convinced citizens that the plague was rendering the entire planet permanently uninhabitable, without needing to show anything other than a few isolated clips that may or may not have anything to do with the situation.

Now, the people are so accustomed to living the way that they have, under constant threat of the plague, that they hardly question the government's rules about having well-fitting paper plague suits available for every household member or other seemingly-benign living adjustments. With enough exposure to it, people begin to forget that the message came to them over the television instead of firsthand, and with no reason to suspect the government of trickery, they believe the messages they've been given.

Mika's discovery of the clean, plague-free world beyond the wall highlights the power that the rich have, to wall off the lower classes and make them believe it is for their own good. Inside the wall, people are packed tightly together in strict classes, with little in-between: the wealthy live in the Golden Turrets, the luxury apartments; the poor live in the slums in tiny fold-down apartments prone to mildew and dampness; the *really* poor live in the Shadows, where they frequently die of illnesses induced by living in mold and dankness. None of the teen characters come from wealthy families, and when teens are rounded up to become an army for the government, the children of the upper-class families are not drafted with them. Children are selected for the draft by a lengthy screening process—the Podfighter tournament—that separates the best fighters from the weakest. Because the prizes are material goods and luxury apartments, the rich teens do not compete, being unmotivated by the promise of prizes they already have.

While class issues do not in themselves make a book a dystopia, it is the government-created class structure that both makes Mika's society look to be running smoothly and sends it crashing down as soon as the balance is disturbed.

30-Second Booktalk:

Mika has never gotten over the death of his twin sister—mostly because he's positive she's not dead. He can *feel* her out there, somewhere, and it's up to him to find her. When the new Podfighter game comes to the arcades, Mika instinctively knows there's something about it that will bring him closer to his missing sister. Podfighter competitions already have pretty high stakes, but for Mika, they just got a little higher.

Readalikes:

Ender's Game (Orson Scott Card) for video games as realistic war simulation

Epic (Conor Kostock) for video gaming

Runaways (Brian K. Vaughan) or *Witch and Wizard* (James Patterson) for teens with mutant powers

Uglies (Scott Westerfeld) for flying sequences and exploring beyond city limits

The Maze Runner (James Dashner) for having safety only inside walls

Inside Out (Maria Snyder) for shocking discoveries about the world outside

Potential Audience:

Middle-school boys may be excited by all the video-game action, but older teens and more avid readers will likely be bored by the lengthy podfighter tournaments and predictable plots.

Collins, Suzanne

The Hunger Games

Scholastic, 2008. 384p. $17.99. 978-0-439-02348-1.
$8.99 pb. 978-0-4390-2352-8. Scholastic Audio, 2008.
$39.95 CD. 978-0-545-09102-2.
$14.99 ebook. 978-0-545-22993-7.

Catching Fire

Scholastic, 2009. 400p. $17.99. 978-0-439-02349-8. Scholastic Audio, 2009.
$39.95 CD. 978-0-545-10141-7.
$17.99 ebook. 978-0-545-22724-7.

Mockingjay

Scholastic, 2010. 400p. $17.99. 978-0-439-02351-1. Scholastic Audio, 2010.
$39.95 CD. 978-0-545-10142-4.
$17.99 ebook. 978-0-545-31780-1

- *The Hunger Games* trilogy

Plot Summary:

As punishment for the uprising in Panem so many years ago, the Capital now demands two Tributes from each district in its annual Hunger Games: a televised battle to the death in a closed arena, pitting teenage boys and girls against each other until only one remains. Contestants are not all on equal footing inside the arena: wealthier districts can afford to train their teens as Career Tributes and send them gifts while they compete, whereas the more struggling districts are forced to rely just on the skills of their tributes.

Katniss Everdeen is from District 12, one of the poorest districts, and feeds her family by illegally hunting game beyond the District's borders. When her sister's name is drawn as District 12's tribute, Katniss volunteers to take her place without a second thought. Before entering the games, she and her fellow District 12 tribute, Peeta, are whisked off on the whirlwind publicity tour in which Peeta discloses his love for Katniss. Katniss chooses to see this disclosure as a bid for audience sympathy, which could earn him extra gifts in the arena.

Twenty-four teens are ushered into the arena, and within the first day that number is cut nearly in half. Katniss's hunting skills protect her, but Peeta—the son of a baker—does not have the same abilities. The star-crossed lovers angle changes things in the arena of ever-changing rules: for the first time, there can be two winners, provided they are from the same district and win as a pair. With this announcement, Katniss searches for Peeta and finds him wounded and ill. Playing the part of a lovesick teen, Katniss nurses him back to health and keeps them both hidden until they are the only tributes left.

According to the previous announcement, the pair should have been declared the winners, but the Gamemakers attempt to force a dramatic conclusion by reversing their rule: one of them must kill the other to end the game. Katniss brings Peeta a handful of poisonous berries, so that they can commit suicide together rather than allowing the Gamekeepers to manipulate them anymore. Before they can follow through, the Gamekeepers agree to name them both winners and release them from the arena. On returning home, Katniss is warned that her small defiance has made many political enemies.

The victory tour at the beginning of *Catching Fire* begins with a visit from President Snow, who is displeased with Katniss's actions in the arena. He instructs Katniss to convince everyone in District 12, and along the tour, that her actions were borne out of love for Peeta rather than any idea to rebel. Unfortunately, nearly every action she takes on the tour is seen as a secret signal to the rebellion brewing among the districts' residents.

Katniss returns home to District 12 in time for the next Hunger Games. This being the seventy-fifth year of the games, a Quarter Quell year, the rules for choosing combatants are different: rather than being chosen from the pool of teenaged residents, they will be chosen from the pool of previous winners. Katniss is the only female winner District 12 has ever seen; Peeta takes the place of the only other male winner, their damaged, alcoholic mentor in the first Games.

Back inside the arena, Katniss and Peeta stay close together, and partner with some of the most intelligent contestants. Together this small group discovers the rhythms of the arena and its hazards, protecting each other from the battery of physical and psychological assaults. With the ability to predict when the lightning storms will hit, they work together to harness that electrical power, using it to fire at the force field that encloses the arena.

Regaining consciousness on the way to District 13, long believed destroyed in the original Panem uprising, Katniss learns that several of her Quarter Quell teammates have been captured by the Capitol. With all that has happened, Katniss agrees to be the face of the rebellion in *Mockingjay*. Along with her friends from the arena, she rescues Peeta and the other captives from the Capitol, but is distressed to find that Peeta has been brainwashed against her and attempts to kill her. He gets medical treatment back in District 13, but his healing process is a slow one.

Katniss's team launches a rebel attack on the Capitol, meaning to start in an unprotected neighborhood, but their mission turns out to be far more dangerous than they'd planned for. On arriving at the Capitol, they get caught up in a violent assault that kills many children and members of the rebel medical team, which included Katniss's sister. Katniss goes straight for President Snow, intending to kill him, but he tells her the attacks were orchestrated by President Coin, the leader of District 13. When her chance comes to execute Snow, she recognizes the truth to what he says and executes Coin instead. Snow is killed in the ensuing riot.

Dystopian Elements:

From the beginning, the *Hunger Games* trilogy is about power: personal power, political power, the power of an individual to rise against a stronger foe. Katniss grows into her power, from being a reluctant entrant into the Games to embracing her role as the face of a rebellion. The Capitol holds an enormous amount of power, forcing its citizens to sacrifice two teens each year in punishment for a rebellion that happened more than half a century before the teens were born.

The Hunger Games has all the markers of a dystopia: a totalitarian government; a redivided United States following a global war; shortages and unequal distribution of food, wealth, even technology. Science has created new animal hybrids with military applications, from the jabberjays meant to spy on rebels and carry conversations back to tracker jackets to wasps whose venom can induce hallucinations and be used in brainwashing. These elements, however, are all background to the story's main themes, centering on the effects of war.

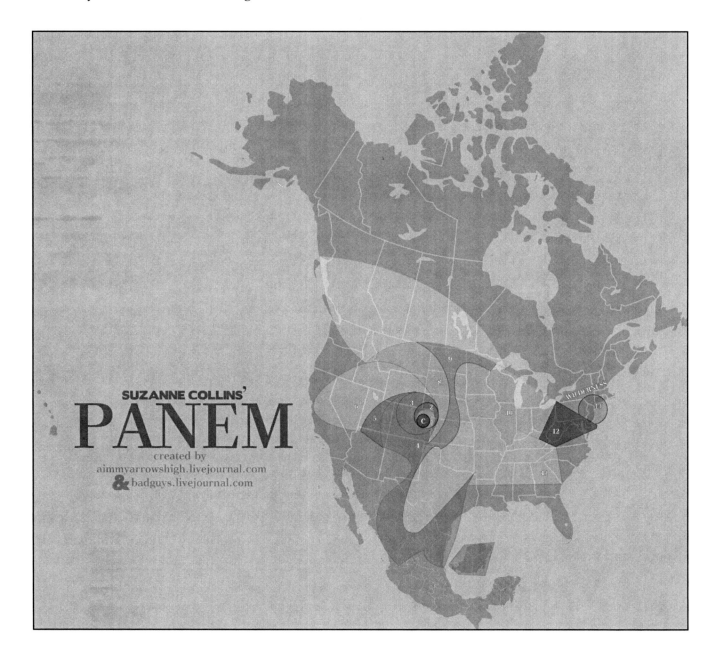

The Capitol instituted the Games as punishment for an uprising, a second war in the Dark Days after the global war led to the restructuring of North America. That war led to the destruction of an entire district, what had been New England and a section of the Mid-Atlantic states[2]. Growing up in the poverty of District 12, drafted into the Games, Katniss is a victim of that long-ago war. Now there is another rebellion brewing, a war of the people against the Capitol, and Katniss is again an unwitting victim, becoming a symbol of rebellion for her small act of personal defiance.

"An overt critique of violence, the series makes warfare deeply personal, forcing readers to contemplate their own roles as desensitized voyeurs," says *The New York Times*[3], commenting on Collins' dual inspirations of televised war coverage juxtaposed against reality television. The packaging of the Tributes for the media tour before the games, and for the Victory Tour after, sends a message that the Games are about spectacle instead of punishment, about fame and glory instead of death and oppression. The series is a commentary on our penchant for reality television, on how easily we overlook brutality in the name of entertainment.

30-Second Booktalk:

Every year, the government selects two tributes from each district to compete in the Hunger Games, a televised battle to the death in an enclosed stadium. Katniss has to hope that the illegal hunting she's been doing for years to feed her family is enough training, because it's all she's got. And the only ally she has inside the arena is her fellow District 12 tribute, who is the only one in the games who *might* retain his humanity by the end.

Readalikes:

Battle Royale (Koushun Takami) for similar battle-to-the-death games

Achewood: The Great Outdoor Fight (Chris Onstad) for similar battle-to-the-death games, though in comic format with crass humor

Chaos Walking trilogy (Patrick Ness) for political maneuverings

Theseus and the Minotaur (mythology) for similar ideas of tributes (and the source material for the series)

Potential Audience:

This compelling series has been capturing high school readers and adults since its inception. Middle school readers have enjoyed it, as well, but the themes of war and violence make this more suited to an older audience.

---

[2] Based on North American geography and resources and evidence in the books. The evolution and logic of the map can be found at http://aimmyarrowshigh.livejournal.com/32461.html?thread=165069. An updated version can be found in "The Panem Companion: An Unofficial Guide to Suzanne Collins' Hunger Games, from Mellark Bakery to Mockingjay" (Smart Pop Books, December 2012).

[3] http://www.nytimes.com/2011/04/10/magazine/mag-10collins-t.html?pagewanted=all

Hautman, Pete

Rash

Simon Pulse, 2007. 249p. $9.99 Trade pb. 978-0-689-86904-4.

- Originally published 2006

-

Plot Summary:

Bo is from a family with a history: both his father and brother are incarcerated for anger-based crimes (road rage and a fistfight, respectively), and Bo is acutely aware of his own struggles with self-control. His rival, Karlohs, intentionally needles him, going so far as to give himself a rash and blame it on Bo. The resulting school-wide psychosomatic rash lands Bo in a heap of trouble, in spite of it not actually being his fault. Name-calling has already put him on probation, so throwing a punch at Karlohs, while satisfying, seals his fate. Bo is off to the Canadian tundra to fill his thirty-six-month sentence in a pizza factory, miles from nowhere and surrounded by hungry polar bears.

Work in the pizza factory isn't unbearable, but it's far from pleasant. However, things take a turn for the better when he's accepted into the factory's highly-selective, highly-illegal football team. Playing football gives Bo the outlet he never knew he'd been looking for, but it's not enough to help him curb his every impulse.

In between Bo's athletic and personal problems, there's the matter of his science-project AI he'd been working on when he was kicked out of school: Bork has somehow, against all odds, developed sentience and a sense of humor, and is now creeping through the WindO as a webghost with legal aspirations.

Dystopian Elements:

The United Safer States of America have outlawed virtually anything dangerous: alcohol, pocketknives, self-mutilation (tattoos and body piercing, mainly), even name-calling, which could damage the victim's feelings. With the number of things now considered crimes, it's no wonder that nearly a quarter of the population is incarcerated, serving their sentences manufacturing goods in factories. The penal system is more about a labor force than corrections, as the USSA relies on the manual labor to keep the major corporations going.

The government has also regulated safety equipment in all high-school athletics: runners must have supportive footwear with shock-absorbing soles, knee pads, and helmets, and all running is done on spongy tracks to reduce risk of injury. Students who have demonstrated anti-social tendencies (including fighting, but also verbal altercations, throwing things, and other displays of temper) are required to take a pill each morning to slow their reactions and give them time to reconsider their actions.

Hautman argues that *Rash* is a logical extension of current safety standards: "I sometimes think we are so obsessed with safety we miss out on much of what life has to offer. If you wanted to be really safe, you would … never play contact sports, or ride a skateboard, or go for a hike in the mountains, or speak to a stranger, or drive a car, or give birth to a child...or do much of anything at all. What if this safety trend continues? What will it be like in another fifty years? How safe do we want to be?"[4] *Rash*'s 2074 time setting points to how quickly the USA became the USSA, moving from current safety measures of seat belts and bicycle helmets to the eventual illegality of french fries—a prescient addition by Hautman when considering the number of cities banning trans fats in restaurants in recent years. (As of the original publication, only the city of Tiburon, California[5], and Montgomery County, Maryland[6], had official bans on trans fats; New York City's mandatory ban took effect December 6 of 2006[7].)

30-Second Booktalk:

When Bo lets his temper get out of hand, he's not surprised to find himself serving a 36-month sentence in a pizza factory on the tundra. What does surprise him is when he makes the elite factory football team—despite football having been outlawed in the United Safer States of America decades ago. The game gives Bo the outlet he never knew he'd been looking for, but it's not enough to help him overcome *all* his fears. There are still those hungry polar bears on the other side of the fence, after all.

Readalikes:

Carter Finally Gets It (Brent Crawford) for football details and humorous style

Be More Chill (Ned Vizzini) for smart-mouthed AI/computer

1984 (George Orwell) for increases in security

Epic (Kostick) for a world in which violence is grounds for exile

Potential Audience:

Sports fans looking for a quick, well-paced science fiction story will find lots to appreciate here. The combination of sarcasm and clever turns of phrase inject levity into the story without it becoming full-on comedy. Readers will root for Bo, despite how many of his problems are entirely of his own making. Eighth grade and up would likely enjoy this (older readers will get more out of it, of course), particularly reluctant reader boys.

---

[4] Copyright Pete Hautman, originally published http://www.petehautman.com/rashguide.html

[5] http://www.bantransfats.com/projecttiburon.html; retrieved 4/21/11

[6] Spivack, Miranda S. "Montgomery Bans Trans Fats in Restaurants, Markets." *The Washington Post* May 16, 2007. http://www.washingtonpost.com/wp-dyn/content/article/2007/05/15/AR2007051501387.html

[7] City of New York. "Health department proposes two changes to city's health code for public comment." Press release (2006-09-26). http://www.nyc.gov/html/doh/html/pr2006/pr093-06.shtml.

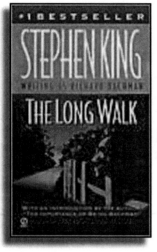

King, Stephen

The Long Walk

Signet, 1999. 370p. $7.99 pb. 978-0-451-19671-2. Penguin Audio, 2010. $39.95 CD. 978-0-14-242783-5.

- Originally published 1979

Plot Summary:

Out of a pool of thousands of applicants, one hundred teenage boys are selected annually to participate in the national sport—the Long Walk—in which the boys must keep a pace of at least four miles per hour or be shot, and the last boy walking wins, anything he wants for the remainder of his life. The walk is unrelenting; it does not stop for darkness, poor weather, or any other reason, making the competition not just one of physical stamina but of overcoming the challenges of sleep deprivation.

Five days into the walk, only two boys remain: Garraty and Stebbins. Stebbins reveals himself to be the illegitimate son of the Major, who runs the Walk. Throughout the walk, Stebbins has shown no signs of physical or mental fatigue, and in the face of such an opponent, Garraty decides to give up and allow Stebbins to win. However, when Garraty attempts to tell Stebbins of his decision, Stebbins collapses and dies, making Garraty the winner. Garraty's mental state is such that he does not seem to realize that the Walk is over, and in spite of the Major's efforts to make him stop, he continues walking, even breaking into a run at the story's conclusion.

Dystopian Elements:

With the story sticking close to the Walk, readers do not get a good look at the society and culture that surround this event. However, through the boys' conversations, we can piece together bits of information that tell the story.

The world of *The Long Walk* is an alternate-history United States, one in which the government has been the victim of a military takeover and replaced with a totalitarian regime, possibly led by the Major. Garraty's father is missing and presumed dead after making some negative comments about the government. The purpose of the Walk is unclear: it may be a way for the government to remind citizens of its power or an attempt to entertain the people with the sadistic game and the possibility of untold riches for the winner.

Participation in the Walk is entirely voluntary; Walkers are given several opportunities to withdraw from competition prior to starting the Walk. The number of bystanders and onlookers foreshadows our current fixation on reality television and competition and our willingness to watch suffering in the name of entertainment.

30-Second Booktalk:

How long can you keep up a steady walking pace of at least four miles per hour? An afternoon? All day? Could you last five days, if your life depended on it? 100 teenage boys have that very hope, applying to be a part of The Long Walk, even though they know that dropping below that speed for more than 30 seconds will mean their death, even though they know that only one of them will win. All they have to do is keep walking.

Readalikes:

The Hunger Games (Suzanne Collins) and *Battle Royale* (Koushun Takashi), for fight-to-the-death competition

Speed (film) for need to keep a certain pace or risk death

The Running Man (Richard Bachman/Stephen King) for other willing participants in deathly games

I Am the Cheese (Robert Cormier) for a long physical journey toward unwanted truths

Potential Audience:

High schoolers will be drawn into the conversations of the teenage boys, and the idea of people willingly volunteering for the competition.

Kostick, Conor

Epic

Viking, 2004. 384p. $17.99 978-0-670-06179-2.
$9.99 pb. 978-0-14-241159-9.
$9.99 ebook. 978-1-101-17653-5.

Plot Summary:

Violence was banned from the world generations before Erik was born. All disputes are handled in Epic, the online role-playing game that functions as real-world economy and judicial system. Everyone plays the game; money gained from slaying monsters in-game buys goods and services in the unclipped world.

Erik is good at the game, but he's run into some trouble recently: to study the great dragon's attack pattern, he's allowed his character to die over and over, sacrificing all of his equipment each time. His parents are disappointed with his frequent losses, as a good performance in the game is Erik's only chance at attending Mikelgard University, especially now that his father has been exiled. But Erik is pretty sure he's figured out the secret to bringing down the dragon, and he convinces his friends to fight with him. Following Erik's direction, they fight as a team, and after many hours, succeed in slaying the creature—only the second time in the history of the game that a dragon has been slain.

Erik and his team acquire the dragon's treasure hold, instantly turning them into the wealthiest players in the game. But the dragon isn't the only near-invincible enemy they must battle: in order to get Erik's father back, they must challenge Central Allocations, their real-world government. But Central Allocations has their own reasons for keeping the poor districts from gaining too much power. Meanwhile, a series of newspaper articles has been published, discussing the successes of these apparent underdogs and the need for a revolution: "We must awaken from this unreal game and demand a new organization of society—one where decisions are taken by vote and not by challenges in the biased fighting arenas."[8]

With their new-found resources, Erik and his friends begin to organize to destabilize the CA. When word gets out in the game, players from all over the world join Erik's army. In spite of heavy losses, Erik's team fights their way to a hidden tower and turns the key to permanently end the game.

Dystopian Elements:

New Earth was built around the idea that there would be no physical violence. Government, resource allocation, justice, and conflict resolution all happen within the fantasy computer game Epic. There is little distinction between in-game and real-world; New Earth's economy is based on in-game currency and requests to the Central Allocations committee are made through challenges in which game characters battle in the game arena.

---

[8] p207, hardcover edition

The Central Allocations committee (CA), though, has had decades to strengthen itself, making it nearly invincible against the teams and individuals who challenge them. When, for the first time, a group from a poor, agricultural district comes close to winning a challenge, the CA calls a draw and agrees to the request for more solar panels. Behind closed doors, the CA meets and agrees: despite the game's provisions to avoid player-characters killing one another, they will override the system to release the Executioner character and eliminate these players who have nearly beaten them. That their power can be so freely abused makes the game—and the real-world society—into a dictatorship instead of democracy; the desire to end violence has instead given rise to a deep inequality and the knowledge that citizens have virtually no recourse against the government.

30-Second Booktalk:

Following yet another death in Epic, Erik creates a new character. On a whim, he chooses a female form, allots all her aptitude points to beauty, and chooses an unusual character class: Swashbuckler. Such an unusual character makes Epic into a whole new game—which is exactly what Erik needs, if he's going to slay the second dragon in Epic's history and challenge the Central Allocation government to release his father from exile.

Readalikes:

Heir Apparent (Vivian Vande Velde) for fully-immersive video games

The Roar (Emma Clayton) for gaming used to gain political control

For the Win (Cory Doctorow) for gamers forming teams to combat government or corporation officials

Saga and *Edda* (Conor Kostick) for more of Erik's adventures in the post-Epic world

Potential Audience:

Middle and high school gamers and fantasy readers will be particularly drawn into the action of *Epic*. The length may turn off more reluctant readers, but once they start, they will likely be hooked by the engrossing plot.

Takami, Koushun, and Yuji Oniki (translator)

Battle Royale

Haika Soru, 2009 (expanded ed.). 632p. $16.99 978-1-4215-2772-7.

- Originally published 1999

Plot Summary:

Forty Japanese high-school juniors are en route to a study trip when the whole busload is gassed. When the teens regain consciousness, they are in a classroom on a small deserted island, being informed about their participation in the Program. The Program is a military research project, ostensibly, but it's more about terrorizing and keeping control over the people. Each year, one class—students in their third year of high school—is selected to compete in the Program, a fight to the death until only one student remains.

The students are fitted with transmitter collars and each given a backpack containing food, water, and a weapon. The weapons are not all equal—one student finds a machine gun; another student receives a fork. One by one, the students are released into the island. Their movements are tracked by the collars; any students attempting to escape or enter a forbidden area will have their collars remotely detonated. All collars will be detonated simultaneously if there have been no deaths in a 24-hour period.

One by one, the students pick each other off until only four remain: one antagonist and a trio that includes Shogo, the lone survivor of a previous Program. Together the trio kills the antagonist, and then Shogo turns on his two remaining classmates, claiming he will kill them, as well. He fires his gun twice into the air, tricking the surveillance microphones, then quickly dismantles their collars. He boards the winner's ship for his second time and smuggles his two friends aboard.

Once on board, Shogo has a shootout with the Program supervisor and some armed soldiers. With the adults killed, Shogo tells his friends how to escape to the United States, then succumbs to his injuries. The last two students return to the mainland and make plans to flee the country, but their safe passage is not assured, as they are spotted boarding a train.

Dystopian Elements:

The Program is billed as a military research initiative, watching how students will fight to save themselves and when—and how—they form and break alliances. That is the official goal of the Program, but the truth is much murkier than that: the randomness of the class chosen, the televised updates on each death, the willingness to kill all the teens if they refuse to kill each other; all these things add up to a culture of fear and terror designed to keep people from organizing insurrections.

The government that forces the Program on its teens is not the focus of the book, but the reader is never able to truly forget that it's there: the Program is the sort of thing that could only happen when the government has taken absolute control and terrorized its citizens into submission. Each of the 40 students in the game is given a back story, giving the reader not only a reason to care about them but an insight into what makes them react the way they do, from letting another student kill them quickly to suicide to vicious fights for survival. Their differing reactions underline the fears and values that they have internalized from their lives prior to the Program and carried to the isolated island with them.

The government's control over its citizens is also evident in its anger at having been outsmarted, with three people surviving through the end of the game and two of them fleeing the country. Readers do not know what ultimately becomes of these two, but there is an implication that government officials will be keeping close tabs on their whereabouts for later punishment.

30-Second Booktalk:

Forty Japanese high school students get detoured on a field trip and wake up in an unfamiliar classroom, where they are informed that their class has been randomly chosen for that year's Program: a fight to the death until only one student remains. Each student is given a backpack containing food, water, and a weapon of varying quality (from machine guns to forks) and released. Alliances are made, then broken; friends are betrayed and killed; one person will win and everyone will lose.

Readalikes:

The Hunger Games (Suzanne Collins) for similar premise

Achewood: The Great Outdoor Fight (Chris Onstad) for similar (though less totalitarian) premise

"The Most Dangerous Game" (Richard Connell) for a short story of hunting a person on an island

Lord of the Flies (William Golding) for students abandoned to survive on an island

Battle Royale (film and manga adaptations) for adaptations of source material to new media

Fight Club (Chuck Palahniuk) for graphically violent battles

The Drifting Classroom (Kazuo Umezo) for a class of Japanese students fighting violently for survival

Potential Audience:

The graphically-described violence is likely to turn off many readers, but strong-stomached fans of horror and gore will be turning pages late into the night. The plot is engrossing and each character, no matter how villainous, is given adequate space in the novel, making each character at least a bit sympathetic. Given its mature content, *Battle Royale* is most appropriate for grades 11 and up.

Chapter 4:

Social Issues

Most people, on hearing the word "dystopia," will automatically think of surveillance, of totalitarian governments, of conspiracies targeting particular people or hiding terrible secrets. As we've seen previously in these pages, there are plenty of dystopias fitting those descriptions. But these are not the only themes that dystopias cover: many dystopias shine a light on a variety of social issues, frequently taking current problems and projecting to—and sometimes past—a logical end.

One of the most well-known dystopias in this category is Margaret Atwood's *The Handmaid's Tale*, in which women have been stripped of all their possessions, financial holdings, even their families and names, to ensure they have no power left over the men who now run the government. Offred—her new name a reflection of the man she now serves—has been taken from her husband and son to be a handmaid for a government official, ideally bearing his children.

Similar themes of classism and reproductive technologies are present in Aldous Huxley's classic *Brave New World*, which deals with assigned social groups and foresees more modern fertility treatments. Reproduction is a central theme of several recent teen dystopias, as well. *Bumped* (Megan McCafferty) assigns reproduction to teens in the wake of an infertility virus that affects adults; it is less about the virus, though, than about the fame and social capital to be gained by "bumping" with sought-after partners. Allie Condie's *Matched* trilogy focuses on a world in which the choices of romantic partners are removed, allowing the government to assign partners with a goal of creating the strongest offspring.

Lauren Oliver's *Delirium* follows similar guidelines of matched partners, but goes a little further by performing surgery on teens to curb emotions like love. Citizens of the titular town in the movie *Pleasantville* have always repressed their emotions; when two modern teenagers get stranded in the 1950s-era sitcom, they force the town to confront their emotions and allow the town—and themselves—to flourish. In the world of Lois Lowry's *The Giver*, the Keeper of Memories holds onto strong emotions and desires, so that the townspeople do not have to experience them. People are expected to minimize their attachments to other people and objects. (The emphasis on distance and conformity is also true of the companion book *Gathering Blue*; these expectations are reversed in the final novel of the series, *Messenger*.)

Conformity is also at the forefront of Scott Westerfeld's *Uglies* trilogy, forcing teens into plastic surgery at age 16 in order to match societal ideals of attractiveness. (The companion book to the trilogy, *Uglies*, takes the opposite approach, using a "fame economy" in which a person's value increases with how much they can stand apart from the crowd, rather than conforming to it.) Honor, the main character in Allegra Goodman's *The Other Side of the Island*, wants nothing more than to be like the other students in spite of her parents' odd teachings; in time she comes to accept the school's propaganda as truth and assimilates into her new home. Tris, the main character in Veronica Roth's *Divergent*, needs to form her own opinions about the other factions instead of blindly accepting what she was taught in her old community.

Gender roles, conformity, emotional overloads: these are issues teens cope with every day. It's easy to believe that life would be better if the difficult choices were made for us. The following seventeen titles show us why that isn't so.

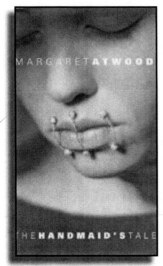

Atwood, Margaret

The Handmaid's Tale

Anchor, 1998. 311p. $15 Trade pb. 978-0-385-49081-8.

- Originally published 1985

Plot Summary:

A supposed terrorist attack has killed the president and most of Congress. In its wake, the Sons of Jacob step in and take control over what was the United States, suspending the constitution on the pretext of restoring order. Women are immediately targeted by the patriarchal group, having their personal assets frozen and their rights stripped away.

Offred remembers her life before the revolution, the life she led with her husband and daughter before their failed attempt to flee to Canada. In this era of declining birth rates and forced female subservience, Offred is taken as a handmaid, a woman used for reproduction. She is currently in her third assignment, working for the Commander. Once a month, they participate in a sexual ritual in which the Commander attempts to impregnate Offred, who lies atop the Commander's wife. Offred's relationship with the Commander is not as clear as the standard handmaid assignment, though; the Commander's high rank allows him to engage her in illegal activities, acquiring her cosmetics and allowing her to read. Meanwhile, the Commander's wife, believing her husband to be sterile (in spite of official Gilead policy stating that only women can be sterile), sets Offred up with her driver, Nick, in the hopes of impregnating Offred.

Offred's relationship with Nick blossoms, and she finds herself enjoying sex with him in spite of what she's been taught about her place. She tells him secrets about her past and what she's learned about the resistance movement Mayday. Soon after, Offred is taken away in a black van under orders from Nick, who tells her that he is part of Mayday and she should trust him. Offred cooperates, unsure whether she is being rescued or captured.

The novel's epilogue is penned by researchers who have found recordings of Offred's story and transcribed them in order to study the Gilead Period. The epilogue implies that the Republic of Gilead was, in fact, overthrown by the resistance movement and a more balanced, equitable society rose in its place.

Dystopian Elements:

When the Sons of Jacob take over the United States—now the Republic of Gilead—among their first actions are the removal of rights from women and "undesireables." African-Americans are relocated to the Midwest; Jews are given the option of converting to Christianity or emigrating to Israel. Women are separated into categories based on their reproductive status: fertile, white women become handmaids, while older, infertile women become the Marthas, performing domestic duties.

Themes of religious persecution, eugenics, and social classes are all present, but the main concern of the novel is the backlash against feminism: at the time of the novel's writing, feminists were launching an attack against pornography, exposing them to accusations of censorship and linking them to the religious right. Atwood based her novel on these attitudes, teased out past the logical conclusions into extremism and ideology. "The thing to remember is that there is nothing new about the society depicted in *The Handmaid's Tale* except the time and place," she says in the Reader's Companion to the 1998 edition.[1] "This is a book about what happens when certain casually held attitudes about women are taken to their logical conclusions."

30-Second Booktalk:

Like the rest of the women, Offred lost everything in the revolution: her financial assets, her family, even her own name, all lost to the new patriarchy. Against her will, she becomes a handmaid, tasked with conceiving the Commander's child. There is a rebellion brewing, the Mayday resistance, and Offred is about to have the decision to join or not join taken from her—just as everything else has been.

Readalikes:

Wither (Lauren DeStefano) for women being used for breeding

Shadow Children series (Margaret Peterson Haddix) for population control

Brave New World (Aldous Huxley) for social classes and reproductive issues

The Declaration (Gemma Malley) for population control

Potential Audience:

Mature themes make this most appropriate for upper-high school and adult readers. Teens who have recently read *Brave New World* in classes may appreciate another look at social classes and reproduction through a different dystopian lens.

---

[1] Available at http://www.randomhouse.com/resources/bookgroup/handmaidstale_bgc.html

Condie, Ally

Matched

Dutton, 2010. 384p. $17.99. 978-0-525-42364-5.
Penguin Audio, 2010. $29.95 CD. 978-0-1424-2863-4.

Crossed

Dutton, 2011. 384p. $17.99. 978-0-525-42365-2.
Penguin Audio. $25.95 CD. 978-1-61176-010-1.

Plot Summary:

Between their seventeenth and eighteenth birthdays, teen girls attend their Match banquets, where they are given their Matches: the boy who has been chosen for them based on genetic and social compatibilities, to ensure that their children will be the absolute best for society. Job classes are similarly determined by the government, guaranteeing that a person's best skills are utilized to the fullest extent possible and that each job in society is done by the worker best able to do it.

Cassia is very excited to attend her own Match banquet, and doubly excited to be matched to her best friend, Xander. This match alone is unique; it's rare that matches are made from the same town. Still, Cassia opens her match files the next morning, curious what information Match officials have on Xander, and she finds far more than she'd anticipated: in addition to Xander's information, there is information on a second match. *Nobody* gets a second match, and as rare as it is to be matched with one person from the same town, Cassia's second match is also a local. As she begins to notice Ky, the Officials notice her, and come to explain that Ky was never meant to be entered into the match pool: it's all been a big mistake. Cassia's curiosity and interest in Ky increase, and as they get to know each other, she finds herself falling for him—and asking questions about the social order she's always accepted.

As Book Two opens, Cassia's questions have led her to the Outer Provinces. With a new friend, she travels through a deserted canyon, searching for Ky and for signs of the Rebellion she's heard about. She hopes that finding Ky will lead her to the rebels she desperately wants to join, the group that will change how Society runs everything. Meanwhile, Ky has his own opinions and goals, and Xander may play a larger role in the story than Cassia expects.

Book 3, *Reached*, will be published in late 2012.

Dystopian Elements:

The Society demands conformity and does not tolerate questions, and free will isn't even a *thing*, really—there are no choices to be made; citizens are assigned everything from lunches to jobs to life partners to death dates. Society Officials make these decisions after extensive research, based on what will be the optimal assignments for the benefit of the Society.

What is the cause of this restrictive environment, though? Society has narrowly avoided being destroyed by a combination of the Warming and a war in the Outer Provinces. Paring down seems the logical solution to keep the population from developing the dangerous ideas that would lead to another war, so Officials have chosen for everyone: optimal matches, best-fit occupations, meals and portions, recreation options. Officials also chose the 100 best examples in several categories to keep: 100 songs, 100 poems, 100 books, 100 paintings. The rest have been destroyed. Cassia never questions this until her grandfather shows her a piece of paper tucked inside a secret compartment in her heirloom compact: a handwritten copy of Dylan Thomas' *Do Not Go Gentle into That Good Night*, a poem decidedly not on the list of 100 Poems. Sharing the poem with Ky leads to her discovery of the black market that surrounds supposed-forgotten works of art, science, technology, and other outlawed knowledge from the time before Society. The limited choices in the arts calls up comparisons to Bradbury's *Fahrenheit 451*, in which reading material is outlawed, with ultimately similar outcomes: small pockets of people devoting themselves, illegally, to preserving these materials.

The archivists' trades for these illegal works are explained more in *Crossed*, which shows the stores of literature and art that farmers, rebels, and other Society outsiders have saved in the mountains. These outsiders have used these materials to pay for things like medicines and information from the archivists and other black-market dealers. *Crossed* focuses on a building rebellion, but there is little discussion of what those forces are rebelling against, be it the lack of choices in Society or the building war in the Outer Provinces.

30-Second Booktalk:

When Cassia gets matched on her 17th birthday, she's thrilled to be matched to her best friend, Xander—and shocked when someone else's information appears in her Match files the next morning. When an Official corners her and confesses that it was a mistake, that Ky was never meant to be entered in the Match pool, her curiosity is piqued. As she and Ky fall for each other, Cassia bristles under the lack of choices in Society, and begins making some dangerous choices of her own.

Readalikes:

The Giver (Lois Lowry) for governmental oversight of all aspects of life and lack of choices

The Hunger Games (Suzanne Collins) for choosing between two strong love interests and for the building rebellion

Delirium (Lauren Oliver) for dystopian romance and lack of choices

Dylan Thomas for readers looking for more of his poetry

Fahrenheit 451 (Ray Bradbury) for censorship/restriction of literature

Potential Audience:

Primarily a romance, though set in a dystopian world, this will mostly appeal to high-school girls looking for dramatic love triangles. With a romance that never strays past kissing, this is perfectly appropriate for middle-school girls as well, though they will be less likely to recognize the dystopian implications of society. The dystopian framework, in which there is very little choice in anything, will speak to teens who find the lack of freedom in the regimented world of high school stifling.

Worth noting is that the only choice allowed in regard to matching is a clause to allow a person to remain single, rather than being matched, and all matches are heterosexual. Presumably this is because the purpose of the Matching system is to ensure the most optimal offspring; still, teens looking for a more encompassing GBLTQ worldview may be disappointed at the lack of representation.

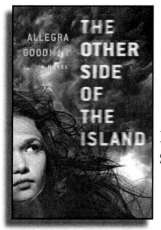

Goodman, Allegra

The Other Side of the Island

Razorbill, 2008. 280p. $16.99. 978-1-59514-195-8.
$8.99 ebook. 978-1-101-05716-2.

Plot Summary:

Honor is ten years old when her family moves to Island 365 in the Tranquil Sea. Her parents tell her it's an *adventure*, moving to this place, where they have no jobs and no money and everything is regulated by the Earth Mother and the Corporation. They live in a damp, ramshackle house near the shoreline, far from the nicer inland neighborhoods where Honor's classmates live.

Honor desperately wants to fit in with the girls at her new school, but it's difficult with parents like hers—parents who aren't willing to do the things they're supposed to, parents who have a second child, parents who name her *Honor* instead of a name with a proper "H" sound like all the other children born in the eighth year post-Enclosure. As Honor grows up on Island 365 and becomes more and more the person her school shapes her to be, she rejects her parents' strange ideas and worries about the unorthodox things they do.

When her parents are taken, Honor is troubled but also unsurprised, as she knows that they have been living dangerous lives in their tiny rebellions. Now 13, Honor and her little brother Quintilian are taken to live at school with the other orphans, other children whose parents were taken. Honor adjusts to her new home as her social standing plummets, reconnecting with an old friend (and now fellow orphan) Helix. Helix has been thinking about the way things work on the Island, and he's certain that the people who have been Taken aren't dead, but rather that they've been made into the Orderlies, the nearly-identical drones who do most of the menial jobs for the Island. Together, Honor and Helix make plans to run away and find their parents.

When the opportunity finally comes, Honor takes it without a second thought. She encounters her father and some other family friends living in the woods, and together they storm the Orderlies' housing compound. Honor finds her mother and brings her back to her father and the others. As her mother comes out of her drugged fog, Honor learns what her parents truly are: not only Unpredictable, but Reverse Engineers, determined to take over the nearby weather station and overthrow the Earth Mother. The adults succeed in the first part; the promise of overthrowing the Earth Mother leaves open the possibility of a sequel.

Dystopian Elements:

From the beginning of the novel, it is clear that Honor's world is one that has survived chaos: more than a half-century earlier, the Flood destroyed everything, leaving only islands where continents once stood. The Earth Mother's solution was to eschew choice and freedom in favor of safety from the elements, slowly enclosing different regions under ceilings in order to create New Weather and block out the destructive forces that had already devastated the world.

However post-apocalyptic the history of Honor's world is, Honor is growing up in a dystopia instead: the Earth Mother made the decision long ago that safety was more important than choice and freedom, and as a result, the only information available is what comes from Earth Mother. Her Corporation controls the weather and the stars in the sky; at her direction, books have all troubling passages (anything sad, relating to bad weather, or otherwise at odds with the Corporation's messages) excised; people who do not readily fall in line are taken from their homes and turned into Orderlies, drugged into subservience and complacency.

Students are taught about the Enclosure, that islands have been ceiled and their weather perfected. However, not all of the information is accurate, as Honor knows when she is told that the Northern Islands—the ones she has recently moved from—no longer have extremes of temperature or anything other than sunny days. In the beginning, she has trouble understanding this revised history, but as she gets older she begins to forget the way she used to live in favor of what she's been taught in school. The students are taught gratitude for all that the Earth Mother and the Corporation have done for them, but the subtle indoctrination also serves as a wedge between children (like Honor) and their Unpredictable parents.

30-Second Booktalk:

Honor and her parents live on Island 365, where the weather is controlled by the Earth Mother Corporation and everyone fits in perfectly—everyone except Honor's parents, who refuse to go along with Earth Mother's rules, and by extension Honor herself. When Honor's parents disappear, it's up to her to find out where they've gone—and what's on the other side of the island for those who won't conform.

Readalikes:

Eye of the Storm (Kate Messner) for corporate control of weather

The Secret under My Skin (Janet McNaughton) for work assignments for low-ranking citizens

1984 (George Orwell) for reeducation of those with rebellious thoughts

The Sky Inside (Clare B. Dunkle) for life in a climate-controlled, domed city

Exodus (Julie Bertagna) for a flooded world

Potential Audience:

The Other Side of the Island follows Honor from age ten until just past her fourteenth birthday. Her struggles to fit in will resonate with tweens and young teens, particularly those in middle school.

Huxley, Aldous

Brave New World

Harper Perennial Modern Classics, 2006. 288p. $14.99 Trade pb. 978-0-06-085052-4.
BBC Audiobooks America, 2007. $29.95 CD. 978-1-60283-336-4.
Modern Library. $8.99 ebook. 978-0-7953-1125-3.

- Originally published 1932

Plot Summary:

Roughly five hundred years from now, the human race is still going strong—stronger than ever, in fact, owing to the precise decanting of new members of society, each new person engineered in a lab to fit in a social caste and fill a particular role. *Family* is a vulgar concept. Sex is for recreation and relaxation (promiscuity is encouraged, even among children). And there is no problem that can't be solved with a tablet or more of the ubiquitous hallucinogenic drug *soma*.

Lenina, a Beta class, wants a normal life, desperately, but she does herself no favors by repeatedly dating only one man, Henry. In a tremendous effort to be more conventional, she chooses another partner: the Alpha-class Bernard, who is close to getting himself sent to Iceland due to his antisocial behaviors. In an effort to impress Lenina, Bernard whisks her on a trip to a Savage Reservation in New Mexico, where they meet Linda (a former member of the World State) and her son John.

Bernard brings them both back to the World State, where Linda engages on a permanent *soma* vacation and John grapples with the wasteful, hedonistic society by which he is now surrounded. His attempts to live a hermetic life after his mother's death are ruined by gawkers who come to watch The Savage, and his shame and horror at his own participation in their society ultimately leads him to suicide.

Dystopian Elements:

At the heart of *Brave New World* is the social order, created at conception and enforced through subliminal messages. Natural reproduction is a thing of the past, families are taboo, and the very mention of the word "mother" is obscene. New members of society are no longer conceived and born, but decanted in Hatching and Conditioning facilities. In the decanting process, chemicals are added to the decanting bottles to ensure that the babies grow into their social classes, from Alpha to Epsilon according to how much chemical the fetus was subjected to. The physical and mental limitations of the lower classes, a result of the chemical tampering, are reinforced with a series of subliminal messages shaping the growing child's ambitions, desires, and social outlook.

The control this conditioning gives the government is not an effort to manipulate society, but merely to stabilize it. This is the reason for many of the platitudes that are sleep-taught to citizens: the economy is held up by the idea that "ending is better than mending" (i.e., it's better to replace a broken item than repair it) and other consumerism-focused ideals; competition among social classes is eliminated by conditioning each class to believe themselves superior to the others.

In his 1958 foreword to *Brave New World*, Huxley remarked that, "A book about the future can interest us only if its prophecies look as though they might conceivably come true." Indeed, his prescience regarding reproductive technology is impressive: in vitro fertilization, in which an egg is fertilized and begins its cell division outside a human body, was not used successfully until 1974, nearly a half a century after Huxley conceived of an entire population of cloned and decanted humans.

30-Second Booktalk:

Bernard is an Alpha, but his desire for solitude and general anti-social behavior has always made him stand out. When Beta-class Lenina shows an interest in him, he tries to impress her by taking her to a Savage reservation—but then he brings a native savage back with him. Bernard's scandalous action has devasting consequences—for Lenina, for the savage, and for Bernard himself, whose need to be an individual could cost him everything he knows.

Readalikes:

Feed (M.T. Anderson) for consumerism

Candor (Pam Bachorz) for subliminal conditioning

We (Yevgeny Zamyatin) for totalitarian messages and comformity

Piano Player (Kurt Vonnegut) for rebellion against an oppressive government

Kids in the Hall: Brain Candy (film) for soma-like GLeeMONEX

Potential Audience:

High school students will likely encounter this in a classroom, but those who don't may be drawn in by the prescience of test-tube babies and technological advances in a book written before their grandparents were born. A good choice to fulfill the "classics" outside-reading assignment, or for mature teens seeking pairings to other dystopian classics encountered in schools.

Kino's Journey

DVD. Color. 325m. Produced and dist. by A.D. Vision, 2009. $39.98. 978-1-4139-0425-3.

- Originally aired between June 18 and November 19, 2003

Plot Summary:

Kino is a traveler, riding her sentient motorcycle (Hermes) across the world. Kino stays three days in each country, long enough to get a feel for the culture but brief enough not to put down any roots.

Each of the thirteen episodes brings Kino to a new country with its own culture and issues: a town where the residents can hear each others' thoughts, leading them all to live in isolation; a country living under the knowledge of the prophesied end of the world; a city in which every visitor must win a battle to the death in order to gain admittance.

The series concludes with Kino visiting a country reputed to despise travelers, but in truth she finds them to be welcoming. On meeting a young girl who reminds Kino of her younger self, Kino toys with the idea of staying more than three days, having finally found a place where she can settle down.

Dystopian Elements:

Each episode brings Kino to a different country, with its own version of dystopia. Most are born out of similar objectives: to establish a community free of the evils that plague other lands. Kino attempts to be an impartial observer in her travels, though her questions to the citizens sometimes make them question the ways they've lived.

Kino's efforts to understand each country she visits give her the opportunity to talk to many people, most of whom are eager to relate their history to a stranger. From countries attempting to facilitate communication by making everyone telepathic (with predictably isolating results) to those that perform a surgery at age 12 which will ensure an adulthood of uncomplaining employment, each culture works to preserve its moral values. However, with such single-minded focus on a particular value comes the erosion of balance—and frequently the erosion of the very value they have set out to ensure, such as communication or peace.

30-Second Booktalk:

Traveling since childhood, Kino has visited many countries, staying in each for only three days before moving on. Kino participates in each culture, helping one community establish a tradition and being thrown into gladiatorial combat in another. With seeing the world the only goal, traveling is the only way of life.

Readalikes:

Delirium (Lauren Oliver) for surgery to usher children into adulthood (episode 4, *Land of Adults*)

The Knife of Never Letting Go (Patrick Ness) for ability to hear others' thoughts (episode 2, *Land of Visible Pain*)

Girl in the Arena (Lise Haines) for gladiatorial combat (episodes 6-7, *Coliseum*)

Kino no Tabi (Keiichi Sigsawa) for original novel on which the show is based

Potential Audience:

With little violence and no romantic subplots, *Kino's Journey* is likely to be an atypical viewing experience for teens. However, high schoolers interested in politics or philosophy will enjoy this quietly-paced series.

Lowry, Lois

The Giver

Delacorte, 1993. 208p. $8.95 pb. 978-0-385-73255-0.
Listening Library, 2003. $28 CD. 978-0-8072-6203-0.
$8.95 ebook. 978-0-547-34590-1.

Plot Summary:

Jonas's society maintains the happiness of its residents by assigning jobs according to skills and talents, matching couples for the most harmonious pairings and placing two children with each matched couple. It's now time for Jonas's Ceremony of 12, at which the Council of Elders will provide him and each of his classmates with their work assignments. Jonas is surprised and confused when his name is skipped in the ceremony, and doubly surprised when the elders call him at the end with a special assignment: Jonas will be the new Receiver of Memories.

The former Receiver of Memories, now The Giver, passes to Jonas the information that the rest of society has forgotten: sadness, music, joy, violence, colors, love, and other strong emotions. To his horror, Jonas also learns what happens when townspeople are Released, long assumed to be exiled from the community but in truth are euthanized.

When Jonas learns that the infant his family has been fostering is going to be Released, he takes the baby and escapes, as the Giver instructed him. In his escape, Jonas releases all the memories he was storing into the community. He struggles to keep the baby safe from cold and hunger, and the novel ends ambiguously with Jonas finding a sled at the top of a hill and sliding down toward some houses.

Dystopian Elements:

The Society promotes harmony among its citizens by ensuring that each person has the best life they can have, assigning jobs according to strengths and matching spouses by personalities and traits. They also control the flow of information—or rather, they assign one person to be the Keeper of Memories, responsible for remembering the town's history in case the information should someday be needed for decision-making purposes.

In promoting harmony and Sameness, the society has lost its emotional depth. There is no emotional pain, because there is no emotional connection. "We can forget pain, I think," Lowry says in her 1994 Newbery Acceptance speech, "and it is comfortable to do so. But I also wonder briefly: is it safe to do that, to forget?"[2] The desire to eliminate everything that could cause harm or distress is a common one in utopias, but it's an idea easily turned around into sterility and emotional distance.

---

[2] http://www.loislowry.com/documents/speeches/pdf_server.php?file=Newbery_Award

Lowry continues:

> I tried to make Jonas's world seem familiar, comfortable, and safe.... I got rid of all the things I fear and dislike; all the violence, prejudice, poverty, and injustice, and I even threw in good manners as a way of life because I liked the idea of it. But [...] we can't live in a walled world, in an "only us, only now" world where we are all the same and feel safe. We would have to sacrifice too much. The richness of color and diversity would disappear; feelings for other humans would no longer be necessary. Choices would be obsolete.[3]

In his training as the Receiver of Memories, Jonas learns the truths that have been hidden from the townspeople, both the good things and the bad, and is burdened by his knowledge. After much consideration, Jonas makes the difficult decision to return these memories and emotions to the community, even though it means exiling himself. In a choice between freedom and safety, he ultimately chooses freedom for himself, and thus imposes freedom on the community.

30-Second Booktalk:

Jonas's world is a happy one: there is no unemployment, no shortage of food, no crime or poverty or discontent. At age twelve, he hears his unusual career assignment: he will be the Keeper of Memories. As he meets with the previous Keeper—now the Giver—Jonas learns many joys and pains that his world has managed to forget. Slowly he understands what this well-ordered society actually costs, and must decide if it's a price he can afford to pay.

Readalikes:

Matched (Ally Condie) and *Delirium* (Lauren Oliver) for lack of societal choice

Messenger (Lois Lowry) as a companion novel

Candor (Pam Bachorz) for a character holding information about society that no one else has

The City of Ember (Jeanne duPrau) for a closed society aimed at a similar reading level

Potential Audience:

In the nearly two decades since its original release, *The Giver* has become a modern classic of teen dystopias, so much so that the majority of upper-elementary and middle-school readers who encounter it will do so in a classroom. The depth of the story will also appeal to high school readers, though the primary audience will be fifth through eighth grades.

---

[3] ibid.

Lowry, Lois

Gathering Blue

Delacorte, 2006. 215p. $8.95 pb. 978-0-385-73256-7.
Houghton Mifflin, 2000. $16 ebook. 978-0-547-34578-9.

- Originally published 2000

Plot Summary:

The Council of Kira's village does not allow for weakness: the sick and infirm are abandoned to die of exposure; children with birth defects are swiftly euthanized. Kira's mother saved her from this fate in spite of her twisted leg and has been protecting Kira from the villagers' scorn for years. When her mother dies, Kira is alone and has reason to fear for her safety.

She is saved, however, by her artistic skills: Kira is a gifted weaver, able to create beautiful and near-prophetic tapestries out of threads and dyes. It is this gift that catches the notice of the Council Elders. Kira and two other village artists are taken to the grand Council Edifice to prepare items—a tapestry, a carving, a song—for the annual Ruin Song Gathering. Through their art, the three learn the history of the Ruin, including the unflattering, dangerous secrets in the village's past. One of those dark secrets is about the three orphaned artists and the Council Elders who are responsible for the deaths of their parents.

Kira is also learning things from her friend Matt, things about a world outside, highlighting the flaws in the village and the life she's always known. Kira could have a life of kindness, ease, and healing, or she could stay and use her art to fix the problems with her society.

Dystopian Elements:

Sometime in the past, the well-ordered society collapsed, leaving communities to reform in its wake. The society of *The Giver* built itself back up with little technology and an avoidance of strong emotions. In contrast, the village of *Gathering Blue* became more primitive, ensuring its utopian ways by removing non-perfection from society altogether.

The council elders keep the villagers relatively ignorant of their history by no longer keeping any books, but instead reciting the history annually in the Ruin Song ceremony. In addition to making it difficult to reinforce this knowledge year-round, the performance of the lengthy song turns some sounds into seeming gibbrish, such as the section a character describes as telling the names of lost places:

Bogo tabal

Timore toron

Totoo now gone[4]

Astute, geographically-familiar readers may identify these places as *Bogota, Baltimore, Toronto,*

[4] *Gathering Blue,* pg171

too now gone. But Kira, and others, do not have the luxury of reading their history and deciphering the words (though they likely would not recognize the place names even if they saw them), or the freedom to regularly or freely discuss their history.

30-Second Booktalk:

Kira's weaving and embroidering skills have caught the attention of the town's elders, and she is given the task of restoring the historical tapestry for the annual Ruin Song Gathering. Kira is taken to the grand Council Edifice to work and learn the dark history of the Ruin while being watched over by the council authorities. In order to properly weave the story, Kira needs a rare pigment—and finding it means leaving the Edifice, despite the Council Elders.

Readalikes:

Madapple (Christina Meldrum) for knowledge of herbs and plants

The Giver (Lois Lowry) for another dystopia in the same time period

Messenger (Lois Lowry) for a better look at the new society Matt talks about

Nation (Terry Pratchett) for a quasi-primitive, yet future, society

Potential Audience:

Teens who enjoyed *The Giver* will likely pick up this next installment by the same author, despite its new setting. As a stand-alone, this will appeal to middle-school students who enjoy the flavor of historical fiction, the plight of an artist, or light dystopias.

Lowry, Lois

Messenger

Delacorte, 2006. 169p. $8.95 pb. 978-0-385-73253-6.
Houghton Mifflin, 2004. $16. ebook. 978-0-547-34589-5.

- Originally published 2003

Plot Summary:

Matty's village is populated entirely by refugees from other communities. Some left willingly to find a new place; others were cast out for alleged misdeeds against society. Matty lives with the elderly Seer, the blind man taken in by the Villagers long ago. The Villagers are kind-hearted and helpful toward each other, particularly toward the disabled; this is initially a shock to Matty, who comes from a community where the disabled and ill are left to die.

The Village is, however, isolated, contained by the Forest that surrounds it. The Forest will issue "warnings" to any who try to pass through, in the form of scratches, poisonous plants, stinging insects, and other minor injuries. The Forest will kill any warned person who dares to pass through a second time. Matty alone passes freely through the Forest, and as a result he becomes the Village's messenger, carrying messages to and from other communities.

Matty's community is changing, though, since the Trade Mart came in. Villagers are trading for items like game stations and sewing machines, and giving up pieces of themselves: their trust, generosity, good health. Those who have traded away their best attributes begin to outnumber those who haven't, and they become hostile and suspicious toward outsiders, eventually voting to build a wall and seal out refugees from other communities. The Seer sends Matty to bring back one last person before the borders close for good: his daughter, Kira. The journey is not an easy one, though, with the Forest attempting to ensnare the travelers. Matty has the power to heal, and at his own expense, uses this gift to heal the Forest and the Villagers, restoring the harmony that used to exist.

Dystopian Elements:

The Leader has established the Village as a utopia, with the villagers readily trading and helping each other. He's been through another kind of utopia, one in which emotions are tightly controlled to allow for a harmonic existence, and he's seen the pitfalls of that approach. In creating his own community, he strives for the opposite: a community in which people are in touch with their emotions and fears, and with each other. It is this tight-knit community that becomes the downfall of the utopia: their isolation provides a sense of security, but the instant that security is threatened, they react by closing themselves off to any other outside interaction.

The Messenger's dystopian elements are more drawn from the contrast between this and the previous volumes in the series than they are on its own story. Still, the contrast provides many ideas to debate and discuss about a so-called perfect society and how easily that perfection can be disrupted.

30-Second Booktalk:

Matty has lived in the village with the blind Seer for a long time, under the benevolent and gentle Leader. But now the town—which had always been welcoming of outsiders—is closing its borders and building a wall to isolate itself. Matty must make one more trip through the hostile forest to bring back the Seer's daughter before the outside is closed off permanently, but the journey is a perilous one and may demand a high price for success.

Readalikes:

The Giver and *Gathering Blue* (Lois Lowry) for insight into characters from the previous novels

Nation (Terry Pratchett) for coming-of-age and building a new society of refugees

Carbon Diaries 2017 (Saci Lloyd) for a different look at border closings

The Village (film) for the perils of an isolated society

Something Wicked This Way Comes (Ray Bradbury) for promises of better lives leading to ruin

Potential Audience:

Middle school students interested in the worlds of *The Giver* and/or *Gathering Blue* will appreciate seeing those two societies blend, and will appreciate seeing what happened to the characters after the events of the previous books.

McCafferty, Megan

Bumped

Balzer + Bray, 2011. 336p. $16.99. 978-0-06-196274-5.
HarperCollins, 2011. $0.99 ebook. 978-0-06-207697-7.

Plot Summary:

By 2035, an infertility virus has infected nearly everybody, rendering them sterile by eighteen. Reproductive ability is now a commodity; girls can line up lucrative contracts with adult couples to have babies for them with designated, professional partners. Melody is just such a girl, the first in her school to go pro and sign such a contract. She's an over-achiever and a trend-setter, but the couple who contracted her services still hasn't found a suitable male—which means Melody is 16 years old, not pregnant, and running out her biological clock. In a stroke of luck, Melody gets matched with the ultra-desirable Jondoe—but it's her identical twin sister Harmony who gets the message.

Harmony was raised in Goodside, an isolated religious community, and has sneaked away from that life in order to find—and save—her sister. Harmony steps into her sister's place in order to stop the transaction from taking place, but succeeds only in getting more deeply involved than anyone could have anticipated, especially since no one is supposed to know of her existence.

Dystopian Elements:

A mere quarter-century from our current time, the infertility virus has rendered all adults sterile, so teens are the only ones who can reproduce. Fertility becomes a commodity, and girls compete to get the most lucrative contracts to have babies for adult couples. The plot is driven by Melody's concerns about her contract and the budding romance between Harmony and Jondoe rather than any of the dystopian elements against which the characters are set, resulting in a light read that touches on several issues but fails to explore any of them in any depth.

The culture of *Bumped*, in which only the most biologically-optimal males are chosen to "bump" (impregnate) the fittest females, would necessarily lead to an increasingly-limited gene pool as generations pass. Reproductive technology appears to have taken a step backwards, too: rather than using in-vitro fertilization or artificially inseminating the teen mothers-to-be, condoms have been outlawed and recreational (as opposed to reproductive) sex among teens is taboo. Teens are encouraged to use drugs to block out the awkwardness of "bumping" with the partners chosen for them.

Celebrity and fame of every bit as motivating in the world of *Bumped* as they are today, with the media stalking the most genetically-desirable teens and following their every move, as is the case when Melody is announced as Jondoe's next partner. This is the main dystopian framework: rather than an overbearing government intruding in couples' personal business, the media drives the frenzy for top males and females, and reinforces the message that Melody, despite her lucrative contract, is nothing until she is pregnant. Her agent and the media have together removed any choices she may have with regard to sex and reproduction, echoing her twin sister Harmony's religious community that arranges marriages as soon as teens hit puberty.

30-Second Booktalk:

Melody is a trend-setter, the first girl in her school to go pro and sign a lucrative pregnancy contract to surrogate for a wealthy adult couple. The couple hasn't found the right male, though, and Melody's time is running out: she's sixteen years old, just two years away from infection with the infertility virus that strikes nearly everyone over eighteen. Melody finally gets matched to sought-after stud Jondoe, but it's Melody's ultra-religious, long-lost twin sister who gets the message—and is desperate to save her from the immorality of bumping for profit.

Readalikes:

The Handmaid's Tale (Margaret Atwood) for women as breeders

Juno (film) for a humorous take on teen pregnancy

Delirium (Lauren Oliver) for lack of choices in romantic partners, and for removing romance from procreation

Potential Audience:

Sexual content is not graphic, but it does drive the plot, making this a decent choice for older teens or adults looking for a light rom-com. Science-fiction elements are subtle enough to be easily ignored by those who typically avoid genre fiction, while the mildly dystopian setting gives genre enthusiasts something to chew on.

Oliver, Lauren

Delirium

HarperCollins, 2011. 448p. $17.99. 978-0-06-172682-8.
$9.99 ebook. 978-0-06-206954-2.

Plot Summary:

It's been sixty-four years since love was identified as the disease *amor deliria nervosa*, and forty-three since science found a cure for it. Lena is looking forward to being Cured, to having the surgery that means she'll never have to be infected or suffer the pains associated with it. She's nervous about her Evaluation, where she'll give the Evaluators all her carefully-rehearsed answers about herself that they'll use to choose four potential matches for her. Despite her preparation, her true opinions slip out of her mouth: confessing her favorite color is the color of sunset, not the safe blue or green; calling *Romeo and Juliet* "beautiful" instead of a frightening cautionary tale. Only a miracle could save this Evaluation—and then the door bursts open, admitting a stampeding herd of cattle. Lena would swear that in the midst of the chaos she hears laughter, and in peering up to the observation deck overlooking her Evaluation room, there's a sandy-haired boy, about her age, laughing.

Even as Lena recovers from the shock of the interrupted evaluation (and is relieved to learn that the results are being disregarded), the boy is still on her mind. She knows, instinctively, that he's an Invalid, someone uncured, and she can't stop thinking about him. She continues her daily life, working in her uncle's store and running with her best friend, but encounters the boy again—and accepts an invitation from him to meet after curfew.

Soon Lena is sneaking off to meet Alex at every opportunity, and realizes that she's been infected with *amor deliria nervosa*. Contracting the disease—falling in love—starts Lena questioning everything she's been told, and wondering if avoiding the pains of love is worth missing out on the joys.

Dystopian Elements:

The best thing about Lena's world is that there is virtually no chance of failure: the Evaluators make every decision about education, employment, and even life partners, all based on a grueling hours-long interview when teens are 17. Like any exam, there are review books and cram sessions, and teens are coached through the best answers, potentially undermining the system.

The control extends beyond seemingly benign life choices, too, into governmental raids of private property to search for contraband or evidence of rebellion. On the night of a raid, Lena says that "private property laws are suspended on raid nights. Pretty much every law is suspended on raid nights."[5] Putting the agents above the law, even encouraging them to use force against any protestation (including the savage beating of a family dog), keeps the citizens in fear and making it unlikely that there will be resistance to the next raid.

---

[5] *Delirium*, p. 202.

The other major element in *Delirium* is the indoctrination: the *The Safety, Health and Happiness Handbook*, or *The Book of Shhh*, is a safety manual, a literary anthology, a science book, and a general life handbook. Every societal rule and belief is detailed in its pages, leaving no room for individual interpretations. Citizens are not supposed to question *The Book of Shhh* or other societal teachings, as Lena knows from the horrified reactions of her Evaluation panel when she describes Shakespeare's *Romeo and Juliet* as "beautiful" instead of as a cautionary tale, or when she names the gray of sunrise her favorite color. Independent, individual thoughts like these are suspicious, grounds for immediate arrest and imprisonment.

30-Second Booktalk:

Decreased appetite, weight loss, lack of concentration, mood swings: all symptoms of *amor deliria nervosa*. Lena is looking forward to being Cured, to getting her match, to having her life's choices settled. But just months before she's to get her cure—on the day of her evaluation, when she'll give the panel the information they need to make those decisions for her—she meets the person who will infect her. It's an ancient infection and deadly dangerous: Lena has fallen in love.

Readalikes:

The Giver (Lois Lowry) and *Matched* (Ally Condie) for governmental assignments of life choices (partners, employment, etc.)

Uglies (Scott Westerfeld) for surgical fixes to "dangerous" thoughts and emotions

Shiver (Maggie Stiefvater) for romance between teen girl and outside-society boy

Equilibrium (film) for elimination of emotion

Potential audience:

With the romantic plot at the forefront, high school girls will clamor for this sci-fi title. The romance is a fairly chaste one, appropriate for 8th grade and up. Boys may be interested in the world setting, but the focus on Lena's relationship may turn off all but the most dedicated male readers. The first in a projected trilogy, *Delirium* will draw in new readers with each successive volume.

Discussion Guide:

http://www.harperteen.com/feature/delirium/pdf/Delirium_discussionguide.pdf

Pleasantville

DVD. Color. 134m. Produced and dist. by Warner Home Video, 2011. $12.97. 978-0-7806-7318-2.

- Written and directed by Gary Ross
- Originally released 1998

Plot Summary:

David and Jennifer are twins, but that's about as far as their similarities go. David has few friends and spends most of his free time watching the 1950s sitcom *Pleasantville*, and plans to spend a night watching the *Pleasantville* marathon. In contrast, Jennifer is building her social status, finally scoring a date with the hottest guy in school to watch a televised concert. In a fight over the television, David and Jennifer accidentally break the remote, rendering the television unusable. At that moment, a television repairman shows up, unbidden, and offers them a new remote that, he says with a knowing wink, will put them right in the show.

The remote does exactly that: on pressing the power button, David and Jennifer find themselves transported into 1950s Pleasantville, the fictional, idyllic suburb of the eponymous sitcom. As Bud and Mary Sue Parker, the twins have very different ideas on how to proceed: David believes in continuing exactly along the show's trajectory, not deviating from any of the show's original values or plots, but Jennifer decides that it is not only okay but preferable for the town's residents to be shaken out of their comfort zones. Jennifer teaches basketball team captain Skip about sex and the knowledge spreads quickly; following this first change, David tells his new classmates about literature, filling in the previously-blank books in the library and sparking an interest in reading and learning. As they develop new passions and interests the Townspeople slowly colorize from their black-and-white selves.

Not everyone in town sees the changes as positive progress, however. Town officials attempt to curtail these changes by forbidding signs of rebellion: rock music, library visits, use of paint colors besides black, white, or gray. In protest, Bud and the soda-shop owner (who has discovered an interest in painting) create a bright, colorful mural on the wall of the police station. At their trial, the judge becomes sufficiently angry to become colorized himself, and the remaining townspeople colorize shortly thereafter. Pleasantville finally connects to the larger world, no longer looping back on itself.

At the movie's conclusion, David uses the remote to send himself back home to his present day, but Jennifer opts to stay in the alternate world to attend college, admitting that she has changed and has better options in Pleasantville than in her "real" life.

Dystopian Elements:

Pleasantville is, at a glance, a fantasy comedy-drama, not something that would ordinarily be considered in any way dystopian. Atypical as it is for the genre, however, the town of Pleasantville is a dystopia: a perfect world in which nothing unpleasant ever happens (even rain never falls) that is slowly revealed to be stifling its residents' imaginations and desires to maintain its easily-managed perfection.

Pleasantville's teens are the first to rebel against the oppression they had been living under, symbolized by their change from black-and-white to color. Intellectual curiosity has been so discouraged that classmates react with shock and confusion when Jennifer asks, on her first day as Mary Sue, what lies beyond Pleasantville's borders. Jennifer is not academically-focused, but even she is horrified to discover that all the books are blank, further discouraging students from forming opinions and questioning their perfect town.

As knowledge of sex, literature, art, and more spread, the town becomes harder to control: riots break out over a nude painting in a shop window and "coloreds" become victims of violence and harassment; husbands and wives turn to other partners; rain pours down on a community that has never witnessed weather that is anything but 72 sunny degrees. While these changes are not good things in themselves, they serve to highlight the lack of free will the townspeople previously had, and the fear they live in as things begin to change.

30-Second Booktalk:

David is something of an expert on the 1950s sitcom *Pleasantville*—which is handy knowledge when he and his twin sister are transported into a fictional suburb of a half-century earlier. Despite David's efforts to avoid disrupting anything in the show's reality, the twins' influence sparks a revolution in the black-and-white town. David is reluctant to mess with the perfection of Pleasantville, but many of the town's teens are ready to make that decision for themselves.

Readalikes:

Blast from the Past (film) for teens catapulted into a different era

Incarceron (Catherine Fisher) for isolated worlds and the play-acting into a different time period

Nomansland (Lesley Hauge) for knowledge of another world changing attitudes and perceptions

Potential Audience:

High schoolers will connect with this movie, particularly with the bulk of its cast being teens in a high-school setting. Teens and adults familiar with 1950s sitcoms (and therefore with the stereotypes of the values of the time) will appreciate some of the sly humor, but even without that background many will enjoy this comedy in spite of its heavy-handed messages regarding racism and freedom of thought.

Roth, Veronica

Divergent

Harper Collins, 2011. 496p. $17.99. 978-0-06-202402-2.

- Originally published 2011

Plot Summary:

In a future Chicago, adults are separated into five classes: Candor (the honest), Abnegation (the selfless), Erudite (the intelligent), Dauntless (the brave), and Amity (the peaceful). At 16, Beatrice goes through the aptitude testing that will tell her what faction she belongs in. Her results are unusual: she could easily fit in any of three factions, marking her Divergent, a very dangerous thing to be. She can stay with Abnegation, where she grew up, move to the brilliant Erudite, long-standing rivals of Abnegation, or abandon her family and become Dauntless, the brave. She chooses this last option and begins the unrelentingly physical training, reinventing herself as Tris to truly become Dauntless. Her surprising aptitude makes her at least one enemy, who is determined to destroy her. As the initiates move deeper into their training, Tris uncovers surprising information about factions—and family— that will affect the whole society if Tris does nothing. Meanwhile, there are some who suspect that she is Divergent, and revealing that secret could mean the end of everything Tris has been working for.

Dystopian Elements:

The social order of Beatrice's world is fairly rigid: there is no fraternizing between the factions, and when children grow up and choose a faction other than the one they were born into, there is the sense of loss, knowing they are unlikely to be with their families again. This rigidity makes something like a caste system, though without the hierarchy. Each faction is known for a particular thing (honesty, peacefulness, intelligence, fearlessness, or selflessness) and each believes their faction to be superior to all others.

The superiority helps to keep the factions apart from each other, dividing society into five distinct parts with little cooperation among them. Early on, divisions were put to good uses: the Abnegation were put in political power, on the grounds that they would selflessly do what was right for society instead of just themselves; Candor's honesty made them trustworthy leaders in law. But over time, resentments grew, and now leaders in other factions are sowing dissent, starting rumors about the misdeeds of Abnegation officials and inciting revolution. With each faction reduced to a single trait, there is little room for distrust: if a Candor says Abnegation is to blame, then it must be a true; if an Erudite says it, they must be basing that conclusion on logic and reasoning. The divisions among the factions make it easy to discount the good that another faction could be doing.

Assigning each person to a faction can also devalue one's personal identity, making them simply a part of that faction instead of a full, dynamic individual in their own rights. Coupled with the beliefs about each factions' strengths and weaknesses, this creates a social system in which only those in power will make decisions, and any lower-status faction members who question those decisions are viewed with suspicion. The factionless—those who chose a faction and did not make it through initiation—are given no voice in government and are dependent on the charity of those in power.

30-Second Booktalk:

Beatrice is nervous about her upcoming aptitude testing and the subsequent choosing ceremony, but she's shocked to learn that her testing results are inconclusive. She could remain with Abnegation, the selfless, or abandon her home and family to join the Dauntless, the brave. Her Divergent traits give her an edge in the brutal Dauntless initiation that could break her, but divergence is also very dangerous—and Tris isn't the only one who knows what she is.

Readalikes:

The Hunger Games (Suzanne Collins) for separated districts

Brave New World (Aldous Huxley) for class system and superiority among classes

Matched (Ally Condie) for training in government-assigned jobs

The Giver (Lois Lowry) for work-assignment ceremonies, and understanding of societal costs

Potential Audience:

Eighth grade and up, particularly teens looking for something very similar in tone to *The Hunger Games*. Tris's romance with the boy who both compels and irritates her is not a central plot point, and the brutal training will give it both boy and girl appeal.

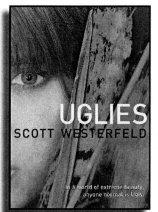

Westerfeld, Scott

Uglies

Simon Pulse, 2011 (reprint ed). 432p. $9.99 pb. 978-1-4424-1981-0.
$9.99 ebook. 978-1-4424-1981-0.

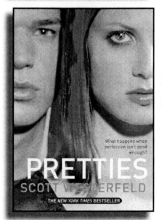

Pretties

Simon Pulse, 2011 (reprint ed). 370p. $9.99 pb. 978-1-4424-1980-3.
$9.99 ebook. 978-1-4169-8734-5.

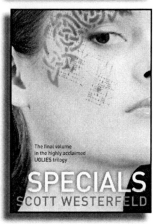

Specials

Simon Pulse, 2011 (reprint ed). 384p. $9.99 pb. 9781442419797.
$9.99 ebook. 9781439106501.

- Originally published 2005-2006

Plot Summary:

Tally Youngblood is looking forward to turning sixteen, when she'll finally get the surgery to become Pretty. The Pretties live across the river in New Pretty Town, where they party and pull pranks and generally have a great time. Tally's best friend is already there, so she sneaks in one night to see him, but is disappointed to find that he barely recognizes her.

On returning from her visit to her former friend, Tally meets Shay, a girl with enthusiasm for her life as an Ugly and some dangerous ideas to stay that way. Shay tells Tally about the Smoke, a community living off the grid and away from the government-enforced rules and procedures. Shay plans to go, and while Tally wants to go with her friend, she's also not willing to give up her chance at the Pretty surgery. It's not so easy for Tally to just let Shay go, though—not when Special Circumstances, the secret police force, wants to find the Smoke and capture its residents. Tally's surgery is withheld until she can infiltrate the group, then activate a tracker to allow the Specials to find them.

After a long journey, Tally finds the group and is accepted into their community. She slowly comes to understand and appreciate their ways, and learns more about the Pretty surgery: specifically, that the surgery involves creating lesions in the Pretties' brains, making them happy and complacent. Armed with this new knowledge, Tally changes her mind about the surgery and decides to stay in the Smoke permanently. Her efforts to destroy the tracker inadvertently activate it, though, and the small community is raided.

Along with one other survivor of the raid, Tally launches a rescue mission to break the Smokies out of Special Circumstances headquarters. There they find that Shay has been turned Pretty, but Maddy, the Smoke's doctor and researcher, might have created a cure. Before testing it on Shay, she would like to test it on a willing subject, so Tally turns herself in to the Specials and demands the surgery to make herself a Pretty.

Pretties picks up with Tally living in New Pretty Town, hoping to be accepted into Shay's clique, the Crims. A former Smoky crashes a party, reminding Tally of what she's given up, and she and another former Smoky, Zane, split a single dose of the Pretty cure. The cure works on both of them, and they have a chance to escape to New Smoke, where their community is attempting to rebuild. When they arrive, the group quickly realizes that there is a tracking device implanted in Zane's tooth, and the group must move on without him to avoid detection. Tally elects to stay behind with him, and when Special Circumstances arrives, they inform Tally that she will become a Special instead of returning to her Pretty life.

Specials, the third volume of the series, begins with Tally and Shay as Cutters, an elite group of Specials, crashing an Ugly party to find members of New Smoke. They succeed in finding a girl, but she escapes capture, and Tally and Shay are injured in the chase. Later, Tally finds Fausto, a Special who was cured. Tally narrowly escapes the meeting before being injected with the cure herself. Shay and the other Specials have been cured, and Tally is locked up as the cure begins to spread across the city. When she is finally released, it is to be "despecialized," but she fights her way out past the surgeons, becoming the last true Special remaining. At the book's conclusion, she returns to the Rusty Ruins, where her story began, to work on curing herself and rebuilding a more stable, less excessive society.

Dystopian Elements:

Evolution has worked to bias humans toward attractive things, and society has worked to make everyone as attractive as possible, giving plastic surgery at age sixteen to make faces more symmetrical and bodies more uniform. The surgery is not an option: everyone must fit the molds. The lack of diversity reinforces the desire for the same beauty standards. The standards are so ubiquitous that Tally visibly recoils from adults who have not had the Pretty procedure. More dangerous than the beauty standards, however, is their mandatory enforcement. Teens are not allowed to opt out of the Pretty surgery, and those who escape to the wild are tracked down and brought back.

Physical attractiveness is not the only thing keeping society complacent: as part of the surgery, surgeons create lesions in the pretties' brains, effectively lobotomizing them into hedonistic, superficial partyers. This makes the New Pretties easy to control, but also makes the Uglies—the teens and children under 16, who have not yet had the surgery—look forward to their own procedures, when they too will be able to have fun all the time without responsibility or concern. Further surgeries can transform people into Specials, weaponizing them as an elite police force and government agency.

The Specials procedure also involves brain lesions, this time causing feelings of superiority, ensuring that the Specials will work to maintain their place at the top of the social hierarchy.

Prior to their surgeries, Uglies can use a simulator to choose their new appearances, but these are virtually the only choices they have. Jobs will be assigned to them, and their lesions will be cured in ways that will allow them to fulfill their new roles. In Tally's case, the surgeries are used as leverage to make her act the way the Specials want her to, removing all remaining choice from her actions.

30-Second Booktalk:

Pretties live in their Pretty cities and have their Pretty parties, and it's all pretty great—no worries, no responsibilities, and best of all, no Uglies. But for those few people who don't want to be made into Pretties, the only option is to leave society all together. Tally Youngblood wants nothing more than to be made Pretty, but her only chance to have the surgery hinges on betraying her friends who have left.

Readalikes:

Surrogates (Robert Venditti) for the ability to change one's appearance

Brave New World (Aldous Huxley) for uniformity of physical appearances

Tankborn (Karen Sandler) for genetic engineering with skill sets and for racism/classism

Potential Audience:

Middle and high school students, both boys and girls, will be drawn into this three-part story. Action/adventure, politics and conspiracy, and light romance are all given equal weight, lending the series wide appeal.

Discussion Guide:

The final chapter of *Specials* is available with Westerfeld's commentary at http://www.simonandschuster.com/specials/kids/behindthepulse/uglies/specialschapterfinalB.pdf

Westerfeld, Scott

Extras

Simon Pulse, 2011 (reprint ed). 416p. $9.99 (pb). 978-1-4424-1978-0.

- Originally published 2007

Plot Summary:

Three years after Tally Youngblood and her friends took down their looks-based society, Aya Fuse is earning her social capital as a kicker, posting news stories to her feed for other citizens to view. Her Japanese city has turned to a fame-based economy, and Aya's low face-rank could cost her many opportunities.

Following a story, Aya finds the Sly Girls, a group of teens who ride the mag-lev trains. Aya begins riding with them, and they soon make a discovery: there's a secret room in the underground tunnel they've been riding through, and it's filled with canisters, all part of a Mass Driver with the potential to destroy the city. Plans to explore the room fully are derailed when Aya becomes the subject of a news story that's just been kicked, speculating on the famous Frizz Mizuno's efforts to talk to her in her dorm. Fame may be the currency in her city, but it makes the Sly Girls nervous and unwilling to trust Aya's discretion.

The next time Aya and the Sly Girls meet, the group reveals that they've known Aya's identity as a kicker for a long time, but the story of what they've found in the tunnel is too important *not* to kick. They launch themselves out of the Mass Driver and parachute to the ground, where the Sly Girls disappear and Aya kicks the story, instantly becoming one of the most famous people in the city.

Aya is very happy with the recent developments, but is unnerved to get a message from Tally Youngblood, the most famous person in the world, urging her to hide until Tally can get there. Once Tally and the other Cutters arrive, they take Aya and her friends to meet David, encountering some opposition along the way. The Cutters destroy the ships of their opposition to facilitate their escape, but the fire gets out of hand. Together, the Cutters and kickers battle the fire until they've saved the city. Aya's face-rank jumps from below 450,000 up to the third-most famous person in the world; her friends see significant boosts as well.

Dystopian Elements:

For today's teens, blogging and internet-fame is commonplace—so much so that it can be difficult to believe that news blogging had only been mainstream for a few years by the time *Extras* was published in 2007. By 2009, two years after the novel's publication, news blogging was beginning to overtake traditional print journalism. With this modern history, it is not difficult to project forward to a society that takes all of its information from the equivalent of a blogosphere, valuing the journalists according to their trustworthiness and the newsworthiness of their stories.

It is also not difficult to project from our current culture how a person's worth is dependent on their fame. Today, celebrities are famous just for being famous, as is the case with Paris Hilton[6] or other reality-television starlets. "We are living in a world now where visibility creates opportunities and reputation builds trust," says Dan Schawbel of *Forbes*. "Building an online presence and managing your reputation (like a brand) will become increasing[ly] effective and yield strong results."[7] A few months after the release of *Extras*, Westerfeld addressed his teenage readers in his blog, saying

> *"We want to know who to trust and who not to trust. Alas, whatever kind of reputation system we use—word of mouth, online, bathroom wall—there's always someone willing and able to abuse it. Pointless celebrities dominate, news channels fabricate, banks collapse, and even best friends lie to us sometimes. [...] But you guys know all this. You're the first generation to grow up with the quasi-reputation economies that are Facebook, Myspace, and Google, all of which show us who has the most friends, links, or comments."[8]*

It's his last point that is particularly noteworthy: today's teens are the first who grew up in this reputation economy, this life in which communications are increasingly virtual. Aya's world is not hard to imagine when looking at our current culture; the only question is whether it would truly take as long as Westerfeld implies to reach that point.

30-Second Booktalk:

In a fame-based economy, having more than 450,000 people more famous than you is a problem. Seeking out a news story about a group that actively wants to remain unknown is a problem. Kicking a news story about a secret weapon that could destroy the city is a *big* problem. And yet that's exactly what Aya plans to do, and she may just save the world by doing it, assuming she doesn't get herself killed instead.

Readalikes:

Uglies series (Scott Westerfeld) for background information on the Cutters and the world setting

Bumped (Megan McCafferty) for the impact of fame

Little Brother (Cory Doctorow) for using blogging and fame to incite revolution

Down and Out in the Magic Kingdom (Cory Doctorow) for reputation economy

Potential Audience:

While this is the fourth book in the *Uglies* series, it functions perfectly well as a stand-alone, focusing on different characters, a different geographical region, and different issues. Still, fans of the original trilogy will be its biggest audience, though teens who appreciate the intersection of action/adventure and technology (as in Cory Doctorow's books) will also find this a riveting read.

---

[6] For commentary on the phenomenon that is Paris Hilton's popularity, see http://chartreuse.wordpress.com/2006/09/18/why-paris-hilton-is-famous-or-understanding-value-in-a-post-madonna-world/ .

[7] http://www.forbes.com/sites/danschawbel/2011/02/28/the-reputation-economy/

[8] http://scottwesterfeld.com/blog/2007/12/reputation-economy-conference/

Part 2: The Apocalypse

What is the apocalypse but an everlasting snow day? —Scott Westerfeld

How will the world end and what will life be like for the survivors? At least since biblical times, people have been imagining the answers to those questions. The imaginings have led to a number of both apocalyptic and post-apocalyptic scenarios in books, movies, television, and other forms of entertainment.

So what sets the apocalypse apart from the post-apocalypse? The answer is as simple and obvious as a function of time: the apocalypse is currently happening; a post-apocalyptic world is creating a new life in the aftermath. Given the nature of time, there is, of course, some blending between the two categories, as characters survive the initial events and make new lives in the changed world.

Apocalyptic and post-apocalyptic tales can provide a certain amount of wish-fulfillment for teens, where they get to see their entire worlds wiped away without a second glance. In a post-apocalypse, they need to resume some kind of normalcy; in an apocalypse, there is only the blend of horror and joy at watching a high school swept away in a disaster, carrying several sources of teen stress along with it. Scott Westerfeld says as much in his essay "Breaking Down "the System'": "It's no wonder that stories about that system exploding, breaking down under its own contradictions, or simply being overrun by zombies are also beloved of teenagers.

"What" is the apocalypse but an everlasting snow day? An excuse to tear up all those college applications, which suddenly aren't going to determine the rest of your life?"[1] How can we argue with the desire to have all our weighty concerns and stresses disappear, even if we know that there will be other challenges ahead?

---

[1] Scott Westerfeld, "Breaking Down 'The System'"
http://www.nytimes.com/roomfordebate/2010/12/26/the-dark-side-of-young-adult-fiction/breaking-down-the-system

Besides the fully-understandable longing to have Friday's algebra test swept from the face of the earth, apocalyptic stories give teens a chance to compare themselves against the heroes: *in dire circumstances, would I survive?* Seeing others survive (or not survive) an apocalyptic event can provide teens with ideas and tips for their own survival should they find themselves in a ruined world. (Whether or not the tips are realistic and practical is irrelevant; it's the conceptual idea of self-sufficiency and power that matters.)

When it comes to blockbuster movies, the apocalypse is far better represented than any post-apocalyptic world, likely owing to the apocalypse's immediacy. As a source of visual interest, a world crumbling before viewers' eyes is much stronger than a more-or-less static image of abandoned, empty ruins. In this next section, we'll be looking at sixteen different views of apocalyptic worlds, ten of which are movies or television shows. This is in no way meant to imply that books do *not* handle the apocalypse as well, only that teen literature tends to be more character-driven, focusing on teens' reactions to the changed world instead of the changes directly.

There are many potential endings to the world, some far more plausible than others. One of the more likely scenarios is a result of military action, as seen in the classic *Twilight Zone* episode "Time Enough at Last," in which a man survives the blast of a hydrogen bomb due to his hiding in a bank vault to read uninterrupted, or Raymond Briggs' graphic novel *When the Wind Blows*, which features an elderly couple attempting to secure their home against a nuclear blast. (A far less likely war scenario is the alien invasion in the 2005 movie adaptation of *War of the Worlds*.)

The world could end on a much smaller scale, beginning with something as microscopic as a virus. This is the case in the 2008 miniseries adaptation of Michael Crichton's *The Andromeda Strain*, in which an extraterrestrial virus is spreading itself rapidly across the United States. More believable is the deadly flu virus that quarantines an entire Canadian island in Megan Crewe's *The Way We Fall*.

Also frighteningly possible is an apocalypse borne of environmental damage, like Saci Lloyd imagines in her *Carbon Diaries* series: in an effort to slow the environmental collapse, the government rations carbon usage, then water. *The Day after Tomorrow*, released in theaters in 2004, sparks drastic weather changes as Earth hurtles toward a new ice age. (Nature can be our worst enemy, as 2008's sci-fi thriller *The Happening* showed; the unrealistic plot involved plant spores driving people to suicide in a series of coordinated attacks around the world.) Celestial events may do us in as well: the 2007 movie *Sunshine* opens on Earth's radically changed climate as the sun dies; "The Midnight Sun" episode of *The Twilight Zone* shows Earth's temperatures rising as it spirals in toward the sun; 1998's *Deep Impact* is about the scramble to save humanity as a giant, life-ending comet bears down on the Earth.

Not every apocalyptic scenario is even a theoretical possibility, though. While the scope of this book aims to stay on the plausible side of science-fictional scenarios, it is impossible to discuss the apocalypse without at least acknowledging the recent trend of zombies. The AMC show *The Walking Dead* (beginning in 2010 and based on the graphic novel series of the same name) opens with our lead character waking up in a hospital overrun with zombies; he does not waste time figuring out the source of the disease before setting out to find his family. Brian Ralph's graphic novel *Daybreak* is similarly unconcerned with the zombies' origins, but features two characters who are still learning to navigate the zombie-filled world. In contrast, Charlie Higson creates a London overrun with zombie adults in his novel *Enemy*; the young teens and children who remain remember watching their parents get sick and turn into zombies.

Can we prepare for an apocalypse? Maybe, if we know it's coming. Luckily there have been some predictions, most notably the supposed Mayan predictions of 2012. This long-forecasted global expiration date was the genesis of 2009's disaster movie *2012*. The basic plot focused on the Earth's destruction through earthquakes, tsunamis, and volcanic eruptions, all caused by solar radiation, but the larger cause is attributed to the Mayan predictions. On the other hand, Neil Gaiman and Terry Pratchett prove that the apocalypse doesn't have to be a drag in their novel *Good Omens*, a send-up of a biblical apocalypse complete with four horsemen and an antichrist (though the antichrist was switched at birth with another boy, and thus has been raised by a normal family).

The authors and creators in this section put the world on hold in sixteen different ways. Whether it's a zombie horde or a simple flu, a comet or a carbon ration, these apocalyptic scenarios will give us much to think about as we prepare ourselves for what might occur.

Chapter 5:

The Apocalypse

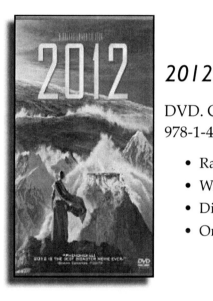

2012

DVD. Color. 158m. Produced and dist. by Columbia/Tri-Star, 2011. $19.99. 978-1-4359-3260-9.

- Rated PG-13
- Written by Roland Emmerich and Harald Kloser
- Directed by Roland Emmerich
- Originally released 2009

Plot Summary:

Geologist Adrian Helmsley is investigating the impact of solar storms on earth, and his conclusions are troubling: the increased radiation from those storms is heating the earth's core, and there's nothing scientists can do to stop or even slow the process. He gets a message to the president, urging him to begin evacuation procedures in order to save some small fraction of the human race.

Novelist Jackson Curtis has sacrificed his family in favor of his writing career, but he's making an effort to reconnect with his kids. He takes them camping in Yellowstone Park, but they are unable to reach the lakeside campsite Curtis plans on, as government security detains them and forces them out of the area. Curtis and his children camp somewhere else in the park, and late at night, Curtis picks up a nearby radio signal: Charlie is broadcasting his end-of-days predictions about Yellowstone and the rest of the United States. When Curtis tracks him down in person, Charlie tells him about the arks that the Chinese have been building for this sort of emergency, a refuge on which the chosen survivors can wait out the apocalypse.

Getting his family to the arks is no easy task as tectonic plates shift around, causing a number of earthquakes and other environmental disasters. Meanwhile, Helmsley and the politicians work on informing the public, herding the chosen people to the arks, fixing last-minute technical difficulties, and figuring out exactly how much time remains before the entirety of earth is swallowed by earthquakes, tsunamis, and volcanoes.

Apocalyptic Elements:

Loosely based on the supposed Mayan prophecy about the world ending on the winter solstice of 2012[1], this disaster movie pulls out all the stops. The increased heat of the Earth's core dislodges parts of the Earth's crust, causing massive earthquakes, which in turn trigger tsunamis. Roads buckle, chasms open, mountains crumble, and our heroes narrowly avoid death time and time again. On the big screen, these disasters are visually impressive, a triumph of a special-effects budget.

In spite of all our cautionary tales about the devastating effects humans have had on the planet, it's both refreshing and troubling to think that there's nothing we can do to prevent a coming apocalypse. In *2012*, the cause of the rise in Earth's core temperature is radiation from solar storms—not global warming, environmental damage, or other human influence. While this takes the burden off us, it also creates a helplessness that will increase the drama of a disaster movie: there is *nothing* we can do to prevent this sort of disaster scenario from happening.

30-Second Booktalk:

Radiation from solar storms has heated the earth's core, destabilizing the surface. Tectonic plates are shifting around, causing earthquakes and tsunamis. Jackson Curtis has heard a rumor of salvation: somewhere, there are arks that will survive the devastation, and all he needs to do is get his family to them. As the roads buckle under his car and the land falls away under their plane, they've only just glimpsed their challenges: how will they get from Los Angeles to the arks—in China?

Readalikes:

The Day after Tomorrow (film) for end-of-days caused by climate issues

Assassin's Creed (game series) for conspiracy surrounding December 21, 2012

The Lost Symbol (Dan Brown) for 2012 doomsday prophecies

Dark Parallel (M.G. Harris) for Mayan mythology and prophecy

Potential Audience:

Primarily boys and fans of action and/or disaster movies. The drama surrounding Curtis's efforts to reconnect with his kids and his jealousy of his ex-wife's new boyfriend will appeal to an older, more adult audience, but this part of the story gets buried under the big-budget explosions.

---

[1] According to the Mayan long-count calendar, the previous world ended after 13 b'ak'tuns (approximately 5,125 years), and the end of the next cycle of 13 b'ak'tuns will fall on December 21, 2012. Modern-day Mayans put little stock in doomsday prophecies; the idea that the world will end on this date is a more modern invention spread through the Internet and speculative documentaries.

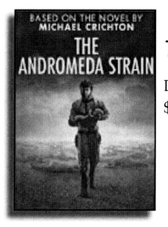

The Andromeda Strain

DVD. Color. 177m. Produced and dist. by Universal Home Video, 2008. $14.98. 978-6-3120-5894-6.

- TV Miniseries
- Written by Robert Schenkkan, based on the novel by Michael Crichton
- Directed by Mikael Salomon
- Originally released 2008

Have the Book

Plot Summary:

Two teenagers witness the crash of a US government satellite and bring the satellite back into town. The town's residents open the satellite, releasing a bioorganism that kills nearly everyone in the vicinity. A military team sent to retrieve the satellite also dies. Wildfire, a team of five scientists called into duty whenever a biological threat is detected, is sent to retrieve the satellite; properly suited, they do so.

The researches begin studying the Andromeda strain inside their underground laboratory. They determine that it has no DNA or amino acids, and they suggest that it may be extraterrestrial in origin. They learn that it is an airborne toxin, and that it causes death within 10 seconds of inhalation.

Unfortunately, all this knowledge does not get the scientists any closer to a cure: Andromeda seems to communicate with other samples of itself, even over great distances, mutating and adapting rapidly to changing treatments and conditions. When the scientists discover that Andromeda's sulfur structure makes it powerless against *Bacillus infernus*, a bacteria found on the ocean floor, they race to culture enough of the bacteria to spray over the infected areas, needing to eradicate Andromeda all at once to prevent it from mutating again.

The miniseries' final scene shows a vial of the Andromeda strain being carefully locked in a satellite, implying that there could be another Andromeda outbreak in Earth's future.

Apocalyptic Elements:

There is very little immunity to Andromeda: the extraterrestrial infection is unlike anything previously seen by scientists, and the few who have survived have virtually nothing in common with each other. With so little to go on, the Wildfire team has no suggestions for the public on keeping themselves safe. Instead, all they can do is hurry their research and track the outbreaks, hoping they can destroy it before it reaches an airport, as one international flight will cause a global pandemic.

Humanity is not completely wiped out by Andromeda; not every region is affected. Andromeda's ability to spread itself and communicate over large distances makes it a serious threat to life on Earth, though, as it continually mutates to infect other organisms. The Wildfire team manages to contain and destroy Andromeda before it can cause a true global apocalypse, but its ability to kill full towns and military bases in minutes poses a threat against humanity should the virus return to Earth.

30-Second Booktalk:

Bringing a crashed satellite back to town wasn't the worst thing the two teens did, but opening it was. Inside the satellite was the deadly Andromeda strain, the airborne toxin that kills inside of ten seconds. Scientists on the Wildfire project are tasked with finding a way to destroy it, but how do you destroy something that doesn't have DNA and can adapt to your efforts almost instantly? Wildfire is running out of time, because Andromeda is about to swallow the whole planet.

Readalikes:

The Andromeda Strain (Michael Crichton) for the original source material (1969)

The Happening (film) for a nearly-unbeatable, seemingly-sentient fatal toxin

Sweet Tooth (Jeff Lemire) for government-sponsored research of infection

Potential Audience:

Teens should be aware that this 2008 miniseries is not an adaptation of Crichton's 1969 novel, nor is it a remake of the 1971 movie; rather, it is considered a "reimagining" of the source material, updating the technology to 21st-century knowledge and reinventing some characters. With that in mind, this miniseries will appeal to amateur biologists and sci-fi fans in high school and beyond.

Briggs, Raymond

When the Wind Blows

Penguin, 1988. 48p. $5.95 pbk. 978-0-14-009419-0. Out of print.

- Originally published 1982

Plot Summary:

The creator of *The Snowman* brings us this short graphic novel account of a retired British couple preparing for a nuclear attack. Jim has picked up a brochure from the public library on how best to build and stock a shelter, and immediately sets about doing so. He takes down doors and sets them at recommended angles to create the structure, paints over the windows, and together he and his wife stock food in their little shelter, too. Jim and Hilda squabble about little things, like the damage the preparations have caused to the paint and curtains and their lack of peanut butter, which neither of them likes, though the brochure says they should stock it.

Their preparations pay off when a nuclear bomb hits London, and Jim and Hilda survive the initial blast within their makeshift shelter. The next morning, they survey the damage: windows blown out, water bottles spilled, water and electricity out, but they are alive and together, so the inconveniences are just that. Over the next few days, though, as they try to go about their lives, they slowly succumb to radiation poisoning, still calm and happy and sweetly dotty just being together.

Apocalyptic Elements:

When the Wind Blows deals with the days immediately surrounding the nuclear attack, with a larger context of a world at war. Originally published in 1982, the book was written and illustrated at the beginning of the increasingly-militaristic second cold war, with Russia viewed as the major threat. The Soviets had recently invaded Afghanistan, a move decried by 34 Islamic nations and protested by the U.N. General Assembly. Briggs never confirms that the Russians are behind the missile launch, but his characters assume it was a "Russkie" attack—though as they get mixed up in their memories of sheltering through World War II, they occasionally blame the Germans. Jim speculates on what each government is doing and can do in the unsteady political situation, but his readings of the newspaper do not confirm any of the players.

The British government produced a series of brochures, *Protect and Survive*, for citizens in 1976, then reprinted it in 1980. They are as Briggs depicts them in his gently-mocking way, suggesting people will survive nuclear fallout inside a lean-to made of household doors and sandbags. (These brochures have been reproduced online at http://www.atomica.co.uk/main.htm.) The speed with which radiation sickness attacks both Jim and Hilda highlights the severity of the attack and the ineffectiveness of their shelter.

30-Second Booktalk:

Jim returns home from the public library with a brochure on how to construct a bomb shelter, following a morning spent reading about a coming war. He immediately sets about building the little shelter for himself and his wife, finishing stocking it with just minutes to go before a nuclear bomb hits. Jim and Hilda retain their good cheer even in the aftermath of the attack, but good cheer may not be enough to weather catastrophe like this.

Readalikes:

Z for Zachariah (Robert C. O'Brien) or *Barefoot Gen* (Keiji Nakazawa) for the aftermath of nuclear war

Gentleman Jim (Raymond Briggs) for an earlier story with these characters

The War Game (film) for a 1967 fictional documentary about the effects of a nuclear attack on a small British town

Potential Audience:

That Jim and Hilda are an older, retired couple limits the teen appeal of this graphic novel, but older teens who grew up with *The Snowman* will likely enjoy seeing some of Briggs's other work. The historical context could make this an interesting supplemental read for classroom discussions of the Cold War and relations with Russia.

Crewe, Megan

The Way We Fall

Hyperion, 2012. 304p. $16.99 978-1-4231-4616-2.

Plot Summary:

Kaelyn is trying to reinvent herself this year, to stop being the old, timid, shy Kaelyn. Before making decisions, she asks herself, "What would the new Kaelyn do?" The new Kaelyn would visit a sick friend and try to strengthen that budding friendship. But that friend has the cough, and the unbearable itching. That friend has the virus. The unnamed virus is infecting more and more people across the small Canadian island, and soon the World Health Organization is called in to quarantine them.

The government has promised that the quarantine won't disrupt day-to-day life on the island: they'll still send ferries with food and medical supplies from the mainland, and communication lines will still be open. Unfortunately, the government has underestimated the demand for the items, and riots break out on the docks as the supply boats get mobbed. More and more people are getting sick, and neither the doctors, the immunologists, nor the WHO has any idea what's causing it or how to cure it. Almost nobody survives the virus, and with food and medical supplies growing scarce, it's starting to look like nobody will survive *not* having the virus, either.

Kaelyn's immunologist father almost never comes from hospital and her brother has disappeared in search of an unguarded path to the mainland; her uncle was killed in the riot and his young daughter is living with them now. When her mother succumbs to the virus at Thanksgiving, Kaelyn sees the beginning of the end. She's trying to hold things together for her family, but her family is falling apart around her. When she begins to itch, she knows that she has the virus, too. Whether she becomes a rare survivor or succumbs is out of her hands.

Apocalyptic Elements:

The modern-day setting keeps this from feeling as bleak as many traditional dystopias or post-apocalypses, and it isn't either one. It is, in its way, apocalyptic, though: the quarantine isolates the island, making the islanders effectively the only people still around. In addition to being physically cut off from the outside world (even supplies are dropped by helicopter, rather than risk supply boats getting too close), communication between the island and the mainland is spotty at best. The unknown virus epidemic is an apocalyptic event, destroying everything and everyone. Things never get quite as desperate as in true apocalyptic books, but there is still looting, hoarding, and scavenging of food and supplies.

30-Second Booktalk:

Kaelyn is trying to reinvent herself this year. The new Kaelyn willingly visits a sick friend, trying to strengthen that budding friendship. But that friend has the cough and the unbearable itching. It's the unnamed virus, infecting more and more people across the small Canadian island, until the whole island is quarantined. Even the World Health Organization is stumped, and unless someone has a breakthrough soon, the whole island will be left to die.

Readalikes:

Life as We Knew It (Susan Beth Pfeffer) for scarcity of both goods and people, epidemic of illnesses, and similarities in tone and scope

Epitaph Road (David Patneaude) for fatal illness wiping out full communities

Matched (Ally Condie) for a seemingly-weak female drawing on inner strength

How I Live Now (Meg Rosoff) for organization in light of disaster

Potential Audience:

Between the light romance, family dramas, and leisurely pace, this will appeal most to high-school girls. Middle schoolers will also appreciate the story, but may not get as much out of the isolation themes.

The Day after Tomorrow

DVD. Color. 123m. Produced and dist. by Fox Home Entertainment, 2007. $14.98. 978-6-3086-8173-8.

- Originally released 2004
- Written by Roland Emmerich and Jeffrey Nachmanoff
- Directed by Roland Emmerich

Plot Summary:

Climatologist Jack Hall presents his findings on global warming at a United Nations conference, but United States officials are unconcerned. Professor Rapson, a Scottish researcher, sees several buoys in the north Atlantic registering massive, sudden temperature changes and concludes that polar ice melting into the ocean is causing big problems with the currents. He contacts Jack, and together they build weather models that predict a new and sudden ice age.

Sam, Jack's teenage son, is in New York City for an academic competition when the weather takes a turn. Giant hail falls in Japan, snow blankets New Dehli, tornadoes touch down in Los Angeles, and severe rains flood New York. Sam calls his father and promises to get on the next train home, only to find that the subways and trains have all been flooded and shut down. The combination of rain and the rising tide flood the city streets, pushing residents and visitors toward safe, high ground: the New York Public Library. Sam and his friends are temporarily safe, but outside the temperature rapidly drops as massive hurricane-like superstorms hold super-cooled air nearby.

With Sam's group unable to get home, Jack and his team set out to rescue the teens. They make it as far as Philadelphia in their truck and have to snowshoe the remainder of the journey. The few people who stayed in the library, rather than attempting a trip south in the bitter cold, have been burning books for heat and raiding vending machines for food. With their circumstances getting more dire, Sam and two friends make the perilous journey outside to scavenge food and medicine. They make it back to the library just ahead of the super-cooled eye of the storm, which instantly freezes everything it passes over. Just after the storm dissipates, Jack and his one remaining team member find the library and dig down until they find a window. Sam and Jack are reunited and Jack radios the government about the group of survivors. The President orders more helicopters dispatched to search for more survivors; Sam's group is evacuated from New York. The final shots of the movie are of astronauts looking down on the northern hemisphere, covered in ice and snow.

Apocalyptic Elements:

As the world is being plagued by a variety of severe weather from hail to tornadoes, life falls apart in nearly as many ways. The storm that freezes New York City is only one of three major storms that have split off. The only geographic region viewers really see is the mid-Atlantic, from Philadelphia to New York City, but it is implied that the situation is roughly the same everywhere in the northern hemisphere: blizzards and freezing temperatures as the storm passes through, leaving behind dozens of feet of snow. Even after the storms dissipate, it will be a long time before the survivors can resume their lives. Society has, quite literally, frozen in its tracks.

Climate change is nothing new: scientists have been monitoring global temperatures for decades, aware that the changes will lead to another ice age. *The Day after Tomorrow* plays on our fears, but the movie's science is flawed. Weather Underground's Director of Meteorology Jeffrey Masters (PhD) debunks the movie, stating that, "The only types of storms planet Earth can manage are the current ordinary hurricanes, blizzards, and thunderstorms. The formation and evolution of the superstorm as described in *The Day after Tomorrow* . . . is a meteorological impossibility."[2]

30-Second Booktalk:

Sam and his friends are excited to compete in an academic competition, but they didn't expect the trip to New York to be as cool as it turns out: a superstorm over New York City causes major flooding before the temperature starts plummeting. As the super-chilled eye of the storm passes over, instantly freezing everything beneath it, Sam finds himself in a sudden ice age from which they might never be rescued.

Readalikes:

Life as We Knew It (Susan Beth Pfeffer) for survival after dramatic climate change

The Coming Global Superstorm (Whitley Streiber and Art Bell) for the pseudoscience book on which the film is loosely based

The Midnight Sun (Twilight Zone episode) for another frozen-world scenario

Trapped (Michael Northrup) for teens sheltering in a building through a severe blizzard

Potential Audience:

The Day after Tomorrow is rated PG-13 for "intense situations of peril," making the film most appropriate for high schoolers. As disaster movies go, this is a fairly gentle choice, featuring no explosions and little person-on-person violence.

---

[2] Masters, Jeffrey, PhD. *The Day after Tomorrow*™: Could it really happen? Weather Underground, Inc. http://www.wunderground.com/resources/education/thedayafter.asp?MR=1 Accessed 11/20/2012.

Deep Impact

Blu-Ray. Color. 121m. Produced and dist. by Paramount, 2011. $14.99. 978-6-3130-5483-1.

- Written by Bruce Joel Rubin and Michael Tolkin
- Directed by Mimi Leder
- Originally released 1998

Plot Summary:

Reporter Jenny Lerner is investigating the sudden resignation of United States Secretary of the Treasury and his connection to a mysterious "Ellie." Lerner's research reveals that Ellie is not a woman, but an extinction-level event (E.L.E.)—specifically, a seven-mile-wide comet that is on a collision path with the Earth and could wipe out all life.

The United States and Russia have been working on building the *Messiah*, a spacecraft that will deliver a nuclear payload into the comet to break it apart and prevent it from destroying the Earth. When the payload is detonated, though, it fails to break the comet into many small parts; instead it breaks it into two smaller comets, each capable of causing global extinction.

In light of this news, governments begin selecting people to live in underground shelters when the comets hit. The United States can shelter one million Americans in the limestone caves of Missouri, 80 percent of whom will be chosen by lottery. With humanity preserved, officials make a last-ditch effort to deflect the two comets; the attempts fail and everyone braces for impact. The smaller comet lands in the Atlantic ocean, sending a tsunami that destroys New York City and much of the coastline on both sides of the Atlantic.

The crew of the *Messiah* knows that they are unlikely to make it back to Earth on their remaining fuel stores, and even if they did, the chances of their survival are slim. With these considerations, they undertake a suicide mission, piloting the ship and its remaining nuclear load into a fissure in the remaining comet. The ship explodes, fragmenting the comet into small pieces that burn up in the Earth's atmosphere, saving humanity.

Apocalyptic Elements:

While the film ends with millions of lives lost and thousands of miles of Atlantic coastline destroyed by the tsunami, *Deep Impact* is mostly a *pre*-apocalyptic movie: the plot is not about coping with a world destroyed, but a world preparing for its destruction. There is no question that the comet will hit the Earth; the only question is of who will survive.

This is not to say no effort is taken to deflect the comet and save humanity. The United States partners with Russia to construct a spacecraft capable of depositing nuclear charges inside the comet to blow it into pieces, but this attempt only fractures it into two comets. With the knowledge that life on Earth is in jeopardy, governments do the next logical thing: find a safe place to house a large number of people who can contribute to society in the aftermath. The United States creates a shelter out of the caves under Missouri and decides it can shelter one million people. In the interest of creating a well-balanced society post-disaster, 800,000 people are chosen by lottery, but the remaining

200,000 are pre-selected to ensure certain things are preserved. Scientists and prominent politicians and officials are included, but teachers and artists are also on the list, showing an understanding of the value of arts and education in everyday lives.

30-Second Booktalk:

High-schooler Leo is at the telescope one night when he notices something odd in the sky. It turns out to be a comet, seven miles across and headed straight for the Earth. The government has a plan to destroy it, but when the plan doesn't work out, it looks like humanity might be doomed.

Readalikes:

Armageddon (film) for similar premise with a more action-heavy execution
The Road (Cormac McCarthy) for the after-effects of a celestial object's collision with Earth
The Day after Tomorrow (film) for the destruction of New York City by tsunami
Life As We Knew It (Susan Beth Pfeffer) for preparations for and aftermath of astronomical disaster

Potential Audience:

A PG-13 rating leaves this disaster movie perfectly appropriate for eighth grade and up, but its quiet, person-focused story will appeal more to introspective high school and college students than to those who traditionally seek disaster movies.

Gaiman, Neil and Terry Pratchett

Good Omens: The Nice and Accurate Prophecies of Agnes Nutter, Witch

HarperCollins, 2006. 412p. $7.99 pb. 978-0-06-085398-3.
$9.99 ebook. 978-0-0619-9112-7.

- Originally published 1990

Plot Summary:

In 1655, Agnes Nutter recorded all her prophecies into a book, the only remaining copy of which is owned by her descendant Anathema Device. One of her prophecies was about the end of the world, which is due next Saturday afternoon.

The Four Horsemen of the Apocalypse have gathered, ready to ride in on their motorcycles. Everyone's been keeping an eye on the Antichrist since he was born eleven years ago. The only problem is that the boy they've been watching—the son of a wealthy diplomat—was switched at birth, and the true Antichrist—Adam—has been living a quiet life with typical parents in the British countryside. Adam doesn't know about his powers, blithely using them to transform the hellhound into a typical scruffy mutt of a dog and grant himself other childhood wishes.

The representatives of good and evil—the angel Aziraphale from the Garden of Eden and the demon Crowley, the serpent from the same garden, respectively—know that it's nearly Judgement Day. They also know that they don't want the world to end, having gotten accustomed to the comforts of Earth and developing an affection for humanity. Anathema Device doesn't want the world to end, either; she's still living in it, after all. Preventing—or at least delaying—the coming Apocalypse means finding the Antichrist, and finding the Antichrist means deciphering the particularly obtuse, possible-drunken prophecies of Agnes Nutter.

Apocalyptic Elements:

Good Omens is unambiguously about the coming apocalypse, but it is not the result of a natural disaster or environmental damage. This is a lighthearted take on the Book of Revelations—a biblical apocalypse that shows a human side to Judgement Day.

The Four Horsemen of the Apocalypse have been given a more modern twist, showing up on motorcycles in this reimagining. Death, War, and Famine are joined now by Pollution, Pestilence having retired after the invention of Penicillin; Famine spends his off hours creating fad diets and tiny-portioned *nouvelle* cuisine.

Even the Antichrist is a result of human error: the boy assumed to be the harbinger of the apocalypse was switched at birth in a hospital mix-up. Instead of being raised as a diplomat's son, he lives an almost idyllic life in the country, raised by completely typical parents. He gets into his fair share of mischief, exasperating his parents and neighbors while remaining beloved by all.

From the first pages, the reader knows that the end of the world is coming, and all the events of the plot are leading up to this point. What really drives the novel is the human element: what it means to be human, how close good and evil can be, the age-old argument of nature versus nurture. The basic premise is straight out of Revelations, but the execution is an affectionate poking at the heaviness of the end of the world.

30-Second Booktalk:

The end of the world is coming. The Antichrist was accidentally switched at birth into a normal family, so he won't be much help. The Four Horsemen of the Apocalypse are ready to ride in on their motorcycles (horses being such antiquated vehicles), but the angel and demon who should be wrestling for control have come to a conclusion: neither actually *wants* the world to end. So much for divine plans.

Readalikes:

Discworld (series) (Terry Pratchett) for similar humor and for more of the character of Death

The Omen (film) for the basis of the tongue-in-cheek ideas of *Good Omens*

The Seventh Sign (film) for the potential birth of the Antichrist and the coming of Judgement Day

Lamb: The Gospel According to Biff, Christ's Childhood Pal (Christopher Moore) for another religious satire

Potential Audience:

High school teens who appreciate sly British humor will be the best audience for this novel, though it has broad appeal to nearly anyone interested in a lighter look at the end of the world.

The Happening

DVD. Color. 91m. Produced and dist. by Fox Home Entertainment, 2009. $14.98. 978-6-3123-9380-1.

- Written and directed by M. Night Shyamalan
- Originally released 2008

Plot Summary:

Starting in Central Park, people are getting confused: repeating themselves, using the wrong words, becoming disoriented—and then they commit suicide. Officials assume that this is a bioterrorism attack, and the neurotoxin quickly spreads through the Northeast: Philadelphia is affected, then Boston, then smaller and smaller towns.

Elliot, a high-school science teacher in Philadelphia, evacuates the city with his wife, Alma, his friend and coworker Julian, and Julian's young daughter Jess. They head toward Harrisburg by train, but the train loses radio contact and lets everyone off in a small Pennsylvania town instead. Julian leaves his daughter with Elliot and goes to find his wife.

With the train stopped and the neurotoxin spreading, the train's passengers begin to move out of the small town, hitching rides with locals who are also fleeing. Elliot, Alma, and Jess find a ride with the owner of a plant nursery; he and Elliot discuss a theory that the plants are releasing this toxin as a defense mechanism against humans, and that the plants are targeting large groups of people. They stop at a crossroads, where travelers from all directions report more suicides in towns behind them. With nowhere else to go, they set out on foot across the fields in small groups.

As their group shrinks, Elliot, Alma, and Jess find themselves traveling alone, and they stop to beg food and shelter from an elderly woman in her isolated house. Mrs. Jones has no contact with the outside world and is unaware of the threat. The next morning, Elliot sees her succumb to the toxin and locks himself in the basement. Using an old talking tube between buildings he urges Alma and Jess to close all the doors and windows in the barn where they've been playing. Elliot and Alma decide that, if they're going to die, they would rather it be together, and they leave the relative safety of their respective buildings. Once they are reunited, they realize that they are unaffected, and that the spreading of the plant toxin has ended as mysteriously as it began.

The movie closes with a similar scene to the movie's opening, only in a different country: people appear confused, freeze in place, and a scream is heard as the first victim commits suicide, implying that the toxin has invaded another region.

Apocalyptic Elements:

Within minutes of a deadly toxin's release in New York City's Central Park, most of the city is frozen in place or driven to suicide, with no explanations. Anywhere that people are gathered in large numbers is a target, and as the day wears on, even individuals are targets. Entire cities are being emptied of their human population literally overnight.

The limited nature of the attack, both in geography and time, may cause some to question *The Happening* as an apocalyptic movie. However, the release of this toxin kills most of the people in the northeastern United States, with an implication that this is only the first of many such attacks around the globe. Long-term, this stands to wipe out a good portion of humanity, leaving the remaining people in a state of anxious paranoia: *Will this happen again? Will I be so lucky a second time?* As director M. Night Shyamalan says in his 2008 conversation with the *New York Daily News*, "[*The Happening*] exists in the paranoia of our society [...], where we're scared of strangers and we're scared of our neighbors and we're scared of letting our kids play outside."[3]

30-Second Booktalk:

Confusion, disorientation, then suicide, all within a few minutes: who is responsible for the deadly neurotoxin spreading through the northeastern United States? Elliot has a theory, but a theory won't help him if he can't keep himself and his family ahead of the wind.

Readalikes:

The Maze Runner (James Dashner) for a toxic environment

"The Monsters Are Due on Maple Street" (Twilight Zone episode, 1960) for paranoia

Nausicaá of the Valley of the Wind (Hayao Miyazaki, manga or film) for plants using toxins for defense

The Road (Cormac McCarthy) for small groups of people traveling in search of safer places

Potential Audience:

With its "R" rating, *The Happening* is aimed at older teens and adults. Plenty of younger teens will enjoy the light-thriller and B-movie aspects of this movie, though plot holes and generally poor writing may strain even the most dedicated fans of bad movies.

---

[3] http://www.nydailynews.com/entertainment/movies/2008/06/08/2008-06-08_shyamalan_back_on_terror_firma.html#ixzz0OlGyryDS

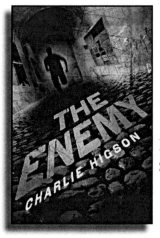

Higson, Charlie ✓

The Enemy

Hyperion, 2009. 448p. $16.99. 978-1-4231-3175-5.
$8.99 pb. 978-1-4231-3312-4.

in system as Charles

Plot Summary:

Nobody knows exactly what happened. A year ago, the sickness infected all the adults—everyone over age sixteen—and turned them into flesh-eating zombies. No one under fourteen has been infected, leaving kids and young teens to pull together into small gangs for their own survival. They barricade themselves in supermarkets, warehouses, former schools, any building that can shelter them and provide some defense against the adults.

One group in particular has been sheltering inside the Waitrose supermarket, but they know their situation is precarious. When Small Sam is taken out of their yard, Arran and Maxie finally have to admit that the zombies—the grown-ups—are getting smarter and more organized. This is confirmed when Arran leads a scavenging party in search of food, and they are ambushed trying to get a vending machine out of a swimming pool—a trap laid by the grown-ups to lure them in. In the resulting battle, one boy is killed and Arran is bitten.

Back at the Waitrose that evening, a boy stands outside their gates and calls to them: there is another group of kids and teens sheltering at Buckingham Palace, and if the Waitrose group can make it across London, they would be welcomed into the safety of the Palace. After some discussion, the Waitrose group agrees and prepares for the journey. As they leave the area, they join with another gang from the nearby Morrison's supermarket.

The Waitrose and Morrison's groups slowly make their way across London, avoiding as many skirmishes as they can with the roving adults. They do have one major battle, though, in which Arran attacks the zombies with such fury that he is mistaken for one of them and killed by friendly fire. In spite of this loss to the group, they eventually make it to Buckingham Palace, where they discover that the seeming utopia is hiding some dark secrets.

The new arrivals must prove their worth to the Palace group before they will be fully welcomed, and in order to do that, they must resolve a territory dispute with a group of local squatters. The Waitrose group wins, but only barely. On returning to the Palace, Maxie voices her concerns about the Palace's leader, David, and the Waitrose group plots an escape. David attempts to stop them, but they leave anyway, taking their chances with the squatters and the roaming zombies—who are growing smarter every day.

Apocalyptic Elements:

The infection began about a year ago, though no one truly knows how or why it only affects adults. The result is a generation of children left to fend for themselves and avoid the flesh-hungry zombie hordes. In the beginning, avoiding them was not difficult, but as the zombies grow smarter and organize, adequate shelters become less secure. Without adults around, all modern conveniences grind to a halt. Electricity becomes spotty; trash does not get collected; children must learn to cook and care for themselves. Several of the teens remember their parents before they turned; a few have memories of needing to kill or escape from their parents before those adults turned on the kids and killed them.

Children and teens under sixteen years old can still be killed by the zombies, but they are not at risk of the infection. There are a few adults who survived the initial infection, as Small Sam discovers: a couple has been living in the subway tunnels, capturing children who wander down and using them for food. When Sam escapes with another captured child, the man who had been keeping them chases them to the surface, where he dies almost instantly, proving that the infection is something in the above-ground air.

The origins of the infection are not fully explored; the companion book (*The Dead*) begins just a few weeks after the infection begins spreading.

30-Second Booktalk:

It's been long enough since the Disaster that the lucky ones have died. Anyone left over 14 is infected, turned into mindless, bloated zombies seeking a quick meal of the living. One group of kids has been holed up in a supermarket for protection, and they know they can't stay there forever. The trek across London to the relative safety of Buckingham Palace isn't going to be as easy as it sounds—and it *sounds* like a bloodbath waiting to happen.

Readalikes:

Zombicorns (John Green) for zombie infection

Gone (Michael Grant), for adult-targeted disappearance and resulting kid-centric world

Forest of Hands and Teeth (Carrie Ryan) for promise of a better, zombie-free world somewhere out there if only you can reach it

Fallout 3 (Video Game) for the side plot of children forming an adult-free society, forcing adults out

The Dead (Charlie Higson) for a prequel to the events of *The Enemy*

Potential Audience:

Filled with non-stop action and plenty of zombie gore, high school boys will be all over this one—and plenty of girls will be right beside them. Middle school readers (and their parents) may be put off by the graphic violence, but strong-stomached horror-movie buffs will clamor for this gritty zombie apocalypse.

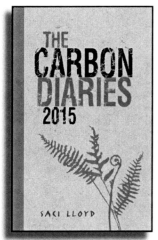

Lloyd, Saci

The Carbon Diaries: 2015

Holiday House, 2009. 330p. $8.95 pb. 978-0-8234-2301-9.

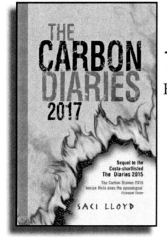

The Carbon Diaries: 2017

Holiday House, 2011. 326p. $8.95 pb. 978-0-8234-2390-3.

- Originally published 2008-2009

Plot Summary:

Laura Brown is not thrilled when London passes out carbon ration cards. Not only will it be that much harder to jam with her band, *the dirty angels*, but now she has to put up with her parents and sister, who are all reacting in strange ways. Her mom is distraught at needing to take the bus instead of driving; her sister (bitchy at the best of times) racks up so much carbon debt that she's enrolled in the mandatory Carbon Offenders program. Dad gets fired from his job, teaching about travel (because who can travel under rationing?) and ultimately finds a future in pig farming.

Laura's got her own things going on—besides the band, she's having issues with her schoolwork (because who can concentrate?) and boys (who are jerks, sweet and beautiful jerks), and mainly the craziness that is her family. Then the climate shifts just a little bit more, and soon carbon won't be the only thing being rationed—droughts across Europe may cause water rationing as well. Luckily, it finally rains—but the rain doesn't stop, and the levies aren't enough to keep London from flooding.

In *Carbon Diaries: 2017*, Laura is attending college in London while her parents make a life for themselves in the country, but two years of rationing are taking a toll on everyone. When her roommates skip the rent payments over break and get evicted, Laura has no place to go but the squats down on the docks. It's dirty and unsafe, but it's free and she'll have a chance to rebuild her carbon balance by living in a place where she won't use any of those points.

Laura is still hanging in, playing gigs with her band and going to school, but things start to fall apart when the government begins severe crackdowns on students rioting and suspected of rioting. *The dirty angels* are offered a tour across Europe with another band, and with nothing holding them to London, they set off in a battered van. On tour, they encounter droughts, riots, water wars, and waves of desperation, as people emigrate from one country only to find things just as bad in the new places. On the *angels'* return to London, they find protest groups, guerrilla armies, and rioters in a face-off with military forces over control of the city. Laura and her friends can either be a part of the revolution, or be crushed beneath it.

Post-Apocalyptic Elements:

The first years of rationing are tough on everybody; it's a huge adjustment to a new way of life. Expectations of privacy are all but forgotten as the government steps in to regulate and monitor carbon usage, going so far as to send over-spenders to the Carbon Offenders Rehabilitation Outreach Centre and make periodic Procedure Review Checkups. Political protests are becoming common by the end of the first book, with citizens protesting Parliament's handling of the rationing and their future plans to weather the environmental crises. By the second book, police and military troops are authorized to use force to quell riots and arrest protesters, curfew breakers, and anyone else suspected of rebellious activity.

The government's strict oversight of everyday lives could qualify this series as a dystopian version of London, but it's more accurate to call this apocalyptic: the world is, almost literally, falling apart. The Prime Minister signs carbon rationing into law in an effort to bring down the UK's carbon emissions and counter global warming, but the damage may have already been done. Storms are flooding London while other regions are under severe water rationing due to drought; malaria and other diseases are on the rise. A new environmental treaty among nations may help countries to mitigate the damage, but the government will have to agree to sign it.

30-Second Booktalk:

The Carbon Diaries: 2015: Carbon rationing is hitting everyone hard: Laura's sister is burning through the family's carbon credits by flying to Spain, their mom is freaked out by riding buses instead of driving her fancy car, and their dad … well, he's thinking of a career move into pig farming. Laura wants her life back, time to jam with her band, and maybe get Ravi next door to notice her. There's a black market in carbon springing up, politics are getting messy, and global warming is kicking off some big storms—like the one threatening to flood London.

The Carbon Diaries: 2017: Two years after the start of carbon rationing, Laura's parents have moved out to the country while she attends college in London. Between living in a squat in a seedy, frequently-flooded neighborhood and the military crackdown on students suspected of rioting, Laura and the rest of the band jump at the chance to go on a European tour. Instead of fame and fortune, they find droughts, water rationing, and the desperation of refugees from worse-off regions. Returning to London gives the band a choice: be part of the revolution, or be crushed beneath it.

Readalikes:

Water Wars (Cameron Stracher) for limited water access

The Limit (Kristen Landon) for government monitoring of commodity usage

Lemonade Mouth (Mark Peter Hughes) for band politics and jamming

Punk Rock Etiquette: The Ultimate How-to Guide for DIY, Punk, Indie, and Underground Bands (Travis Nichols) for punk band culture

Potential Audience:

A good choice for budding environmentalists or those into music/punk/band scenes. The novels are perfectly appropriate for seventh grade and up, though high schoolers will get more out of them.

"The Midnight Sun" *The Twilight Zone*

Blu-Ray Black & White. 950m. Produced and dist. by Image Entertainment, 2011. $99.98. 978-6-3139-9501-1.

- Originally aired 1961

Plot Summary:

Norma is a painter, painting burning city after burning city. Her inspiration is her everyday world: the Earth has slipped in its orbit and gotten a little closer to the sun. Most people have left the city, either moving north in search of cooler weather or dying in the heat. Norma's only company in her apartment building is her landlady.

The two women are struggling in the heat and with the new restrictions: electricity is being strictly conserved; water is only turned on for an hour each day. The landlady begins to crack under the pressure of the intense heat, demanding that Norma paint something other than burning cities. They are interrupted by footsteps in the hall, and despite Norma's threatening him with a gun, the man breaks in and drinks all their water. He apologizes, assuring them that he meant them no physical harm, but his thirst drove him to looting.

Norma shows the landlady her latest painting: a cool waterfall. Delighted, the landlady claims she can feel the cool spray, then collapses on the floor and dies. The temperature pushes past 120 degrees, breaking the thermometer, and Norma's oil paintings begin melting. Norma also collapses.

The scene changes to the apartment at night, with a raging blizzard outside and Norma with a raging fever inside. The intense heat was only a dream; in reality, the Earth is moving away from the sun, causing temperatures to plummet into a near ice age.

Apocalyptic Elements:

In the aftermath of an unspecified event, the Earth has slipped in its orbit, circling ever-closer to the sun. As a result, the temperatures are rising, killing millions of people. Food and water are scarce, and the luxuries of air conditioning are in short supply as electricity is restricted. The heat has some deadly physical effects, but takes a mental toll on the survivors as well: the radio weatherman breaks down on the air, and the landlady hallucinates when viewing Norma's painting of a lake and waterfall.

The reality is just as bad: the Earth has actually moved away from the sun, causing temperatures to plummet and the city to be blanketed in snow. There is still the implication that the city has emptied. Dangerously, Norma is ill, and while there is still a doctor available, for how long can the viewer reasonably expect that to be the case? Currently the thermometer is reading -10 degrees, which, while dangerously cold, is not far off from the average winter temperatures in parts of Canada and other northern countries.

Whether it will be excessive heat or extreme cold, it is clear that survival is tenuous at best. The Earth is steadily moving away from the sun (or towards it, in the dream), which will result in the temperatures continuing to get more extreme until they are, literally, unendurable.

30-Second Booktalk:

It's hot, and getting hotter. There is no air conditioning, no fans, and for twenty-three hours a day, no water. Norma and her landlady are the last ones left in their apartment building after everyone else has either gone north or died. The city is boiling and the Earth slides toward the sun. And the mercury continues to rise.

Readalikes:

Life As We Knew It (Susan Beth Pfeffer) for climate change in the wake of astronomical disasters

2012 (film) and *Sunshine* (film) for climate change

The Sky Inside (Clare B. Dunkle) for a world too hot and dangerous to survive in

Potential Audience:

Twilight Zone fans will probably recognize this, one of the more well-known episodes. Middle and high school teens will be drawn into the brief story and surprised by the ending's reversal of the plot.

Ralph, Brian

Daybreak

- Drawn & Quarterly, 2011. 160p. $21.95 978-1-77046-055-3.
- Originally published in three pamphlets, 2006-2008

Plot Summary:

Daybreak opens with an older teen directly addressing the reader, involving "you" in the plot. The one-armed teen invites you back to his shelter for the night to get out of the dark, and once inside, he offers food and water.

After a good night's sleep, you wake to find the teen has waited for you before heading off to scavenge for the day. He shows you to an abandoned storehouse and you both take the opportunity to raid the pantry shelves. Unfortunately, while inside, the storehouse is surrounded by the zombie hoard. The teen barricades the two of you in a smaller room off the main room while you discuss strategy. Escape is all but impossible; the longer you wait, the larger the crowd outside will become. The teen has an idea, and quickly stuffs and dresses burlap sacks into decoys, then prepares to burst through the door and fight through the zombie hoard. He pushes a few into the room you just vacated, and the two of you prepare to make your exit. At that moment the building collapses, blown up by an older survivalist who is apologetic but unwilling to take in these two refugees before him.

You and the one-armed boy make your way across the ravaged land, crossing through a junkyard and sheltering in abandoned truck cabs to avoid the approaching zombies. On the other side of the chasm, you are spotted and captured by an old man who has plans for you—similar to the plans he had for his wife, whose head he keeps in the passenger seat of his van, or the plans for the zombies he's captured, whom he uses like guard dogs to his apartment. When the boy goes up to the apartment to investigate, he is bitten by several of the zombies before he manages to clear the room of them completely. By the time you get to him, he knows what's happened and what's likely to happen to him, and he tells you that. "It's ok. When it's time, you do what you need to do. But just be sure of it. I don't want you hacking my head off in my sleep."[4]

You leave for a bit, and come back to check on him again. He is still in reasonably good spirits, but knows that his end is near. The ending panels are ambiguous; the boy's expression betrays no fear, confusion, or acceptance of his fate, and the final pages fade to black.

Apocalyptic Elements:

The reader never learns how the zombies came to be, only that they have swarmed to the extent that it is now unusual to see actual people. What's left is a world picked over, a place where scavenging is the only way to live. The zombies have taken over the darkness: nighttime, windowless spaces, rainy days.

---

[4] p.130

The few remaining humans are almost all interested solely in their own survival: the first one you and the boy encounter seals himself inside his armored tank to wait out the approaching rain, leaving his dog outside and telling the boy to keep him rather than re-open the hatch and risk letting anyone else inside. The other man is using zombies as watchdogs and refers to them as his family, though it is unclear whether these are family members who were turned into zombies or the other way around. Either way, there is a palpable loneliness surrounding the man, suggesting that he has been without other humans for a long time.

30-Second Booktalk:

Falling asleep is usually a bad idea. You wake up this time to find a one-armed teen leaning over you. He seems friendly, and offers you food and shelter. He's willing to help you. And frankly, you could use his help, because it's been a long time since you've seen anyone actually alive, and it's a little surprising you've survived this long on your own.

Readalikes:

Zombicorns (John Green) for travel through a zombie-infested world with an unlikely ally

The Forest of Hands and Teeth (Carrie Ryan) for another zombie apocalypse with only mild violence

The Eleventh Plague (Jeff Hirsch) for scavenging while traveling and distrust of other people

Sweet Tooth (Jeff Lemire) for post-apocalyptic travel and graphic novel format with semi-cute illustration style

Potential Audience:

The first-person perspective of this graphic novel is an excellent hook, drawing readers into the story whether they wish to be or not. The boy's indiscriminate age gives him appeal with teens and adults; his preference for junk food over more substantial fare suggests he is a teen instead of an adult, but there are few other clues provided. Most of the zombies are off-panel and there are few violent images, making this a good choice for teens down to eighth or ninth grade.

Sunshine

DVD. Color. 110m. Produced and dist. by Fox Home Entertainment, 2009. $14.98. 978-6-3116-7891-6.

- Directed by Danny Boyle
- Written by Alex Garland
- Originally released 2007

Plot Summary:

In the year 2057, the sun is dying, and life on Earth will be over unless it can be reignited. Seven years ago, the *Icarus I* was sent to deliver a stellar bomb directly into the sun, but that ship failed in its mission. Now the *Icarus II* has the same mission, and has used up the remaining materials on earth to make a second bomb.

The *Icarus II* is on track to deliver its payload and complete its mission when the crew picks up a sound: the distress beacon of the *Icarus I*. After careful consideration of the potential risks and benefits, the captain decides to change course to meet the disabled ship, as they could double the chances of the missions' success by launching that ship's payload as well as their own.

The *Icarus II* couples with the derelict *Icarus I*, and four crew members board and explore. Inside, they find a sabotaged computer system that won't allow the ship to move or launch its payload and a video of the *Icarus I* captain stating that the mission was being purposefully abandoned to comply with God's will. Suddenly they get word that the ship's airlocks have decoupled, and the men are stranded. They attempt a dangerous return to their ship, bursting open the derelict's airlock and counting on the vacuum effect to return them to their own ship. Of the four who had gone over, only two make it back aboard the *Icarus II*.

With the number of crew deaths, the remaining oxygen should allow enough time for the delivery of the payload into the sun. The computer system states otherwise, alerting the crew to the presence of an extra person: the captain of the *Icarus I* was responsible for the destruction of the airlocks and has sneaked aboard, intent on stopping the *Icarus II* from completing the same mission that his own ship had abandoned. After disabling the computer system, the *Icarus I*'s captain tracks down and kills the remaining crew members until only two are left: Capa, the physicist, and pilot Cassie. Capa manages to manually launch the payload, and after a near-fatal fight with the captain, sets the bomb to detonate, completing the mission and reigniting the sun.

Apocalyptic Elements:

According to current understanding of nuclear fission, the sun will continue on in its current state for another five billion years. However, the sun in *Sunshine* is burning out within the next half-century. The blame is placed on a "Q-ball" (a theoretical particle being researched by the European Organization for Nuclear Research [CERN]), a sort of "blob" of matter left over from the Big Bang that disrupts the normal matter around it.[5]

---

[5] A likely cause as suggested by CERN scientist Brian Cox, science advisor to the film, in the commentary track.

The sun's impending death has changed the climate in such a way as to make the planet inhospitable to life, and the creation of the *Icarus II*'s payload used up most of the remaining resources. The multi-ethnic crew also emphasizes that this is a global problem, not an isolated issue of one particular country or continent. Reigniting the sun is humanity's last, best hope at survival.

The majority of the movie is spent on board the spaceship, but a brief scene at the end takes place back on a dark, snow-covered Earth. With a caption over the screen informing the viewer that the time is "8 minutes later" [than the detonation of the payload], the sky brightens, implying that the mission was successful and the newly-reignited sun's light has made the 8-minute trip from the sun to the Earth. This hopeful image, one bursting with promise for all living things, concludes the film.

30-Second Booktalk:

Seven years ago, the *Icarus* failed in its mission to release a bomb into the dying sun to reignite it. Now the *Icarus II* has the same mission, with an additional attempt to salvage the payload from the *Icarus I* while they're at it. But the first mission's failure was not accidental, and someone wants to ensure the second mission's failure, as well.

Readalikes:

"Midnight Sun" (*The Twilight Zone*), for rapid climate change

2001: A Space Odyssey (film) for the sentient computer system

Life as We Knew It (Susan Beth Pfeffer) for rapid climate change

The Scorch Trials (James Dashner) for solar flares damaging Earth's climate

Potential Audience:

Sunshine is an intriguing, thought-provoking science-fiction movie with appeal to adults and upper high-school students, particularly science-minded types. Those watching for the science elements will be disappointed when the last third of the movie becomes more of a slasher/thriller, but there are plenty of crossover fans of both sci-fi and horror. *Sunshine* is rated R for violence and language.

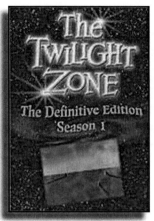

"Time Enough at Last" *The Twilight Zone*

Blu-Ray. Black & White. 182m. Produced and dist. by Image Entertainment, 2010. $99.98. 978-6-3137-7029-8.

- Originally aired 1959

Plot Summary:

Henry Bemis loves nothing more than reading a good book. His desire to spend all his time with books annoys his wife, who does not understand or approve of his love of reading, and his boss, as Bemis reads while working as a bank teller.

To escape the stares and snickers, Henry takes his lunch break in the bank's vault, where he can read undisturbed. On this day, he settles in with his sandwich and the newspaper, taking note of the headline that proclaims "H-Bomb Capable of Total Destruction." No sooner has he read the headline when the vault shakes violently, and Bemis is knocked unconscious.

Sometime later, Bemis wakes and fumbles around for his glasses, without which he can't see a thing. Cautiously, he opens the vault and steps outside, and is shocked to find that the shaking in the vault was caused by the detonation of a nuclear bomb. The bank, along with everyone in it, is gone; the surrounding city is in ruins. Bemis was saved by being inside the vault, but now that he is alone in the world, he quickly falls into despair and contemplates suicide.

Lifting a scavenged revolver to his head, he spots something in the distance: the public library has survived the bombing. On further exploration, many of the books also survived. Bemis is the only man left in the world and there is food enough to last him the rest of his life. With no commitments or obligations, he can spend every waking minute reading. He bends to pick up his first book and his glasses fall off, shattering on the floor. All but blind, he cries out "That's not fair. That's not fair at all. There was time now. There was all the time I needed...! That's not fair!"

Apocalyptic Elements:

When Bemis settles in for his lunch break, the front page of his newspaper warns about the destructive power of a hydrogen bomb, foreshadowing the events of only a few minutes later. The bomb that drops indeed causes near-total destruction, leveling buildings, eradicating life, and providing Bemis with the one thing he needs above everything else: time.

Bemis unwittingly finds shelter from the bomb in the bank vault, where he hides to avoid the sneers of the non-readers who surround him. It worked nicely as a bomb shelter, sparing his life while everyone not in the vault was killed in the blast. There is no explanation for the survival of the library, except as a stroke of good luck for Bemis. There is also no concern about radioactive fallout as a result of the bomb; in reality Bemis would likely die from radiation poisoning within days.

While the bomb is responsible for destroying most of the world, it is the loss of his glasses that truly destroys Bemis's life. All but blind without the thick lenses, he is unable to read the books that survived, making his life not worth living. However, in a landscape so recently changed by this violent event, blindness could very easily kill him long before boredom ever could. Without his vision, scavenging food will be difficult and even navigating the debris-strewn streets could be deadly.

30-Second Booktalk:

Henry's bank-teller job and wife leave him precious little time to read. To guard what reading time he can get, he takes his lunch breaks hidden in the vault of his bank. That's where he is when the bomb detonates, destroying nearly everything in the world except Henry... and the public library. Finally, Henry can spend as much time turning pages as he wants. It's a good thing his glasses survived the bombing, too.

Readalikes:

I Am Legend (film) for being the last person on earth after a disaster

Fahrenheit 451 (Ray Bradbury) for a protagonist surrounded by those who scorn books and reading

Z for Zachariah (Robert C. O'Brien) for being the last person following a nuclear attack

Blindness (Jose Saramago) for navigating an empty world without vision

Potential audience:

One of the most famous *Twilight Zone* episodes, "Time Enough at Last" is probably already familiar to most teens. Whether they already know the story or not, teens will be sucked into Henry's delight at finally being able to indulge his love of reading and will cringe with him at life's irony when it is all taken away from him. Even today, *The Twilight Zone's* O. Henry-like plots entertain people of all ages, from upper-elementary school-aged children through adults, and the series is perfectly appropriate for middle and high school students.

The Walking Dead, Season 1

DVD. Color. 292m. Produced and dist. by Anchor Bay/Starz, 2011. $39.98. 978-6-3140-1441-4.

- TV Series originally aired 2010

Plot Summary:

Deputy Rick Grimes was shot in the line of duty. When he wakes from the resultant coma, he's alone in the hospital. *Completely* alone—no doctors, nurses, or even other patients. He soon discovers that, while he was comatose, the world was overrun with the walking dead.

He leaves the hospital and finds that his wife and young son are missing. Grimes arms himself and sets out to find them in the most logical place: Atlanta, where his wife had family and the Centers for Disease Control has set up a quarantined safe zone. When he gets there, though, he finds that the city is not the protected oasis of safety he'd heard about, and he is almost immediately swarmed by "walkers."

Rick is rescued from his perilous situation by Glenn, a member of a local survivors' camp. Glenn takes Rick back to a department store, where a scavenging group has gathered. As the walkers swarm, Rick and Glenn lead an escape and get the scavengers safely back to camp. Once returned, Rick meets the other survivors, and is overjoyed to discover his wife and son among them.

Following a walker attack on the camp that leaves several of the group members dead, the remaining survivors head for the CDC. When they arrive, they find a scientist contemplating suicide: he's isolated himself to study the Walker Virus, but has just lost his only sample. He takes the survivors in and provides them showers and food, then explains what he's learned about how the virus affects the brain. Meanwhile, the building is counting down to its decontamination process: a self-destruct sequence that will launch when the power supply is exhausted, lest the carefully-stored disease samples be released into the world. The survivors escape just before the building is destroyed, ending the first season.

Apocalyptic Elements:

Rick re-enters the world to find it irrevocably changed: where once there were living people, there are now scores of zombies, the Walking Dead. Viewers are not given an explanation of what, exactly, happened to the world, but are left to fill in the blanks in light of the current situation.

When the walker virus began, the Centers for Disease Control attempted to quarantine the city of Atlanta, creating a safe place for refugees to gather. However, the presence of so many people clustered together makes for a quick-spreading disease once the barrier is breached. As a result, what should have been a safe place is instead packed with the walkers, the refugees who sought safety and were turned into zombies instead.

In spite of the walkers, survivors are attempting to live their lives. Banded together for safety, they continue to forge relationships, raise children, continue their domestic troubles. They mourn the loss of loved ones while allowing new people to join their camps. Survivors have not yet been able to settle into new lives away from the ever-present threat of the walkers. They are still adjusting to the new reality, learning about the walkers and hoping to see the end of each day, leaving little time to work on rebuilding their previous lives or make significant progress on a new society.

30-Second Booktalk:

Rick has just woken up out of a coma to find himself alone: alone in his room, alone in the hospital, alone in the town. That's not *quite* true: there are the walkers, the zombies who overran the town while he slept. They overran much more than just one town. Rick's wife and son are gone. Finding them is his only goal. Surviving is the only thing that matters.

Readalikes:

The Walking Dead (Robert Kirkman) for the graphic novel series on which the show is based

The Enemy (Charlie Higson) for action-heavy zombie battles

The Andromeda Strain (film) for isolated scientists researching sudden plagues

Epitaph Road (David Patneaude) for creation of small camps of survivors

Potential Audience:

Zombie aficionados are likely already familiar with this series, either through its AMC broadcast or through the original graphic novels. Due to the violence and sexual content, the series is most appropriate for ages sixteen and up.

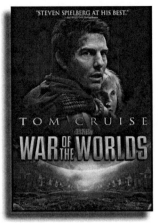

War of the Worlds

Blu-Ray. Color. 117m. Produced and dist. by Paramount Home Video, 2011. $22.99. 978-6-3135-7162-8.

- Written by Josh Friedman and David Koepp (based on the original novel by H.G. Wells)
- Directed by Steven Spielberg
- Originally released 2005

Plot Summary:

Ray's ex-wife Mary Ann drops off their two children, Rachel and Robbie, for the weekend while she travels to Boston to visit her parents. Ray is unaccustomed to caring for his children and mostly leaves them to their own devices. While Ray is napping, teenage Robbie takes Ray's car and goes to visit his friends. On waking, Ray goes out to find him, but instead finds a strange cloud emitting a series of lightning strikes. When the lightning subsides, Ray investigates the hole in the pavement caused by all the lightning strikes. Out of the hole comes a giant machine on three spindly legs: a tripod that immediately begins firing a heat ray, vaporizing everything in its path. Ray escapes, gathers both his kids, and finds a car to drive them away from the city for safety.

They shelter at Mary Ann's house for the night, hiding in a boiler room to avoid detection and destruction. In the morning, they find that the tripod has knocked a plane out of the sky; its engine is now in the house. A news team is already there, and they show Ray footage from other cities being destroyed by the same tripods.

Ray and his children head for Boston, but along the way encounter another group of tripods. Robbie leaves his father and sister to join the military in fighting the invaders. From a precarious shelter, Ray and Rachel see the machines spreading a red weed on the ground and fertilizing it with human blood and tissue.

Rachel is taken by one of the tripods, and Ray chases after her, snatching a handful of grenades before getting himself taken into the tripod. He leaves the grenades in the body cavity, and the other captives help to pull him back out. The grenades detonate, destroying the tripod and setting the captives free.

Ray and Rachel finally make it to Boston, where they find both Mary Ann and Robbie. The red weed is dying and the remaining tripods are acting strangely, and nearby soldiers are able to destroy it. A voiceover explains that the alien tripods are dying of an infection caused by germs on Earth to which the aliens had no immunity.

Apocalyptic Elements:

The War of the Worlds was originally written in 1898, long before environmental concerns sparked humans' imaginations in ways the world could end. While an alien invasion is certainly less realistic a conclusion to humanity than our more modern concerns, it is no less frightening in its literary presentation.

The aliens in the movie (and in the source material) are unambiguously hostile; there is no doubt as to their intentions. They begin their time on Earth by vaporizing all in the vicinity, then essentially terraforming the planet to cover it in the red weed familiar to them from their home world, killing humans to use as fertilizer.

At its heart, though, this can be viewed as an anti-war movie, in spite of its military action and violence. Few people fight back against the aliens, choosing instead to flee. It also highlights isolation, as people rarely stop to help each other, and those who do offer help are generally worse off for it in the end (such as the mechanic who fixes a car that Ray then steals from him, or the man who shelters Ray and Rachel only to be killed when Ray fears the man's rantings will give away their location). Survival becomes a matter of every man for himself, as no amount of cooperation will destroy the alien tripods. Ultimately the aliens are brought down by simple biology, a germ to which they have no resistance, allowing nature to save the day rather than any military action.

30-Second Booktalk:

Ray is out searching for his son when the lightning starts: dozens of strikes, all hitting the same spot. Where the ground has been split open, a three-legged machine comes out—and almost instantly vaporizes the crowd with its heat gun. If Ray is going to keep his kids safe, he needs to gather them quickly and get them to a place where the alien tripods aren't—if there are places like that left.

Readalikes:

The War of the Worlds (H.G. Wells) for the source material

Pod (Stephen Wallenfels) for alien invasion

2012 (film) for an estranged father trying to save his children and reunite his family

To Serve Man (Twilight Zone episode) for another hostile alien invasion

Potential Audience:

High school teens will be the best audience for this sci-fi action movie, rated PG-13 for violence and disturbing images. Teens familiar with the source material, or the Orson Welles radio play, will appreciate seeing another, more visual representation of the same material.

Part 3: Post-Apocalypse

This is the way the world ends
Not with a bang but a whimper. —T.S. Eliot

The world has ended. Everyone you once knew is gone, eliminated in an unspecified disaster. In a great stroke of luck, you've survived. Food is scarce, limited to whatever canned goods you can scavenge. Water supplies might be contaminated. Most of your friends and family have died, either in the initial event or in the subsequent days, weeks, years. A great stroke of luck, indeed.

This is the post-apocalyptic world: whatever destroyed civilization did it long enough ago that it's a memory now, something in the survivors' history rather than something they are still grappling with. Our characters have survived it or were born into the changed world. Life is about living in the changed world, not merely coping with it. That is what distinguishes the post-apocalyptic period from the merely apocalyptic: the ability to not just *make* a new life, but to *live* a life without the crutches of modern society to lean on.

"The beauty of post-apocalyptic work is that it boils us down to the essence of who we are," says blogger My Friend Amy in her post "Women, Children, and the Apocalypse."[1] In the immediacy of the apocalypse, we still frequently see characters assigned to their rigid categories: the smart one, the jock, the rebel. But once the world has ended, those old labels cease to matter. Suddenly the jock has good ideas on food distribution; the nerdy kid can chop firewood longer than anyone. In many cases, the social hierarchies have broken down in favor of having a society that *works* rather than one based on popularity.

---

[1] http://www.myfriendamysblog.com/2010/08/women-children-and-apocalypse.html

Philip Reeve attributes the recent popularity of the genre to this idea. "[The] strong hero or heroine survives by intelligence, resourcefulness, and good old-fashioned pluck. ... The settings may be nihilistic, but the message that an individual can make a difference and that courage and ingenuity can triumph even in the most dreadful circumstances, is anything but."[2] What teen does not wish to make a difference, to triumph over the adversity of their lives? The ability to be part of a community, to still have friendships and love interests, all without internet connectivity and cell phones can demonstrate a strength that teens aspire to. The world may have ended, but that doesn't mean it's doomed: it's up to teens to shape the new society into something sustainable.

The idea of that sort of power can be intoxicating, but what is the appeal of gaining that power within the context of a post-apocalyptic world? Why not change the landscape of a regular, realistic, present-day high school instead? "I suspect that young adults crave stories of broken futures because they themselves are uneasily aware that their world is falling apart," says Paolo Bacagalupi. "The truth of the world around us is changing, and so the literature is morphing to reflect it. Teens want to read something that isn't a lie."[3] Giving fictional teens the power to fix a world ravaged by war, disease, or environmental disasters means giving readers (and viewers) the tools to cope with the real-world problems that they are all too aware of.

In this section, we'll look at the three major categories of real-world problems that could wipe out civilization and force us to start over. The first section highlights the long-term effects of wars. Fears of nuclear fallout force some societies to move into deep shelters or isolated locations. Wars can alter the biology of a region, which would in turn shape society's reemergence and rebuilding. Those are just the effects on the physical world; more pressing are the effects of war on people. The threat of global annihilation can be enough to force leaders to move their towns and communities or to block out refugees. There are also the effects wars can have on the individuals, particularly those who were prisoners in wartime or otherwise persecuted.

The second threat to humanity is one that keeps popping up in the news: pandemics. Viruses and plagues can move quickly and wipe out whole civilizations, before scientists can develop a vaccine or even track disease vectors. Many post-apocalyptic books and movies that begin with viruses go beyond the basic "lots of people got sick and died," taking the stories to more science-fictional heights of cloning, zombies, or the rise of new races of people. Other creators stick with a straight-up humanity-ending illness, and these can be even more frightening due to their plausibility.

Wars and plagues can end the world, but mostly because they end *people*. The last category focuses on environmental ruin and natural disasters, the sorts of events that destroy the world instead of its population. Humans have to find ways to keep themselves alive when the world has been pulled out from under them, sometimes literally. In some cases, the apocalypse was our fault: global warming, weather manipulation, mishandling of resources. More terrifying is the apocalypse we never see coming and couldn't avoid even if we did, such as astronomical events or tsunamis. Creating a functional society in the wake of these disasters means overcoming the biases of the way things were in addition to the new challenges presented by the irreparably changed world.

This is the new reality. In an apocalyptic event, there's still the chaos of the original event, still the hope of rescue. The post-apocalyptic world is one in which people have stopped waiting on help that may never come and begin relying only on themselves. This is not to say that it is a world without

[2] Philip Reeve, "The Worst Is Yet to Come: Dystopias are grim, humorless, and hopeless—and incredibly appealing to today's teens". http://www.slj.com/slj/printissue/currentissue/891276-427/the_worst_is_yet_to.html.csp

[3] Paolo Bacigalupi, "Craving Truth-telling" http://www.nytimes.com/roomfordebate/2010/12/26/the-dark-side-of-young-adult-fiction/craving-truth-telling

hope; there's a new sort of hope, a hope that teens will be able to rely on themselves instead of waiting for others to do things for them. It's the truth Bacigalupi references above: teens identify with these stories because they recognize the desire to solve the world's problems. And when the world ends, who better to survive than the people who want to set civilization back to rights? Their survival may be the great stroke of luck humanity will count on.

Chapter 6:

War

There are more than seventy wars that are considered of major significance since humans started recording such things; nearly half of these have occurred since the American Revolution.[1] The pace of global conflict has been picking up speed, and if the pace continues, how many more conflicts will have been fought by the next century? As a species, what have we gained, lost, learned from these conflicts?

There is no arguing that war is destructive, splitting families, communities, even countries apart. Robert C. O'Brien's *Z for Zachariah* splits a family when Ann Burden's parents and brother never come back after setting out in search of other survivors from a nuclear blast. L.J. Adlington's *The Diary of Pelly D* shows what happens when an entire community is forced into classes according to genetic codes, quickly and efficiently separating people into a rigid class structure. *Legend* by Marie Lu takes place in a far future, long after a war has divided the United States into two still-warring territories, the western Republic and eastern Colonies.

The destructive properties of war are not limited to merely fracturing societal units: war can destroy a society altogether, forcing the people to find new ways to move on in the changed world. For Jeanne DuPrau's characters, moving on means finding a way to rebuild their society: one group creates the titular City of Ember deep underground, outfitted to support a community for two hundred years; the other group establishes their above-ground village in *The People of Sparks*. (No indication is given of how Sparks came into being; it is possible that the village was founded by survivors of the war.)

While societies can break down under the stresses of war, so can people. *The Compound* by S.A. Bodeen features a father who has commissioned, at great personal expense, a fully-functional bomb shelter that will sustain his family for over a decade—but then seals part of his family outside of it in his haste to lock the door, and keeps the others from escaping when the shelter begins to fail. V, the main character of Alan Moore's *V for Vendetta*, becomes something of a vigilante anarchist after being the victim of wartime experimentation.

Nausicaä and the Valley of the Wind, written and directed by Hayao Miyazaki, shows the effect that wars have had on an entire planet. The first war was fought over a thousand years ago and culminated in the Seven Days of Fire, which severely poisoned the world's ecosystem. Now the world stands at the edge of a new war, one being waged for control of a deadly weapon that could, in the wrong hands, destroy the planet once again. This kind of global ruination is also seen in Anders Nilsen's graphic novel *Dogs and Water*, in which a solitary man wanders through a desolate world. Masamune Shirow's graphic novel series *Appleseed* opens on a young couple holed up in an abandoned city, unaware that the war they've been sheltering from ended long ago. *The Boy at the End of the World* (Greg van Eekhout) shows an Earth that has begun to repair itself after humans have gracefully made their exit, waiting for Fisher and the other preserved humans and animals to be pulled from suspended animation.

Wars change country borders, governments, attitudes, people. The following ten authors show how much is changed in wars, and in their wake, what our society can—and will—become.

---

[1] http://ehistory.osu.edu/world/WarsList.cfm

Adlington, L.J. ✓

The Diary of Pelly D

Greenwillow Books, 2008. 304p. $8.99 (pb). 978-0-06-076617-7.

- Originally published 2005

Plot Summary:

Toni V is working on clearing rubble from the war so, that the City Five can be rebuilt. He knows that he isn't supposed to take anything he finds, so he's already taking a chance just by keeping the diary he dug up from under the city plaza.

The diary once belonged to Pelly D, a girl about his age. Pelly was everything Toni is not: wealthy, privileged, socially connected. Because of her charmed life, she is completely unconcerned when the government suggests genetic testing to sort people into their proper categories: Atsumi, Mazzini, or Galrezi. There are no social differences among them, no advantage to being a particular class over any other—not at first. But soon the classes begin to stratify, with the Atsumis gaining all the power and status and the Galrezis being stripped of their homes, their belongings, their dignity as their hands are stamped according to their inferior rank. As Pelly's rights and options are slowly stripped away, Toni gets more caught up in her story, and more determined to expose the buried secrets of his society's history.

Post-Apocalyptic Elements:

Long before Toni's time, before Pelly's time, humans left the polluted Earth behind and settled on the new planet, dubbed "Home From Home." A new planet to settle did not solve the basic problems of human nature, though, and the world Toni is toiling in is one ravaged by war, not environmental decay.

In Pelly's time, City Five is going to war with City One over water: City One is nearly out, and to speed along an irrigation project, people of lesser gene lines are sent from City Five to help. With need of more labor than was readily available, the government mandates that all citizens have their gene lines identified, and the rights and privileges of those lesser lines are slowly whittled away. The process is so gradual that Pelly doesn't notice, but it is nearly impossible for Toni to overlook as he reads Pelly's words.

From one perspective, this is a dystopia, an effort to perfect society by grouping its citizens by traits to allow the best distribution of tasks and privileges. This is also an apocalypse, as Pelly experiences her world fall apart around her, taking away everything she has piece by piece until the genocide is complete. More than either of these, Toni's world—the main setting of the novel—is post-apocalyptic, existing after the gene tagging that destroyed Pelly's people and after the war that followed. Toni's world is not attempting to make sense of what happened; they are, for the most part, ignorant of their shameful history. The war has destroyed even knowledge of itself in City Five, and without Pelly's action to hide her diary in the town square, the future generation—Toni's—would never know the truth about it at all.

30-Second Booktalk:

In clearing rubble after a war, Toni finds Pelly D's diary. Back before the war, before the gene tagging, she was the most popular girl in school, setting trends and dating the hottest guy. But then Pelly submits to the DNA testing—but despite the government's assurances that all three gene classes have much to offer society, Pelly's class is not the favored one. Toni has a lot to learn about his society's history, and Pelly is the only one who can teach him.

Readalikes:

The Diary of a Young Girl (Anne Frank) for a true holocaust story

Cherry Heaven (L.J. Adlington) for another story set in the same world

The Wave (Todd Strasser) for another holocaust parallel, showing how easily a movement gets started

Brave New World (Aldous Huxley) for classifications based on genetic makeups

Potential Audience:

The heavy subject matter will pair well with a holocaust unit, showing how easily a society can get caught up in following rules no matter what the cost. Eighth graders and up will find plenty of discussion fodder here, though the book may be a little on-the-nose in its parallels to Anne Frank's *The Diary of a Young Girl* to provide much enjoyment for an individual read.

Bodeen, S.A.

The Compound

Square Fish, 2009. 272p. $17.99. 978-0-312-37015-2.
$9.99 pb. 978-0-312-57860-2.
Brilliance Corporation, 2008. $24.95 MP3-CD. 978-1-4233-6559-4.
Google eBooks, $9.99. 978-1-4299-8383-9.

- Originally published 2008

Plot Summary:

Eli's family is out hiking when they get word from one of his billionaire father's assistants: a nuclear bomb has been launched. From where they currently are, they have, at best, about 40 minutes to find shelter before the fallout reaches them. Eli's father knows a place, and hurries his family along to the underground shelter he's secretly constructed. They make it inside with minutes to spare, locking the hatch and preparing to spend their next fifteen years inside while the planet becomes habitable again.

That was six years ago. Eli appreciated his father's paranoia and forethought in building this giant compound, complete with an artificially-lit greenhouse, plentiful food stores, even livestock. But there are two things missing: Eli's grandmother and twin brother, Eddie, who had gone back to their camp for Eddie's asthma medication and didn't make it to the shelter in time.

The compound was designed to sustain their family for fifteen years, but they may not make it that long. The spare light bulbs for the greenhouse have been smashed, and makes some of their food stores have been contaminated. When Eli asks his father about these problems, he gets evasive answers, when he doesn't get outright lies. There's even sporadic internet access, but with the nuclear bomb above, who would be using the internet?

Eli is shocked to have that question answered: Eddie. Eddie, who didn't make it to the shelter, and yet wasn't killed in the blast or the fallout. Eddie, who tells Eli that there *was* no nuclear explosion. With their father's lies beginning to fall into place, Eli recognizes that his family is not safe in the compound with their father anymore, and it's time to lead an escape.

Post-Apocalyptic Elements:

With the bulk of the story taking place six years after a nuclear bomb, *Compound* falls neatly into the post-apocalyptic category: an act of war has fundamentally changed the way Eli and his family live. They now live in a fallout shelter, surviving on the foresight of a man who was prepared to live in the closed system for more than a decade.

Custom-built shelters currently exist[2], at prices Eli's billionaire father can easily afford, though few if any suggest they are capable of sustaining life for fifteen years. Feasibility isn't the biggest issue, though; Eli's father has already proven that he can have a shelter built to his specifications. The bigger concern is the toll that the prolonged isolation will take on the family. Locked inside the compound for six years, Eli's father exhibits signs of extreme cabin fever[3]: paranoia, restlessness, irritability, distrust. As he slips further into his own madness, he sabotages the supplies and food stores, jeopardizing his own safety as well as his family's.

The phenomenon of cabin fever is related to the fiction staple of Ocean Madness[4] (and its cousin, Space Madness), in which a character trapped at sea (or in space) for a prolonged period slowly goes insane. While cabin fever is recognized by psychologists, the terms Ocean Madness and Space Madness are rarely used outside of discussions of these fictional occurrences. Still, they are relevant to this book; while Eli's family is neither at sea nor in space, they are still trapped together with unchanging scenery, breeding a kind of claustrophobia that can induce paranoid delusions in anybody.

30-Second Booktalk:

When a nuclear bomb is launched, Eli's family has, at most, about 40 minutes to find shelter. Luckily, they're not far from their underground compound that can support them for the next fifteen years while they wait for the radiation to clear. Now six years in, the food stores have been contaminated—or sabotaged. There's only one way out—and the person who knows it is the one who won't let them leave.

Readalikes:

Blast from the Past (film) for a comedic take on life in a bomb shelter

Z for Zachariah (Robert C. O'Brien) for isolation after a nuclear disaster

Enclave (Ann Aguirre) for a subterranean culture

The Shining (Stephen King) for an extreme case of cabin fever

Potential Audience:

Eli's voice and struggles will appeal to middle-school boys in particular, though there is nothing here that would alienate girls. High school readers will be intrigued by the subplot of the "nursery," where babies are effectively farmed to grow spare organs for any family members who may need them.

---

[2] Examples at http://www.popularmechanics.com/technology/engineering/architecture/4325649
[3] http://www.psychology-lexicon.com/cms/glossary/glossary-c/cabin-fever.html
[4] http://tvtropes.org/pmwiki/pmwiki.php/Main/OceanMadness

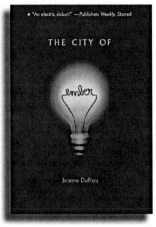

DuPrau, Jeanne

The City of Ember

Random House, 2003. 288p. $16.99. 978-0-375-82273-5.
Yearling Books, 2008. $6.99 pb. 978-0-385-73628-2.
Listening Library, 2006. $30 CD. 978-0-7393-3167-5.

Plot Summary:

The Builders created the City of Ember deep underground, outfitted with enough supplies to sustain the community for 200 years while the Earth's surface was uninhabitable due to a nuclear war[5]. The first mayor of the new city was given a locked box to be passed down through generations, though none of them knew that the box—containing instructions on returning to the surface—was set to automatically open after 200 years.

Two hundred forty-one years have now passed since Ember was first founded, and supplies are dwindling, having sustained a community nearly a half-century longer than planned. Lina and Doon are given their job assignments, Lina ultimately becoming a messenger and Doon a pipeworks laborer. In her travels, Lina finds a box with a paper in it. After much effort, she and Doon decipher the torn letter, discovering that it contains the instructions for leaving Ember behind.

Together, Lina and Doon search through the pipeworks to find the exit, eventually coming to an underground river with boats. At the end of their boat ride, they find a journal detailing the city's history, then make a steep climb to reach the world outside. In a cave, they find a cliff; staring into the abyss they see the twinkling lights of Ember far below. They are shocked to learn they had been living underground, and they tie the exit directions around a rock and drop it over the cliff for Ember's residents to find.

Post-Apocalyptic Elements:

Within the pages of *The City of Ember*, there is no explanation of what drove Ember's founders underground; those explanations come later, in the prequel *The Prophet of Yonwood*. However, Ember's creation deep underground and outfitting to sustain life for 200 years implies that the surface would suffer a catastrophic event (while radiation levels from an atomic bomb detonation will decrease to safe levels within five years, some level of contamination will exist for some time after that[6]). Also, Ember's original population of 100 adults and 100 children would allow for sufficient genetic variation for reproduction (minimum viable population is generally considered 100-150 individuals[7]).

---

[5] See *The Prophet of Yonwood*, Jeanne DuPrau, 2008
[6] http://www.nti.org/h_learnmore/nuctutorial/chapter02_06.html
[7] Minimum viable population size, Lochran W. Traill, Barry W. Brook, and Corey J. A. Bradshaw; http://www.eoearth.org/article/Minimum_viable_population_size?topic=58074

Beyond the issues of potential nuclear fallout, though, are the issues of supplies. Ember's supplies are held in stockrooms that run under nearly the entire city, and greenhouses supply the city's produce and oxygen-creating vegetation. The population of Ember has swollen to over 400 people, with supplies and equipment that have already lasted at least two decades more than intended. The failure of an infrastructure that has supported the city for centuries will cause a somewhat anti-climactic apocalypse, one caused by a slow progression of events rather than one catastrophic incident.

30-Second Booktalk:

Ember has been running smoothly for almost 250 years, an oasis of light surrounded by inky blackness in all directions. But now supplies are dwindling, and Lina and Doon are the only ones who are concerned. When Lina finds an old paper cryptically labeled "Instructions for Egress," they know that something is up, and their city is no longer a safe place to live. Can they convince the rest of the townspeople of that? And how do they get out?

Readalikes:

The People of Sparks, *The Prophet of Yonwood*, and *The Diamond of Darkhold* (Jeanne DuPrau) for the past, present, and future of Ember and its citizens

The City of Ember (film) for the movie adaptation

Enclave (Ann Aguirre) for exploration of an above-ground world

The Giver (Lois Lowry) for work assignments

Potential Audience:

The City of Ember is an assigned read in many middle schools, so many younger teens will find this via reading lists. However, the intriguing premise and relateable characters will overcome the "school" stigma to appeal to upper-elementary through early high school readers.

DuPrau, Jeanne ✓

The People of Sparks

Random House, 2004. 352p. $16.99. 978-0-375-82824-9.
Yearling, 2005. $6.99 pb. 978-0-375-82825-6.
Listening Library, 2006. $30 CD. 978-0-7393-3169-9.
Google eBooks. $6.99. 978-0-375-89050-5.

Plot Summary:

After a harrowing journey, Ember's 417 citizens have found their way to the surface. For days they wander in the open air before finding a small village. Sparks is already experiencing food shortages and other challenges, but with some reluctance they agree to let the Emberites stay for six months, to teach them how to grow food, build shelters, survive.

It isn't long before the people of Sparks begin resenting the drain the Emberites place on their limited resources, and the amount of help the Emberites need in order to live on the surface. The tensions between the two groups grow when the Emberites are repeatedly vandalized and the quality of the food they are provided declines. The Emberites are already aware that they have overstayed their welcome when the people of Sparks move them all into a dilapidated hotel and give them one more month to move out to form their own village.

The cycle of resentments finally turns around when Sparks' town hall catches fire. While most Emberites refuse to help, Lina runs to help the people of Sparks, and it is her willingness that encourages other Emberites to join the effort. Lina's friend Doon, her partner in finding a way out of Ember, runs into the building to rescue a young boy trapped inside, and it is his heroic effort that brings the two communities together.

Following the fire, Doon combines a scavenged light bulb with knowledge from an old science textbook to rediscover electrical currents, providing hope for a brighter future for both Sparks and Ember.

Post-Apocalyptic Elements:

As in *The City of Ember*, the cause of the initial devastation is never revealed (though the prequel, *The Prophet of Yonwood*, makes clear that it was a nuclear war). However, Sparks is going through some new issues, among them the additional strain the Emberites are placing on their limited resources.

With Sparks' supplies already stretched to their limit, it is no surprise that they are reluctant to take in a full community of refugees. The Emberites do not make any particular efforts to integrate themselves into their temporary community, being ignorant of the scavenging and agricultural tasks and procedures that keep Sparks running. The people of Sparks view the Emberites as lazy and entitled; the Emberites see Sparks as selfish and unwilling to help them, in spite of all evidence to the contrary.

The Emberites, having spent their whole lives sheltered underground with supplies freely available, experience a bit of dependency syndrome once they are forced to surface: their entire lives have been ripped away with no hope of ever going back to the world from which they came, and their problems (chiefly, how to survive in this new world) are not ones they believe they can solve on their own. They lean heavily on the small village of Sparks, unwilling to give up their old ways of life or take any sense of ownership over the tasks the people of Sparks attempt to help them with.

Dependency syndrome is common in developing countries and communities, where charitable organizations will provide (for example) a well, or food, but the community never takes ownership of the new resource and therefore lets it fall into disrepair, waiting instead for another charitable organization to help again. It is also common after disasters, for similar reasons: "Emergency responses focus on meeting immediate needs as quickly and efficiently as possible. Governments . . . [assume] that local people are unlikely to have the knowledge or competence to contribute anything useful. [. . .] [S]olutions are frequently out of touch with people's real needs... "victims" seem unwilling to do anything for themselves."[8] This is fitting with the dynamic between the people of Sparks and the Emberites, with Sparks attempting to fix the immediate needs and teach the Emberites about survival but instead being put off by the time commitment and the Emberites' unwillingness to help themselves.

30-Second Booktalk:

When the whole world is new to you, finding someone who can help is a fantastic stroke of luck. But when the town you find is full of people who don't want you there—people who are struggling to survive just like you—there are going to be conflicts. Lina, Doon, and the rest of the Emberites have been given six months to learn how to survive on their own, *if* the people of Sparks don't kick them out early.

Readalikes:

City of Ember, *The Prophet of Yonwood*, and *The Diamond of Darkhold* (Jeanne DuPrau) for the rest of the Ember series

Enclave (Ann Aguirre) for adjustment to a new life above ground

Restoring Harmony (Joélle Anthony) for food and material shortages

Potential audience:

While the Books of Ember are all one series, of which this is the second book, each title stands perfectly well on its own. Lina and Doon are still major characters, so middle schoolers who enjoyed the first book will be drawn into this second installment. Enough material from the previous book is summarized to give teens new to the series the necessary background.

---

[8] "Making Space for Children: Planning for Post-Disaster Reconstruction with Children and Their Families." Published by Save the Children, 2007. http://sca.savethechildren.se/Documents/Resources/Making%20Space%20for%20Children%20(ENGLISH).pdf

Lu, Marie

Legend

Putnam Juvenile, 2011. 336p. $17.99. 978-0-399-25675-2.
Penguin Audiobooks, 2011, $25.95. 978-1-61176-008-8.
Google eBooks. $10.99. 978-1-101-54595-9.

Plot Summary:

June is a military genius, having aced her exams and graduated early from the academy. Her genius has given her special privileges—exemptions from punishments when she scales the building and performs other stunts, for example. Her brother, Metias, gets the phone call each time June would face disciplinary action, but as he is the best soldier in the military, he too has special privileges. Shortly before June's graduation from the academy, Metias is on guard duty outside a hospital, where notorious criminal Day has staged a heist. Metias is killed in the line of duty as Day escapes, and in her grief, June is given her first assignment: track down the elusive Day.

Day, in contrast to June, failed all his exams and has been living on the streets ever since. He smuggles his gambling winnings to his brother, the only member of Day's family who knows he's still alive, to help his mother and brothers make ends meet. His little brother is sick, possibly with the plague, and his family is too poor to afford the medicines that the Republic funnels into wealthier neighborhoods. Day's hospital heist was an effort to acquire the plague cure that the Republic is unwilling to provide.

Working undercover and following her few leads, June tracks Day, searching every back alley and fighting match she finds. She inadvertently spars with an expert fighter, emerging the victor thanks to her military training, and her injuries are treated by a kind girl who has been living on the streets with an older, protective boy. June and the boy—both traveling under aliases and assumed identities—make an excellent team, and their relationship begins to grow. Everything comes crashing down when June suddenly realizes that the boy who has saved her, protected her, and fought along side her, is none other than the criminal who killed her brother.

With mixed feelings, June reports Day's location, leading to his capture at his family's home. With Day locked in prison, June begins sifting through his records. She is shocked to find that he did not in fact fail his exams, but rather answered every question perfectly, yet the Republic still flagged his file and sent him to the labor camps instead of the training academy. Armed with this new knowledge, she goes to Day under the pretense of interrogating him, and together they figure out the many ways the Republic has lied to them and how deep the conspiracies go. The two plot their escape, breaking Day out only minutes before his scheduled execution.

Post-Apocalyptic Elements:

Legend is a mixture of post-apocalyptic and dystopian: the strict government overreaches into personal lives, breaks into people's homes and inspects the residents for illnesses. The government knows what to look for in its plague inspections, because they have been experimenting with different plague formulations, purposely unleashing its new strains in disadvantaged areas where the residents lack the means to fight back or purchase expensive cures. The educational testing, designed to find the best and brightest pupils for the military training academies, performs this function well—but when Day, a student from a poor neighborhood, aces the exams, his socioeconomic background brands him a threat instead of an asset, and he is sent to a labor camp instead of military strategy training.

The labor camp, it turns out, is less about working children than about human experimentation. Day has his eyes biopsied, looking for the source of his sharp vision; his knee opened, to determine what keeps him agile; his heartrate slowed to nearly death, to learn how little he can survive on. Other children in the "labor camps" are examined for imperfections, or are victims of plague experiments, new strains being tested for deadliness and contagiousness.

These strains of plague are infecting whole communities, with the worst outcomes in poorer neighborhoods where the victims can't afford the treatments. The families struggling to get by in these areas are under constant surveillance, regularly inspected for signs of plague by government officials. Day's family lives in one of these areas. With the threat of illness overhead, everyday life becomes about survival in End Times, a looming apocalypse.

But none of the above elements would be possible if not for the war. The war is currently raging between the western Republic states—from the west coast to West Texas—and the eastern Colonies—from the east coast to Eastern Texas. The war, like many wars, is waged over land ownership, with the Colonies desiring to annex the Republic and become one union. The Colonies lost a lot of their own land in the floods, more land than the Republic did. Parts of the Republic, particularly in the Los Angeles area, are still underwater. The flooding destroyed thousands of data centers, forcing technology backwards into less efficient databases and devices.

While *Legend* does not specify exactly what caused the flooding, it is implied that the floods came sometime after an event that split the United States in two. Whether the event was a war, a natural disaster, or something else is unclear, but the event was far enough in the past that a coin from 1990 is referred to as "Evidence. See the name? United States. It was *real*."[9] The Republic and the Colonies have both rebuilt themselves into their own countries with only a few flooded areas to remind them of their post-apocalyptic landscape, but the current war could spell a second apocalypse.

30-Second Booktalk:

June is a military genius, having aced her exams and graduated early from the academy. Her first assignment: track down the elusive Day, the Republic's most-wanted criminal and her brother's killer. June wants to avenge her brother's death. Day wants to buy the cure to the plague that's ripping through his family's neighborhood. June is about to find out exactly what the Republic government is capable of—and that's something Day has known all along.

Readalikes:

The Lab (Jack Heath) for fast pacing and super-agent storyline

Ender's Game (Orson Scott Card) for military genius and strategy

The Way We Fall (Megan Crewe) for a government-manufactured plague

Potential Audience:

Primarily high school, but middle school students will also enjoy the action-heavy sequences. Following two very different characters—the military strategist and the criminal, the well-off girl and the boy from the slums—will appeal to a variety of teens.

---

[9] p229 (ARC)

Nausicaá of the Valley of the Wind

Blu-Ray. Color. 118m. Produced and dist. by Walt Disney Studios Home Entertainment, 2011. $39.99. 978-6-3139-9243-0. $29.99 DVD. 978-0-7888-2400-5.

- Written and directed by Hayao Miyazaki
- Originally released 1984 (Japan), 2005 (US, uncut and redubbed version)

Plot Summary:

A millennium after the Seven Days of Fire, the great war that destroyed both civilization and the ecosystem, Lord Yupa travels the earth in search of the foretold "man in blue," the legendary person who has the power to reunite man and nature. Inspired by Lord Yupa's travels, the Princess Nausicaá also travels and searches, though for different things: Nausicaá is a skilled fighter, but also a budding naturalist, collecting and identifying everything from poisonous spores to insects. It is these insects that give her people pause, though, as the giant insects that roam the Toxic Jungle have overrun and destroyed whole cities as the jungle spreads itself further into the surrounding area.

Late one stormy night, an airship crashes nearby, despite Nausiccaá's best efforts to guide it to safety. In the wreckage, Nausicaá finds a prisoner, the Princess Lastelle of Pejite. Lastelle confesses that the ship is carrying an embryo of a Giant Warrior, the insect that was instrumental in the Seven Days of Fire one thousand years ago, and she urges Nausicaá to destroy it. Rival nation Tolmekia stole the embryo from the Pejite who had discovered it, and now that their airship has crashed, the Tolmekia swarm into Nausicaá's valley to secure the embryo and take over the Valley of the Wind.

Princess Kushana of Tolmekia takes Nausicaá and several others hostage on a return trip to Pejite. Following airship battles and the discovery of clean soil and water beneath the Toxic Jungle, Nausicaá ultimately finds herself on a ship of Pejite refugees. To her horror, she learns that they are planning to lure the Ohm, the giant insects of the jungle, to her valley to destroy the Tolmekians and reclaim the Giant Warrior. Nausicaá escapes on her glider to warn the Tolmekians and save her valley from the stampeding Ohm.

She soon discovers that the Pejite have incited the stampede by stealing a baby Ohm, dangling it from their airship just ahead of the herd. In her efforts to help the baby, Nausicaá is gravely wounded, but her sacrifice does not go unnoticed: the raging Ohm begin to calm, and several reach out their tentacles to heal her injuries. When she awakens and stands to face her people, her dress, stained blue with the baby Ohm's blood, marks her as the foretold Man in Blue.

Post-Apocalyptic Elements:

A thousand years ago, Nausicaá's world fought a Great War, a war that culminated in the Seven Days of Fire. Those seven days destroyed the world's ecosystem, throwing everything out of balance. In the wake of the damage, a great jungle feeds on the pollutants left behind, taking over much of the earth's surface with its poisonous spores. Only a few populated cities remain unclaimed by the jungle, Nausicaá's among them. The jungle is protected not only by its poison gasses but also by the Ohms, giant insects that will swarm and attack when threatened.

Centuries after the Great War, the remaining enclaves of civilization are still threatened by the spreading of the Toxic Jungle, the spores that could infect crops and water supplies, and the Ohm that could overrun their cities at any moment. These are far from the only threats, though. After all the damage the original war caused, there is a new war being waged, a battle between the Tolmekians and the rival Pejite to claim a Great Warrior embryo. The very existence of the embryo is a threat to the remaining cities, as whoever has the embryo could easily grow the insect to a mature form and use it to dominate another war like the one that destroyed the world so long ago.

While the film has a strong message of environmentalism, there are also comparisons to today's threats of nuclear war and the importance of our current Nuclear Non-Proliferation Treaty. Just the knowledge that this potentially-world-annihilating weapon exists is unsettling enough; the knowledge that it is in the wrong hands, poised to create a new apocalypse, is terrifying.

Nausicaá's world has regrown itself since the Great War, going from a post-apocalypse immediately after the war to a workable civilization a thousand years later. However, with this new threat looming, they are on the brink of a second apocalypse.

30-Second Booktalk:

The winds in Nausicaá's valley have been enough to keep the spores from the nearby Toxic Jungle from settling there, but her people are about to be overrun by a different threat: the Tolmekian army is on their way to recapture the Giant Warrior embryo that they'd stolen from the Pejite people and lost in an airship crash in the valley. To defend the Valley of the Wind, Nausicaá will have to use everything she's learned about the Toxic Jungle and about the giant insects who are stampeding toward the Valley.

Readalikes:

Nausicaá of the Valley of the Wind, volumes 1-7 (Hayao Miyazaki), for the source material

Princess Mononoke (film) for another Miyazaki movie dealing with environmental issues

The Happening (film) for plants releasing deadly toxins as defense measure

Z for Zachariah (Robert C. O'Brien) for a valley protected from airborne toxins

Potential Audience:

Manga and anime fans will likely already be familiar with Miyazaki's work, and these teens will be the most obvious audience. However, Nausicaá will also appeal to middle- and high-school teens who are concerned about long-term environmental impacts of current practices, and to teens who appreciate female-centric adventure stories.

Moore, Alan, and David Lloyd (ill.)

V For Vendetta

- Vertigo, 2008. 296p. $19.99. 978-1-4012-0841-7.
- Originally published 1988

Plot Summary:

Evey first meets V when he saves her from being raped and killed by the fingermen, London's secret-police force. Evey trusts this mysterious stranger in the cloak and Guy Fawkes mask and tells him her whole story, starting from the nuclear war in the 1980s that spawned the current fascist government that executed her father as a political prisoner.

V's detonation of a bomb planted at London's Old Bailey court building puts him in the crosshairs of Eric Finch's investigation, determined to find the vigilante. Meanwhile, V has a full agenda: after destroying the Houses of Parliament, he targets three individuals active in the Party: Prothero, the party's "Voice of Fate" in the propaganda broadcasts; Lilliman, a priest; and Surridge, a doctor who was once involved with Finch. All three had ties to the Larkhill concentration camp where V had been a prisoner.

Evey and V are still close, but she has begun questioning him. After a confrontation, he abandons her. A string of subsequent events lead to her being framed for a party member's murder and thrown in jail. Her interrogation and torture nearly break her, but she finds strength in the letter written by a woman in a nearby cell, a woman who has been jailed for homosexuality. Evey refuses to cooperate with the officials, at which point she is released and learns that the imprisonment was another of V's methods, this one forcing her into similar conditions to those that shaped him.

A year later, V bombs another building, this time effectively destroying all government. He has not yet created the anarchy he desires, but only chaos. He allows himself to be shot and manages to make it back to his lair, where he dies in Evey's arms. Evey dons a spare mask and cloak and speaks to the crowds as V, warning them of the imminent destruction of Downing Street and sparking an insurrection. She returns underground to load V's body onto a subway train laden with explosives and set to detonate under Downing Street.

Dystopian Elements:

Floods and crop failures have destabilized the country, and with much of the world destroyed in the nuclear war in the 1980s, London's government has been jettisoned in favor of a fascist regime. The new leaders rule by fear, killing opponents in concentration camps and remaking London as a police state, complete with surveillance cameras and listening devices nearly everywhere.

The political dichotomy aside, *V for Vendetta* draws as much from history as from visions of the future. The atrocities committed at the concentration camp in the name of medical experimentation, and the imprisonment of homosexuals and ethnic minorities, draws as much from World War II and the holocaust as it does from Moore's predictions of England's political future. (In his preface to DC's reissue of the book, Moore notes ruefully that, "The simple fact that much of the historical background of the story proceeds from a predicted Conservative defeat in the 1982 General Election should tell you how reliable we were in our roles as Cassandras."[10]) In fact, Moore's original conception of the book involved a 1930s setting; heeding the objections of artist and co-creator David Lloyd, Moore reenvisioned the story in the near future rather than the recent past. "Since both Dave and myself share a similar brand of political pessimism, the future would be pretty grim, bleak and totalitarian.... With disturbingly little difficulty it was easy for me to plot the course from that point up until the fascist takeover in the post-holocaust Britain of the 1990s."[11]

30-Second Booktalk:

"Remember, remember, the fifth of November." It's Guy Fawkes day, and V has big plans. Destroying the judicial building is only the beginning: he will make the people overthrow the fascist government in favor of anarchy. Even death won't stop him from achieving his goals.

Readalikes:

1984 (George Orwell) for surveillance

V for Vendetta (film) for movie adaptation

Night (Elie Wiesel) for the effects of life in a concentration camp

The Carbon Diaries (Saci Lloyd) for a post-flood Britain

Potential Audience:

High school and older readers with an understanding of fascism will get the most out of this, but plenty of teens will be drawn in by the plot's many secrets and revelations. Sexual content and violence push this into upper high school or adult collections.

---

[10] Reprinted in the 1989 paperback edition of V for Vendetta, page 6.
[11] From Warrior Magazine, October 1983; reprinted in the 1989 paperback edition of V for Vendetta, page 270-271.

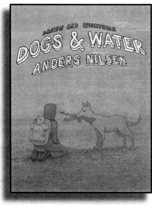

Nilsen, Anders

Dogs and Water

Drawn & Quarterly, 2007. 96p. $19.95 978-1-897299-08-1.

Plot Summary:

A young man travels across a barren landscape, escaping from and searching for nothing in particular. He travels light, with only a small backpack of supplies and a stuffed teddy bear for company. He talks to the bear and vents his rage on it as they travel aimlessly, but even after beating it with a stone, he remains protective of the toy, sewing up the damage and fist-fighting animals who attempt to carry it off. The traveler encounters several animals—first deer, who he fights off when a small herd surrounds him and acts aggressively, and later dogs, who take him in as one of their pack. He leaves the company of the pack when the dogs find a dead human body and pick over the remains.

Not far off, he finds someone else: a man, collapsed and bleeding near a large pipe and a crashed helicopter. The injured man explains that he and his team had just repaired the pipe after a bombing and were taking off when their helicopter was shot down. The injured man is paralyzed and begs the traveler to shoot him, but the traveler cannot bring himself to do it. While thinking it over, the injured man is approached by a boy with a rifle. Neither man is willing to kill the boy. The traveler finally shoots the injured man, then offers the boy some food and water. The boy, though, is uninterested in the offer and takes the traveler's boots instead, then asks for the bear. The traveler considers for a long moment before finally agreeing. The boy rides off, leaving the traveler more alone than he has ever been. Slowly he buries the other man's body, then shoulders his pack and begins his next journey.

Post-Apocalyptic Elements:

This brief graphic novel never specifies that it is set in a post-apocalyptic world; the man is equally likely to be crossing an unpopulated desert, a war zone, or a world that has been completely destroyed. There is a sense that the young man has been traveling alone for some time, given his attachment to the teddy bear and his surprise at finding the helicopter pilot. In the opening scene, he remarks to the bear that, "We haven't seen a car for about two weeks, let alone any flowers or trees or houses... we could go on forever and get nowhere."[12]

On his journey, the man finds a small cluster of houses and pushes a door open to shelter inside. Beyond the door, the house only has half its walls and part of a roof, the rest having crumbled and been abandoned. Occasional corners jut out of the earth, suggesting that houses once dotted this whole landscape. The damage could be from long neglect or from a more recent bombing. The helicopter

---

[12] *Dogs and Water*, p6-7

pilot gives the only indication that there has been a war of some sort that has destroyed the land, as he tells the young man about repairing a pipe that was bombed and having his helicopter shot down.

Overall, *Dogs and Water* is not a clear-cut post-apocalyptic graphic novel. The events that created the bleak landscape—war, neglect, a dream?—are open to interpretation.

30-Second Booktalk:

A young man travels through an empty world with only a small backpack and a teddy bear. He has no destination to reach, no journey to complete, and no goal beyond survival. By day, the world is flat, dry, empty; at night, in his dreams, he floats across a vast ocean in a failing lifeboat. Dog packs, aggressive deer, and an injured helicopter pilot all help to give the man's aimless journey some direction.

Readalikes:

The Road (Cormac McCarthy) for a walk through a post-apocalyptic landscape

Rash (Pete Hautman) for a walk through barren world and fighting with wild animals

Louis (Metaphrog) series for a dreamy comic with a vague sense of a post-apocalyptic world

Flood (Eric Drooker) for a non-linear graphic narrative of a man swept away by water

Potential Audience:

This dreamy graphic novel does not have a clear-cut narrative, making it more of a challenge for younger readers. Upper-high school and college students will likely be drawn into this bleak and yet hopeful story, identifying with the protagonist's directionlessness as they teeter on the brink of adulthood.

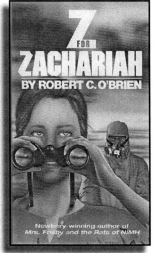

O'Brien, Robert C.

Z for Zachariah

Simon Pulse, 2007. 240p. $8.99 pb. 978-1-4169-3921-4.

- Originally published 1975

Plot Summary:

After the war ends, Ann Burden's father and brother travel to a neighboring town for information. They come back to report that everyone in that town is dead: families, animals, birds that had been flying overhead, all dead in their homes or on the streets. The next day, they set out again. This time, it's supposed to be just her parents; Ann and her brother are to stay home to feed their animals and stay near in case the phone comes back on and someone tries to call.

It's a few hours before Ann realizes that her brother sneaked away to go with them after all, and soon it's clear that none of them are coming back. At sixteen years old, Ann is the last person still alive on earth, the last person not affected by the nuclear radiation that has poisoned the rest of the planet. For a year, she's been surviving in her valley, the one place the radiation did not settle on, alone in the world.

But she's *not* alone: a stranger in a radiation-proof suit comes into her valley, intruding on the peace and security she's built up. He's a scientist, but neither his knowledge nor his suit save him from making a terrible mistake. Ann nurses him through the radiation poisoning, and when he recovers, the two make plans for how to cultivate and share the valley.

As time progresses, though, it is clear that Mr. Loomis is not to be trusted. His behavior becomes increasingly violent, ending in a cat-and-mouse game around the valley in which he shoots Ann in the leg to prevent her from leaving. She manages to evade him, then steals his radiation suit and prepares to abandon her valley. In a final confrontation, she tells Loomis that she refuses to be his prisoner or to allow herself to be hunted. She leaves the valley in search of other survivors, and Loomis tells her he's seen birds circling to the west, suggesting there may still be a living town.

Post-Apocalyptic Elements:

The war destroyed nearly everything. Toward the end, the enemy was dropping nerve gas, bacteria, and other antipersonnel weapons; it could be one of these or something different that has killed every living thing surrounding the valley and poisoning a stream that runs through it. The valley only survived due to its geography: outside winds blow right over, rather than through, effectively giving the valley its own weather system.

This is the world that Ann has now spent a year in: isolated in every way, knowing that leaving her valley would be deadly. She has spent her time learning how to live in her destroyed world and piece together a life out of what remains, and every bit of that is thrown into turmoil by the arrival of the dangerous stranger. When he drives her out of her home, she is left to journey through the deserted, radioactive wasteland that used to be the surrounding, thriving communities. With only the supplies she can bring along, she'll have to find a way to survive, just as the stranger did before finding her valley.

30-Second Booktalk:

Following a nuclear war, sixteen-year-old Ann Burden learns to survive alone in the untouched valley—until the day a stranger wearing a radiation-proof suit comes over the hill. When the stranger makes a crucial mistake, Ann nurses him back to health—making a crucial mistake of her own.

Readalikes:

Sweet Tooth (Jeff Lemire) for surviving alone in an isolated location

The Boy at the End of the World (Greg van Eekhout) for survival as the last person on Earth

When the Wind Blows (Raymond Briggs) for the effects of radiation poisoning

The Way We Fall (Megan Crewe) for geographic isolation

Nausicaá and the Valley of the Wind (HayaoMiyazaki) for a geography that creates its own weather system

Potential audience:

Middle- and high-school students will be engrossed by this classic, which holds up well in spite of its age. The updated cover's bold colors and striking image of a gas mask capture the book's suspense and well represents this sci-fi thriller.

Shirow, Masamune

Appleseed:The Promethean Challenge

Dark Horse Comics, 1995. 192p. $16.95. 978-1-56971-070-8.

- Originally published 1985

Plot Summary:

After World War III, soldier Deunan and her cyborg partner Briareos have been living in an abandoned city, making their plans for their future survival in Badside. They've been on their own for some time, so it's a shock to discover that there's someone else in their city, a hulking cybernetic machine who has been taking surveillance photos and monitoring the couple. Together, Deunan and Briareos take down the creature and open the battle armor.

The girl inside the armor, Hitomi, has been sent from Aegis, the Central Management Bureau, to collect them. This is the first Deunan and Bri have heard of the end of the war, and of the new political organizations. Arriving in the new city of Olympus, the travelers find jobs with ESWAT (Extra Special Weapons and Tactics). Maybe they were just picked up because Athena, the head of Olympus government, wants to gather everyone from the surrounding Badside areas, but it certainly seems like she was looking specifically for Deunan. Eighty percent of the city's population is bioroids, people with at least some artificial parts, and the artificial intelligence is beginning to undermine the utopian vision of the city.

Post-Apocalyptic Elements:

Most of the world has been destroyed in the third World War: populations have been decimated; cities destroyed, abandoned, left to decay. The world that Deunan and Bri are living in at the start of the book is, unambiguously, post-apocalyptic as a result of the war: not only was the city they are living in abandoned, Bri finds traces of biochemical weapons in the surrounding desert. This concerns Deunan, as the food they have already scavenged from the area could easily poison them, but Bri assures her that the chemicals used were rapidly-dispersing nerve gasses, long gone before the pair arrived to take what they could. Communication links have been down long enough that they are unaware that the war has ended, and a new organization has risen up.

Outside of this decimated city, though, the world has moved on from this post-apocalyptic state: new cities have been created, Earth unified by a new Central Management Bureau. The CMB, called Aegis, allows the individual countries to do what they like, within the confines of disarmament deals and the oversight of trading and economies. "Functional simplicity, structural complexity: the best life for all," Aegis-headquarters city Olympus declares, and they achieve that through extensive use of cybernetics. Buildings designed to minimize winter shadows, optical fibers that bring sunlight indoors, opto-electronics to facilitate registration procedures—all part of the "people first" philosophy of the city. The city is, by most definitions, a utopia: technology removes most sources of stress from people's lives, and the city aims to keep those lives happy and productive.

The problem—what turns the utopia into a dystopia—is that the technology that keeps the city running smoothly is mostly bioroids, artificial intelligence beings who have other plans than to keep the humans happy. The death of so much of the human population in the war was only the first step in AI evolution, and the AI in the Olympus council recognize that the human race is unstable at best, a mere three generations away from losing biological vitality.

The series oscillates between post-apocalyptic and dystopian themes and plots, but in the end, none of it would be possible without the apocalyptic war that began it all.

30-Second Booktalk:

Soldier Deunan and her cyborg partner, Briareos, have been hiding out in an abandoned city through the end of World War Three. Now there's someone new prowling around: a girl in battle armor, who takes them back to the new city of Olympus. Deunan and Bri, unaware that the war ended or that these new governments have been established, are awed by their new city, while still being plenty skeptical of what all the perfection might be hiding.

Readalikes:

Prometheus Unbound, Prometheus Unbound, and *The Promethean Balance* (Masamune Shirow) for the rest of the *Appleseed* story

Surrogates (Robert Venditti) for humans using other technological "bodies" in their daily lives

Blade Runner and *A.I.* (films) for the rise of androids to take over the world

Potential Audience:

Appleseed is a classic of cyberpunk graphic novels, still popular among manga fans today. Minor nudity and themes of conspiracy and military strategy make *Appleseed* best suited toward upper high-school and adult collections.

van Eekhout, Greg

The Boy at the End of the World

Bloomsbury, 2011. 212p. $16.99. 978-1-59990-524-2.

Plot Summary:

Fisher wakes up knowing only his name and that he is alone in a dangerous world. The young teen has just been born out of suspended animation, roused by a damaged robot named Click while the ark that housed them both was being attacked. Every other pod on the ark has been destroyed, killing off the humans and animals that had been carefully preserved with the hopes of repopulating Earth. If Fisher is going to help repopulate the planet, though, he's aware that he'll need to find other people—and that means surviving that long.

Fisher and Click set out for the south, following evidence that suggests Fisher's ark was not the only one. On finding the Southern Ark, Fisher and Click are wary of the effusively-welcoming Intelligence, a robot made from millions of tiny nanobots. Intelligence was tasked with protecting and preserving the humans and animals in their pods, but the Intelligence has taken his instructions far too literally: he has turned off the suspended animation and injected each body with cell-repairing nano-worms, keeping the humans and animals from dying by keeping them from living. The Intelligence is determined to do the same to Fisher, but Fisher and Click manage to narrowly escape with their lives.

The trip to a possible Western Ark is long and arduous, made even more difficult by the presence of a thieving, super-intelligent prairie dog named Zapper. Fisher saves the unlucky animal from drowning, though, and wins Zapper's loyalty. Zapper is part of a colony that lives near the Western Ark, and she is willing to show Fisher the way, though the Ark is forbidden territory for the prairie dogs. Fisher's rescue of Zapper earns him the favor of most of the colony, and he is accompanied to the ark with a small army of prairie dogs. They fight off the Gadgets to allow Fisher opportunity to get inside the ark and awaken some of its humans.

Once that moment comes, though, Fisher and Click learn a terrifying truth: an Intelligence nanobot has stowed away inside Fisher's head, breaking free only to wriggle inside Click and take over the robot's operation. The Intelligence controls Click, demanding that he power down several pods before attacking Fisher and preserving him in an empty pod. Click fights the control, urging Fisher to destroy him before the Intelligence destroys any option of a repopulated Earth. With great reluctance, Fisher does so.

The book concludes with Fisher waking a girl his age from suspended animation, making her aware that she is not alone in this new world.

Post-Apocalyptic Elements:

When humans dominated the Earth, our achievements in technology, agriculture, and other areas had a disastrous effect on the planet: farming practices stripped nutrients from the soil; manufacturing polluted the air and waters; deadly new diseases were unleashed on humans and animals alike. The scarcity of resources led to war, and war led to the further destruction of humankind and the Earth. Attempts to fix one problem gave rise to other problems, until the only solution was not a solution at all: preserve what life forms could be preserved and leave them in suspended animation until such time that the Earth could again support life.

This is the world into which Fisher is born: the only humans are floating in bubbling gel, waiting to be pulled from their suspended states. Finding them will require long journeys through landscapes unfamiliar to the newly-aware Fisher and to Click, whose rudimentary geography programming is centuries out of date. Without humans, the Earth has returned to a mostly-wild place; Texas has turned into a desert; the Mississippi river is several hundred miles shorter than it used to be.

Fisher's world is one of long-term effects of human progress, and our efforts to repair isolated parts of the intricately-linked natural world. While the natural world struggles to recover from centuries of damage, technology continues to assert itself, the artificial intelligence adapting, learning, even extrapolating in new and dangerous ways.

30-Second Booktalk:

His name is Fisher. The world is dangerous. And he's the only one in it. These are the things Fisher knows immediately upon waking up, upon being born from the survival pod ages after all the other humans have died. The journey to find any other humans will require Fisher to outsmart robots, evade the deadly gadgets, and win over a colony of warrior prairie dogs—all in a world that has been completely destroyed.

Readalikes:

Hatchet (Gary Paulson) for survivalist adventure

The City of Ember (Jeanne DuPrau) for journeys to find other humans

The Carbon Diaries (Saci Lloyd) for the impacts of environmental damage

The World Without Us (Alan Weisman) for a look at how the Earth will repair itself when humans are gone

Potential Audience:

Adventure-seeking upper-elementary and middle schoolers will appreciate the post-apocalyptic landscape and Fisher's journey to find other humans. "Green" teens will recognize the environmental messages that are obvious and cautionary without being didactic.

Chapter 7:

Virus & Plague

In early 2003, the first cases of Severe Acute Respiratory Syndrome (SARS) were reported in China. Within months, the virus infected more than 8000 people in dozens of countries across four continents.[1] The World Health Organization named 2009's H1N1 flu a pandemic when it reached seventy-four countries within two months of its first outbreaks.[2]

With two pandemics in such recent memory, it's no surprise that authors have been imagining what life would become in the wake of an even more extensive outbreak—or how the outbreak would begin. Some pandemics begin with noble intentions; some end in zombies. The plagues can significantly reduce the population in one go or destroy reproduction opportunities, or they can *increase* the population by creating an entire new race of people. In this chapter, we'll be looking at ten different takes on how viruses and plagues can change—or end—the world.

In the 2007 film *I Am Legend*, scientists have developed a cure for cancer. What begins as a medical breakthrough mutates into a virus that quickly eradicates most of the population. Similarly, Lauren DeStefano begins her Chemical Garden trilogy with a cure for cancer and other diseases, but that tampering with genetic code has a unintended effect: while the generation that found the cure is aging gracefully, their children are dying by their 25th birthdays.

In Fiona Smyth's graphic novel *The Never Weres*, cloning may be humanity's only hope for survival after the barren virus struck more than ten years earlier. Yorick, the lead character in the graphic novel series *Y: The Last Man* (Brian K. Vaughan), has somehow survived the sudden extermination of every male on the planet—and as the series progresses, we learn that the virus is connected to research on human cloning.

The plague that spawned Snowman's story in Margaret Atwood's *Oryx and Crake* also began with good intentions, though not to the benefit of humankind. In an effort to save the planet (instead of humanity), Crake unleashes a virus that all but eliminates humans, making room for the new race of people he's created. The graphic novel series *Sweet Tooth* by Jeff Lemire shows Gus, a nine-year-old deer-child, as something of a scientific curiosity. It's not his hybrid status that makes him as unusual—since the virus struck, all children born are at least part animal—but that he's older than all the others. John Green's novella *Zombicorns* does not create a new race of people but changes the existing ones: any who have eaten the infected corn have become "z'd up," an entire population of people concerned only with the proliferation of corn.

Ann Aguirre's *Enclave* and Jeff Hirsch's *The Eleventh Plague* both feature man-made viruses, unleashed as biological weapons against unwitting populations. These acts of war are echoed in Anna Sheehan's *A Long, Long Sleep*, in which Rose emerges from 60 years in stasis to find a world completely remade after the Dark Times of disease and the reemergence of bubonic plague.

From well-meaning science to weaponized flu: we may only be a cough away from our own extinction. Below, ten creators speculate on a virus that could wipe us off the planet—and who knows how many more there could truly be.

---

[1] http://www.cdc.gov/ncidod/sars/factsheet.htm
[2] http://www.who.int/csr/disease/swineflu/frequently_asked_questions/about_disease/en/index.html

Aguirre, Ann

Enclave

Feiwel and Friends, 2011. 259p. $16.99 978-0-312-65008-7.
Macmillan Young Listeners. $29.99 CD. 978-1-4272-1120-0.
Google eBooks, $9.99. 978-1-4299-5036-7.

Plot Summary:

Girl15 is looking forward to her Naming: she's finally becoming the Huntress she's been training to be, fulfilling her lifelong ambition. The newly-christened Deuce gets paired with Fade, the loner-outsider who makes no pretense of goodwill towards anyone. Together they patrol the tunnels of their subterranean world, searching for food and avoiding the mindless, hungry, vaguely human-shaped creatures they call freaks.

On a recon mission to a nearby enclave, Deuce and Fade are surrounded, and they have a troubling realization: the freaks are getting smarter. They're organizing, strategizing, no longer simple killing and eating machines. This is bad, and will mean trouble for their Enclave. And the trouble will get worse if the officials won't listen to them. Still, they pass their information along and continue to patrol as usual, waiting for a decision to be made.

Following another long day of hunting and patrolling, Deuce and Fade return to the enclave to find that one of Deuce's best friends, a Breeder, is accused of hoarding: storing artifacts in his private quarters, rather than turning them over to the enclave's archivist/historian. Deuce knows that Stone would never do such a thing, that the book he's accused of hoarding was planted to allow the officials to remind everyone the consequences of such actions. Before Stone can be banished from the enclave, Deuce claims the book as her own, and Fade claims to have planted it. Immediately the pair is exiled, forced to survive on their own in the tunnels without the safety of the enclave to help them.

Deuce's underground world becomes a memory as she's forced topside for the first time in her life. Fade knows the surface world, though, and helps his partner navigate the dangers of this brightly-lit world, all that remains of a city. Fade's father told him of a settlement north of the city that would be safe, and the pair heads that direction, but they'll have to evade the gang whose territory they pass through—and then evade the freaks that have made it to the surface in search of food.

Dystopian Elements:

In her Author's Note, Aguirre talks about her inspiration for *Enclave*, setting her story after a manufactured plague and projecting what cities might be like from post-Katrina New Orleans. This became her topside world, a New York City ruled by violent, territorial gangs after the population has been decimated by an unstoppable virus. To escape the virus and the violence on the surface, others have fled into the ruins of the subway system, living off scavenged goods and trades with other subterranean communities.

As Deuce's community is set up, there are three main career options for teens to choose in a ceremony when they come of age: Breeders (procreation and childcare), Builders (carpentry, engineering, and maintenance), or Hunters (hunting, security, and trade runs). There is a distinct hierarchy among them, with Hunters are at the top and Breeders at the bottom, and everyone in the Enclave recognizes their respective stations. The classism among the three major work assignments is clear enough, but there is one more class: the elders, and specifically the Wordkeeper. The Wordkeeper is the Enclave's archivist and historian, and his knowledge is not to be questioned; also unquestionable are the elders who make all decisions for the Enclave and are unwilling to believe the bad news that Deuce and Fade bring back from their recon mission to a nearby settlement.

While Part 1 ("Down Below") of the book is dystopian, with its carefully-controlled government and strict social hierarchy, Part 2 ("Topside") switches to a post-apocalyptic world, in which a man-made plague wiped out New York City and much of the surrounding areas. Deuce and Fade struggle to make it through the remains of the world, scavenging the discarded sunglasses, canned foods, and other goods that would have survived the deadly virus while avoiding the violently territorial gangs that have taken over the city streets. This is all unsettling enough, but when the Freaks from underground come up to the surface in search of food, the plot morphs into a straight-up zombie story.

30-Second Booktalk:

Deuce, a new Huntress, gets paired with Fade, the loner-outsider who hates everyone in the enclave. Together they patrol the tunnels of their subterranean world, On a recon mission to a nearby enclave, Deuce and Fade are surrounded by freaks, the mindless creatures who will kill and eat anything, and they have a troubling realization: the freaks are getting smarter. This is bad, and will get worse if the Enclave officials won't believe them.

Readalikes:

The City of Ember (Jeane DuPrau) for underground society and the need to explore the surface

Divergent (Veronica Roth) for choosing career paths and an unapologetically battle-ready heroine

The Forest of Hands and Teeth (Carrie Ryan) and *The Enemy* (Charlie Higson) for attempts to find a safe haven through zombie-infested areas

Potential Audience:

Fight scenes and action sequences keep the plot moving, and the lack of graphic descriptions make this a good choice for middle schoolers. Science fiction and zombie fans will enjoy this novel, though some readers may be put off by the change from the dystopian underground society to the zombie-apocalypse topside.

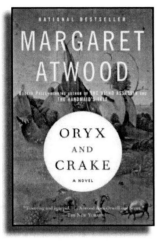

Atwood, Margaret

Oryx and Crake

Anchor Books, 2003. 416p. $15. 978-0-385-72167-7.
Google eBooks. $11.99. 978-1-4000-7898-1.

Plot Summary:

The man known only as Snowman has been living near a group of human-like Crakers, trading his knowledge for their resources in the bleak post-apocalyptic landscape they all inhabit now. Snowman's story, however, began years ago, when he was a child named Jimmy.

As a boy and teen, Jimmy played at the online trivia game Extinctathon with his best friend, who gave himself the name Crake. With their expansive knowledge of extinct plants and animals, they advanced through the game's levels quickly. By the time they left for college, Crake had made it to the level of Grandmaster.

While Jimmy studied humanities in college—a scorned career path leading only to propaganda production—Crake pursued bioengineering. After college, with a high-power position at a biotechnology company, Crake began work on his life's mission: he created the Crakers, genetically engineered humans who eat only grass and leaves and have limited breeding seasons, with the mission of creating a peaceful society that will exist harmoniously with each other and with the earth.

Crake also created a virus that would wipe out nearly all of humanity and leave only the Crakers behind—and Jimmy, whom Crake secretly inoculated so that Jimmy could be the caretaker for the Craker civilization. Crake's plan was meant altruistically: he truly meant to save humankind from a slow, painful death and preserve intelligent life by way of the Crakers. When Jimmy confronted Crake about this plan, the two fought, and Jimmy shot Crake. Jimmy's questions about this new world, and his role as protector of the Crakers, remain forever unanswered.

Later, as Snowman, he finds three true humans camping nearby. He debates how—and if—he should approach, factoring in the safety of the Craker settlement. His final decision is not revealed, allowing the reader to assign meaning toward his final thought that it is "time to go."

Post-Apocalyptic Elements:

When the book opens, the reader only knows that Snowman is the last human, though he lives near a settlement of human-like Crakers. As the story unfolds, we learn what actually happened to the other humans: hidden in vaccines was a virus, genetically modified to become a pandemic.

The Crakers are the results of biological engineering and a desire to make an intelligent race that would coexist with the environment for an indefinite time, taking no more than the environment can easily provide—specifically, grasses and leaves. Other bioengineered life forms include the pigoons (pigs with balloon-shaped bodies to accommodate the extra organs they grow for human transplantation) and rakunks (blends of raccoons and skunks). Meanwhile, natural plants and animals are going extinct, tracked by the Extinctathon game Jimmy and Crake frequently played as teens.

The questions left behind at the novel's conclusion are, in Atwood's words, "What if we continue down the road we're already on? How slippery is the slope? What are our saving graces? … It's not a question of our inventions—all human inventions are merely tools—but of what might be done with them."[3] These are valuable questions to ask, given current technological trends and capabilities as well as the proliferation of particularly-virulent flu strains and other contagious diseases.

The novel's frame story, of Snowman caring for the Crakers, shows a bit of life in the aftermath of Crake's virus. Snowman is creating the new world along with the Crakers, including creating a new religion based on Crake as their godly creator and Oryx, the prostitute who became both Jimmy's and Crake's love interest, as the protector of animals. Even this small bit of invented theology suggests the story of Adam and Eve, and the beginning of a new world.

30-Second Booktalk:

Crake has always been interested in extinct animals and ways to preserve life. It's an interest that takes him right into a career as a bioengineer, and leads him to create his own new race of people, the Crakers. But in order for his peaceful, herbivorous human-like creatures to live in harmony with nature and preserve intelligent life, the existing humans need to be spared their long, slow decline. He has a plan for that, too.

Readalikes:

The Year of the Flood (Margaret Atwood) for a companion to the events of *Oryx and Crake*

The Hunger Games (Suzanne Collins) for genetically-engineered hybrid animals

Sweet Tooth (Jeff Lemire) for the creation of a new race of people

The Road (Cormac McCarthy) for similarities in tone

Potential Audience:

Students interested in biology and extinction will find much of interest in Atwood's novel. Grades 10 and up will get the most out of this novel.

---

[3] Atwood, Margaret. "Writing *Oryx and Crake*." 2003. Accessed via Archive.org, http://web.archive.org/web/20090327103531/ http://www.randomhouse.com/features/atwood/essay.html, 11/3/2011.

DeStefano, Lauren

Wither

Simon & Schuster, 2011. 368p. $17.99. 978-1-4424-0905-7.
Google eBooks. $9.99. 978-1-4424-0911-8.

- Chemical Garden trilogy, Book 1

Plot Summary:

The remaining First Generations are around seventy years old: they are the generation that found a cure for cancer and manipulated our genetic code to ensure perfect lives free of disease. In doing so, however, they also unleashed a deadly virus in all future generations, a virus that kills males at age twenty-five and females at twenty. To ensure humanity's survival, teenage girls are frequently abducted and sold to the highest bidders to be wives to wealthy young men and have their babies while First Generations continue to search for an antidote to the virus.

At sixteen, Rhine is taken, stolen by Gatherers and crowded into a van with other stolen girls. She and two others are chosen out of that van to be wives for Linden Ashby, to keep him company and bear his children until the virus takes them all, just as it did his first wife and true love. Rhine is desperate to escape, to get back to Manhattan and her twin brother, to leave behind the opulent fakery of Linden's world and return to what she knows is real.

Rhine's younger sister-wife, Cecily, takes readily to marriage, eager to please him in any way she can and become a mother to his children; her older sister-wife, Jenna, remains emotionally distant from Linden but becomes a true friend to Rhine. Rhine herself is uncertain: she's quickly becoming Linden's favorite, but she still has no desire to be married to him and fulfill that role. Instead, her affections are growing in a different, dangerous direction, and her father-in-law will stop at nothing to ensure Rhine's cooperation.

Post-Apocalyptic Elements:

As this is the first book in a projected trilogy, it's difficult to say what post-apocalyptic elements will be prevalent through the series. In the first book, there are passing references to an environmental apocalypse that flooded six of seven continents (North America being the only remaining land mass). Government has mostly turned its back on the run-down cities and their orphans.

Nearly a century prior to the novel's events, scientists had a breakthrough in medical research: cancer was cured, and human genetic code was manipulated to ensure that children had long, disease-free lives. Two decades later, a deadly virus claimed all females at age 20 and males at 25, a side effect of the scientists' tinkering with genetics. Teen pregnancy is literally the only way to keep the human race going.

With most of the novel taking place within the mansions' grounds, the reader can forget the post-apocalyptic landscape, can forget that most of the Earth is flooded. The flooding and ruination will likely play larger roles in the next two books, in which Rhine is out of the Ashby mansion, though this is, at this writing, conjecture.

30-Second Booktalk:

The First Generations successfully manipulated genetic code to ensure their children had perfect lives, free of cancer and other aging diseases. Two decades later, they learned they'd also unleashed a virus that kills men at age twenty-five and women at twenty. Sixteen-year-old Rhine has been stolen to be one of three sister-wives to the wealthy Linden, to bear his children to ensure humanity's survival. Being a bride thrusts Rhine into a life of luxury, but it's not enough to overcome her desire to escape, even when an attempt could kill her.

Readalikes:

Bumped (Megan McCafferty) for a lighter take on enforced breeding among teens

The Handmaid's Tale (Margaret Atwood) for polygamy and breeding

Ship Breaker (Paolo Bacigalupi) for similar tone and need to escape

The Chosen One (Carol Lynch Williams) for polygamy and teen brides

I Am Legend (film) for a cure for cancer becoming a humanity-ending virus

Potential audience:

Older teens looking for more substance than the other recent dystopian romances may enjoy this, though romance is not at the forefront. While the main premise of the book involves child brides and teen pregnancy, there is little discussion of it, and the main character rebuffs all advances, keeping the novel appropriate for 9th grade and up.

Discussion Guide:

Website and trailer available at: http://thechemicalgardenbooks.com/wither/?page_id=34

Green, John

Zombicorns

Self-published, 2011. Available for free download at http://dft.ba/-zombicornpdf (pdf format) or http://dft.ba/-zombicorndoc (Word .doc)

Plot Summary:

Mia is the last surviving member of her family. Her parents and sister have all been Z'd up, infected with the virus spread by, of all things, corn. It's not quite right to call them zombies; they're not undead, exactly, but rather slaves to the corn, planting and tending the corn plants to the exclusion of anything else. Nobody's lurching around threatening to eat Mia's brain, but if the Z'd up catch her, they're likely to force-feed her that same corn and make her a devotee to the cornfields as well.

Mia's not totally alone in the world. She's stuck around Chicago to keep an eye on her little sister, making sure she gets the protein and food she needs to survive, even though Mia knows that Holly isn't really Holly anymore. Mia has her dog, Mr. President, a stray she took in after the rest of the world fell apart. Then she finds Caroline hiding out in a library vault, and while the girls have certain ideological differences about the infected, they develop the kind of friendship that only comes of being the last two living people in Chicago.

The girls scout around the city for supplies, but to Caroline it's all a game: she plans to leave Chicago and head north, hoping to cross into an agriculturally-unfriendly part of Canada where the Z'd haven't gathered. Mia doesn't believe such places exist, and she prefers to stay in Chicago near her sister anyway. Caroline tries to stress the importance of leaving Chicago, explaining that, "There's no survival here, Mia. Maybe there's survival up north and maybe not, but we're definitely not gonna find it here."[4]

The novella concludes with Mia's thoughts on the evolution of the Z and on humanness in general, writing her story and her musings in her "Re/Accounting of human life post-virus."

Post-Apocalyptic Elements:

"That which nourishes me, extinguishes me," the Romans said, and the Devotion131Y strain of corn is doing the same thing: anyone who has eaten the D131Y is infected with AMRV [the acronym is never defined]. AMRV makes people feel protective over the corn, planting more and more of it and carefully tending the new cornfields. Mia mentions that the D131Y corn has spread its virus across the United States. Emigration to Europe had been possible with a weeks-long maritime quarantine, but she speculates that the virus has found its way into other countries, so that the infection is now world-wide. It's been just over a year since Mia's family succumbed; there has been plenty of time for the virus to encroach on the rest of the world.

---

[4] p72

While Green did not do research before embarking on this hastily-written novella, it can spark discussion on sustainable agriculture and healthy eating. How much corn is too much? At what point do Americans become slaves to the corn that makes up so much of our diet? How does that impact our health? Obviously we have not become the zombies Green suggests, but as corn becomes a bigger percentage of our food supply, it has an increasingly negative effect on public health.

30-Second Booktalk:

It all started with the corn. Corn that can be anything, from sugar to plastic. Corn that wants there to be *more* corn. Corn that caused the Zapocalypse. The Z'd up won't try to eat your brains—only force-feed you the Devotion131Y corn variety that will make you a thoroughly devoted tender of the corn, as well. Mia is the last surviving member of her family, and maybe the last surviving person in Chicago. And she has her reasons for staying.

Readalikes:

In Defense of Food (Michael Pollan) for information about the bioengineering of food products

King Corn (film) for an in-depth look at corn production

Vlog Brothers (YouTube channel; http://www.youtube.com/user/vlogbrothers) for more of Green's kinetic energy

Sweet Tooth (Jeff Lemire) for a new race of people evolving

Potential Audience:

"Nerdfighters," John Green's legion of fans, will surely flock to this zombie-apocalypse novella Green penned to benefit the Harry Potter Alliance. Zombie-apocalypse devotees and those interested in the bioengineering of, and the many uses for, corn in American food production will be willing to give this a cursory skim as well.

Discussion Guide:

John Green reads the beginning of *Zombicorns* at: http://www.youtube.com/watch?v=4ZgfxrvC6ro

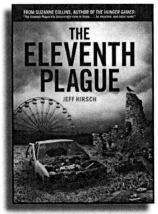

Hirsch, Jeff

The Eleventh Plague

Scholastic, 2011. 278p. $17.99. 978-0-545-29014-2.
$34.99 (CD). 978-0-545-35396-0.
Google eBooks. $17.99. 978-0-545-38809-2.

Plot Summary:

Stephen is a scavenger, traveling the post-Collapse landscape with his dad and ex-Marine grandfather. His father and grandfather have never seen eye-to-eye about how to survive, with his father preferring to help others whenever possible and his grandfather erring toward isolation. But now his grandfather is dead, and Stephen and his dad are making their own way.

In their scavenging, Stephen and his father find an old plane, a lucky find as they seek shelter for the night. While huddled inside, more people come in: slavers, with two prisoners in tow. Stephen's father attacks, setting the prisoners free and wounding the slavers, but their run to freedom has tragic consequences: Stephen's father falls from a small cliff and gets swept away in the river. Stephen manages to pull him out and save him from drowning, but the crushed skull presents a much larger problem.

Stephen and his father are discovered by a small band of men from a nearby settlement, and reluctantly Stephen agrees to join them. His father, still in a coma, is patched up and watched over by the town's only medical professional. She takes Stephen in as one of her own children, sending him to school with the others and assigning him chores.

Stephen's experience in the outside world makes him distrustful of this pre-Collapse life, and he's barely spent any time in Settler's Landing before he's making plans to leave. Before he can depart, though, he participates in what should be a harmless prank—but instead it ignites a war between Settler's Landing and the nearby town of Fort Leonard. With the violence on his conscience, Stephen is doubly resolute in his plans to leave, only to recognize his obligation to set things back to rights. Ultimately he decides to give up his peripatetic life in favor of contributing to a stable community.

Post-Apocalyptic Elements:

The Collapse was brought about long before Stephen's birth: what should have been a minor international incident (the detainment of two Americans in China) started a conflict that became a war. In the war, the United States launched nuclear weapons at China; China retaliated by unleashing a biological weapon. What they released was a particularly virulent strain of flu, P11H3. P11, or the Eleventh Plague, killed millions of people worldwide, and with all those people dead, hospitals, schools, power stations, and other vital services shut down. The cycle of deaths leading to shuttered services leading to deaths continued until civilization had been all but extinguished.

There are many things that contributed to this worldwide destruction: nuclear war, biological weapons, contagions, shortages. By the time the events of the novel take place, though, the shortages are the biggest lasting result. Survivors are no longer concerned about P11 or radiation fallout, but the food and supply shortages make every day a struggle. Finding an industrial-sized can of pears makes Stephen and his father marvel at their luck: they could trade the can for medicine, other food, winter clothes, and other valuables, but such a deliciously rare treat is worth just as much as the goods they could trade for.

The people of Settler's Landing carefully gather whatever supplies they find in the area, and hunt for their food. The long-standing dispute with Fort Leonard could erupt into a war, an echo of the events that caused the Collapse. As the world grows smaller, the potential grows for each skirmish to destroy what's left of civilization.

30-Second Booktalk:

Stephen is from a family of scavengers, taking what they can find and living off the post-Collapse land. Survival is difficult, but there are always people willing to help. Stephen is lucky enough to find some of these people when his father is gravely injured, but staying in this peaceful community permanently is completely out of the question—especially after a prank goes wrong and incites a new war, and Stephen knows that it's his fault.

Readalikes:

The Road (Cormac McCarthy), for aimless travel through a post-apocalyptic landscape

Restoring Harmony (Joélle Anthony) for traveling and joining new communities

Chaos Walking trilogy (Patrick Ness) for war-mongering leaders and joining new communities

Potential Audience:

All things considered, this is a fairly gentle post-apocalyptic war book, with violence that is neither gratuitous nor graphic. Most appropriate for seventh through tenth grades, this could be a good choice for book discussions, or for teens who prefer their post-apocalyptic wars a little more hopeful.

I Am Legend

DVD. Color. 100m. Produced and dist. by Warner Home Video, 2011. $14.98. 978-0-7806-7394-6.

- Written by Mark Protosevich and Akiva Goldsman
- Based on the 1954 novel by Richard Matheson
- Directed by Francis Lawrence
- Originally released 2007

Plot Summary:

Three years ago, humanity cheered when a cure for cancer was discovered. Unfortunately, something went wrong, and the cure for cancer unleashed a terrible virus. Those who are not killed become Infected—bloodthirsty monsters that cannot bear the light.

Dr. Robert Neville is the last man standing in New York City, somehow immune to both airborne and contact-based strains of the virus. Each day, Neville and his German Shepard Sam make their rounds through the city, hunting and scavenging for food and searching for other survivors. At night, he and Sam lock down their house with reinforced doors and shutters, keeping the Infected at bay.

Neville uses some of his time in the evenings to research a cure for the virus: starting with infected rats, he has been using different compounds of his own immune blood, trying to isolate the parts that will turn the Infected back into humans. With one compound that looks promising, he captures an Infected and tests his possible cure, only to find that it kills the host instead of just the virus. Disappointed, he revives her and returns to his research.

Meanwhile, the Infected are getting smarter, and one has set a snare trap for Neville, similar to the one Neville used to catch the Infected he has been testing. In the ensuing battle, Sam is injured, and Neville has to strangle his dog before he is attacked. In his grief, Neville attacks a group of Infecteds the following evening. He is injured in the attack, and rescued by a woman, Anna, and her son, who are traveling to a survivors' compound in Vermont.

Anna and her son have taken Neville back to his home, but she did not take his usual precautions in covering the trail. The Infecteds track them, mobbing the house the following evening. Neville and the two travelers are cornered in his basement laboratory when Anna notices that the Infected Neville attempted to cure looks, in fact, cured. Working quickly, Neville draws a vial of blood from the previously-Infected woman and tells Anna to take it with her, that the cure is in there. She and her son escape through a coal chute while Neville releases a grenade, killing the horde of Infecteds and himself.

The movie concludes with Anna and her son reaching the survivors' colony and handing over the vial. A voice-over explains that the future generations will be Neville's legacy, and his fight to eradicate the virus will make him a legend.

Post-Apocalyptic Elements:

When a cure for cancer goes wrong, humanity is pushed nearly to extinction by the resultant rabies-like virus. Most of the world's population has been killed or Infected within three years of the virus's genesis, leaving New York City all but abandoned. There are plenty of Infecteds inhabiting it, of course, and a number of animals run wild, but Neville is the only remaining human.

Neville has clearly spent much time isolated in the city, holding conversations with department-store mannequins he's arranged in a DVD store and along his path. It is the discovery of one of his mannequins in a new location, moved by an Infected showing greater intellect than the others that causes him to be caught in a snare trap. Neville's grip on reality loosening, he demands of the mannequin "Fred, if you're real, you better tell me right now!" before shooting it. This isolation and its effects were one of the director's chief goals in making the movie. "Something's always really excited me about that," [Lawrence] said. "What that's like psychologically — to have experienced that much loss, to be without people or any kind of social interaction for that long."[5] The psychological effects of solitude and isolation have been well documented, primarily studied among prison inmates[6].

30-Second Booktalk:

When a deadly virus kills most of humanity, Robert Neville is the last man left in New York City, possibly in the world. For all the research he's done, he's no closer to a cure, and each day the Infecteds get a little stronger, a little smarter, and a little more likely to kill him.

Readalikes:

I Am Legend (Richard Matheson) for the original story

The Omega Man (1971 film) for an earlier adaptation of the source material

The Forest of Hands and Teeth (Carrie Ryan) for zombie-like viral infections

The Way We Fall (Megan Crewe) for isolation and quarantine in a viral outbreak

Wither (Lauren DeStefano) for a cure for cancer resulting in an apocalyptic virus

Potential Audience:

Rated PG-13, *I Am Legend* is a good choice for roughly eighth grade and up. Violence is not graphically depicted on-screen (though there are some fight scenes), and the movie is suspenseful. Not for the most delicate viewers, but zombie enthusiasts and thriller fans will find much to like here.

---

[5] http://www.nytimes.com/2007/11/04/movies/moviesspecial/04halb.html?ref=moviesspecial [retrieved 9/18/2011]
[6] http://www.prisoncommission.org/statements/grassian_stuart_long.pdf and
http://serendip.brynmawr.edu/exchange/node/1898

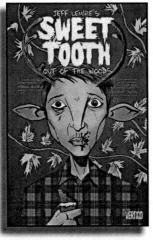

Lemire, Jeff

Out of the Deep Woods

Vertigo, 2009. 128p. $9.99 978-1-4012-2696-1.

In Captivity

Vertigo, 2010. 144p. $12.99 978-1-4012-2854-5.

Animal Armies

Vertigo, 2011. 144p. $14.99. 978-1-4012-3170-5.

- *Sweet Tooth* series
- Originally published 2009-2011 (ongoing)

Plot Summary:

Several years ago, a virus began wiping out whole populations. The last surviving adults know their days are numbered. Strangely, children born after the start of the virus are all hybrids: part human, part animal, and not susceptible to the virus.

Gus is nine years old and has lived in isolation with his father all his life. His mother died when he was too little to remember, and his father is dying now. He warns Gus about leaving their camp, but after his death, Gus has no choice: hunters have found him, and it's only with the help of a mysterious, dangerous stranger that Gus survives the encounter. Jepperd promises to take Gus to the preserve, where hybrid children are safe, and Gus really has no option but to believe him.

Volume 2, *In Captivity*, begins with Gus trapped in the "preserve," where he meets several other animal-kid hybrids also locked up in the prison camp. Wendy, a pig-girl, is one of the few who can speak, and she tells him what actually happens there: someone comes to get the hybrid kids, and they don't come back. Soon Gus is taken to talk with the doctor, who believes that something in Gus's past will explain the plague. Meanwhile, Jepperd considers his own past, remembering his late wife and child and coming to terms with his betrayal of Gus.

Animal Armies shows Jepperd attempting to atone for what he's done—starting with rescuing the hybrid kids, in particular Gus. To free them, he'll need a militia, and he joins forces with an animal-worshiping cult. Meanwhile, Gus and the other hybrid kids are attempting their own escape.

Post-Apocalyptic Elements:

The world has crumbled, and the population is significantly reduced. The virus that infected so many had another side effect: since it began, every pregnancy has resulted in a hybrid child, part human and part animal. The proportions are unpredictable: some are more animal than human, incapable of speech; others (like Gus) are mostly human, with only a few animal characteristics (Gus's antlers, e.g.) that mark them as different.

The post-apocalyptic elements are clearer in the second book, in which the reader sees flashbacks of Jepperd's life and what brought him to betray Gus. Cities have been decimated; Jepperd and his wife are wandering in search of a better, safer place, free of the virus. On their journey, Jepperd learns that his wife is pregnant, and while he doesn't believe the rumors of the hybrid children, nor can he rule them out. When salvation is offered in the form of a government camp, they jump at the chance, only to learn that the hybrid children are being taken away for experimentation in the hopes of using their immunities to the virus to find a cure.

This series is ongoing, so readers still lack answers to the big questions in this post-apocalyptic world: was Gus the first hybrid child? What makes him, or any of the others, immune to the virus? And how far does the government's reach go?

30-Second Booktalk:

About a decade ago, a deadly virus struck, wiping out entire populations. All children born since then are immune—and are human-animal hybrids. Gus is a 9-year-old deer-child, rescued from hunters after his father's death by a mysterious, dangerous stranger. Jepperd promises to take Gus to the preserve, where hybrid children are safe, and Gus really has no choice but to believe him. But Jepperd has his own reasons for going back there, and helping a young boy isn't one of them.

Readalikes:

The Road (Cormac McCarthy) for the travel to an assumed safe haven

Z for Zachariah (Robert C. O'Brien) for the need to trust a stranger for survival

The Roar (Emma Clayton) or *X-Men* (Marvel Comics) for mutations

Potential Audience:

Eighth graders would certainly understand the whole story easily, but the frequent (though not graphic) violence may push this into high school territory.

Sheehan, Anna

A Long, Long Sleep

Candlewick, 2011. 342p. $16.99 978-0-7636-5260-9.
Candlewick on Brilliance Audio. $19.99 MP3-CD. 978-1-4558-2052-8.
$24.99 CD. 978-1-4558-2050-4.
Adobe Digital Editions eBook. $16.99. 978-0-7636-5605-8.

Plot Summary:

Rose has just been pulled out of stasis by someone she's never met, awakening to a world she doesn't recognize and can't understand. It's been over sixty years since she was last out of her stasis tube. Everyone she's ever known is long dead, victims of the Dark Times that killed millions of people. She gives her name, Rosalinda Fitzroy, to the boy who rescues her, and he is shocked: the lone heir to the multinational UniCorp has survived, after all this time!

Rose's recovery in this new world is not easy: in her new school (where she is always behind in all her classes), she learns the gruesome details of the Dark Times of plague and disease that she slept through; at home, there is a robotic assassin with orders to capture or kill her, and it has been carefully tracking her every movement.

But along the way she's learning things, coming to understand what happened to her. That it's been just over a century since her birth, but she's only 16 years old, thanks to the amount of time her parents kept her in stasis. That her parents were killed in a helicopter crash only 30 years ago, nine years after the end of the Dark Times, and that they had never let her out of stasis. That Xavier, her soul mate, was also killed in the Dark Times, and that they only ever had one year together, being chronically out of phase with each other due to her stasis. That she's falling for a new boy before getting over Xavier. That she has one new friend who honestly wants to help her, even though she—as the heir of UniCorp—technically owns him and his alien-hybrid siblings.

Top priority, though, is disabling the robotic assassin, which can only be done by discovering who sent it and what its orders are. She thinks she tracks it to the acting president of UniCorp, a weaselly man eager to keep control for himself, but the assassin destroys him in its efforts to get to her. The discovery that it was sent by her own father is a blow that shakes Rose to her core and provides her the strength to fight back and destroy the assassin, allowing her a true chance at living her own life for the first time in her century-long sixteen years.

Post-Apocalyptic Elements:

In the time that Rose spent in her stasis tube, she missed the Dark Times and the reconstruction from them. The Dark Times began with a tuberculosis epidemic, followed by a strain of bubonic plague. Millions of people worldwide were killed. Recovery has taken some time, but the world has actually become a far better place in the wake of such a disaster: with the population reduced so dramatically, unemployment is virtually unheard of. Because nearly everyone is gainfully employed, poverty is a thing of the past, and without poverty, there are far fewer desperate people, so violent crime and thefts have also dropped off dramatically.

There is no arguing that this world has become something of a utopia, overseen by one major multinational company. There is nothing in the company's handling, though, that turns this seemingly-perfect world into a dystopia; all perfection is simply born out of the balance between population and societal resources. Post-apocalyptic worlds are usually very bleak, featuring struggles to survive, but in this case the tuberculosis epidemic and plague actually *corrected* the problems countries have been struggling with.

There are some references to civil rights of half-alien hybrid teens and their status as property of UniCorp, but these issues are not fully explored. However, it is just enough to emphasize that not every social ill in the world has been eliminated.

30-Second Booktalk:

What's it like to wake up to a world you don't recognize? Rose has been asleep in her stasis tube for over sixty years when she's finally discovered. She missed the Dark Times and their recovery; shes missed the deaths of her parents, and most of all she misses Xavier, the love of her life and soul mate. She's lived sixteen years in the century since she was born. And there's a robotic assassin after her, determined she keep all her family's secrets to herself.

Readalikes:

Across the Universe (Beth Revis) for time spent in suspended animation

Sleeping Beauty (traditional; Charles Perrault or The Brothers Grimm) for original story

The Boy at the End of the World (Greg van Eekhout) for waking to a radically-changed world

Reincarnation (Suzanne Weyn) for a romance across time

Cinder (Marissa Meyer) for fairy-tale-turned-dystopia

Potential Audience:

This *Sleeping Beauty* retelling will primarily interest girls in 8th grade and higher, though some of the science-fiction elements will appeal to boys as well. Some readers will be frustrated by the unresolved romance between Rose and Xavier, but there are enough other romantic threads in the story to hold readers' interest regardless. Short chapters and quick pacing make this compellingly readable.

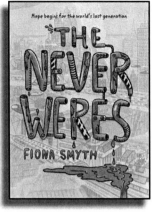

Smyth, Fiona

The Never Weres

Annick Press, 2011. $12.95 Trade pb. 978-1-55451-284-3.

Plot Summary:

Three tenth-graders—Mia, Xian, and Jesse—are among the last generation on Earth. The Barren virus struck fifteen years ago, leaving humanity no way to go on without cloning. Unfortunately, attempts at human cloning have thus far all gone very, very wrong, and subsequent attempts have been outlawed.

Xian's scavenging through old subway tunnels yields a mystery: an odd symbol on walls closest to an abandoned lab. Mia notices the same symbol in old news footage about a missing teenager from sixty years earlier. Jesse's geneticist mom is familiar with the lab and the experiments that were done there. It's not long before they know there's a connection between the lab and the missing girl. Mia works in a senior center, assisting an elderly woman in the early stages of dementia with an art project that turns out to be a map of the tunnels, and the trio interviews her to learn how—and why—she knew all the tunnels and lab locations. Caught in her dementia, the old woman calls Mia "Ames" and begs her not to leave.

Meanwhile, the body of the missing teen has been found, and with it an old USB drive. Xian puts her computer skills to use and pulls the data off the ancient device, and the story is pieced together: the one cloning success was with a terminally ill teenage girl and her rapidly-aged clone. The original girl, Amelia, died while the clone escaped the lab, had a life, and then moved into an old-age home, where she makes artwork out of the subway tunnels with Mia. The discovery of the one clone provides a breakthrough in the research, and humanity is saved through new cloning.

Post-Apocalyptic Elements:

In the wake of the Barren Virus, there have been no new births on earth for fifteen years. Elementary schools stand empty; childcare facilities are now senior centers. The only way to bring children back into the world—the only way to save humanity—is through cloning, but even the best human cloning efforts have resulted in failure.

The logistics of the cloning efforts aside, there are ethical concerns about cloning, both in the book and present-day. Currently, attempts to clone mammals have met with a very low (0.1-3 percent) success rate[7], and among the few successes, 30 percent of the clones born alive experience debilitating medical problems.[8] In the time frame of the book, these sorts of problems have not yet been overcome, with the exception of one experiment in rapidly aging a clone to match the age of the genetic donor.

---

[7] http://learn.genetics.utah.edu/content/tech/cloning/cloningrisks/
[8] http://www.ornl.gov/sci/techresources/Human_Genome/elsi/cloning.shtml

The American Medical Association outlines its reasoning for being against cloning, emphasizing the medical community's lack of understanding on how animal cloning works.[9] Still, in a world where the alternative is to watch humanity slowly slide into old age and extinction, it is no surprise that the scientific and medical communities would begin experimenting with a way to save the human species.

30-Second Booktalk:

The youngest people left on earth are in high school. The barren virus struck over a decade ago, and the only hope for humanity's survival is cloning. A teenage girl, gone missing a half-century ago, could hold the keys—if three intrepid 10th graders can crack through the mysteries surrounding her disappearance.

Readalikes:

Epitaph Road (David Patneaude) for virus affecting birth rates of children

Bumped (Megan McCafferty) or *Wither* (Lauren DeStefano) for virus affecting childbearing

Sweet Tooth (Jeff Lemire) for a new race of children

Potential Audience:

Warm, casual artwork keeps this both accessible and appealing to middle-schoolers. The text borders on overly expository and occasionally redundant, which may turn off older readers.

---

[9] http://www.ama-assn.org/ama/pub/physician-resources/medical-science/genetics-molecular-medicine/related-policy-topics/stem-cell-research/human-cloning.page

Vaughan, Brian K.

Y: The Last Man: Unmanned (volume 1)

Vertigo, 2003. 128p. $12.99. 978-1-56389-980-5.

Plot Summary:

In the first book of this 10-volume series, the reader is introduced to amateur escape artist Yorick Brown, on the phone with his girlfriend. While Yorick talks to Beth, something happens across the globe: every male simultaneously dies of an unknown cause. The mysterious plague has no boundaries, affecting humans and animals equally: any living thing with a Y chromosome is killed.

Every male, that is, except for Yorick and his pet monkey Ampersand. Yorick goes to Washington, D.C., in search of his mother, a prominent member of Congress. He also meets the new president, the former Secretary of Agriculture—the highest-ranking woman in office after all the men died—who assigns a special agent (named 355) to protect Yorick. Yorick and 355 set out to find the scientist who may know something about the virus and why Yorick was the only man to survive.

Yorick and 355 make their way to Boston to meet with Dr. Mann, encountering the radical, man-hating Daughters of the Amazon on the way. The Daughters of the Amazon have nothing on the other group that's hunting Yorick, though: an Israeli military group who aim to capture Yorick and use him as leverage against their enemies. When the military group finds Dr. Mann's lab empty, they burn it, forcing Yorick, 355, and Dr. Mann to head out for California in search of Dr. Mann's backups of data and samples.

Post-Apocalyptic Elements:

The introduction to the second book of the series provides statistics: in the wake of the virus that eliminated all men, approximately 48 percent of the global population disappeared. That 48 percent included well over 90 percent of commercial pilots and truck drivers, mechanics, and construction workers. Eighty-five percent of government officials are dead, worldwide.[10]

As the series progresses, the reader learns more about the source of the virus, how it targeted only men, and how Yorick and his pet monkey survived. In this first book, though, the reader gets an overview of the new shape of the world: it's a confused, chaotic place, with so many people suddenly gone. The former Secretary of Agriculture only reluctantly accepts the presidency of the United States; travel becomes difficult without the benefit of pilots, train conductors, and ship captains.

---

[10] *Y: The Last Man: Cycles*, p3

For Yorick, as the last man on Earth, life is even more dangerous: he has an obligation to survive and procreate if the human race is to continue, but militant groups of women (such as the Daughters of the Amazon) revel in this new female-centric world and would kill Yorick if given the opportunity. Yorick also has value to the Israeli military group, whose leader has been tracking Yorick with the goal of capturing him as leverage against Israel's enemies.

There is no discussion of how the plague will affect the global ecosystem in the absence of male animals: the plague affected all males regardless of species, and the lack of breeding pairs will lead to the extinction of cattle, sheep, dogs, and other work and food animals in one generation. There is no discussion of this aspect, though the series ends with vignettes that prove the advancement of human cloning; one can presume that animal cloning was perfected in this time as well.

30-Second Booktalk:

Yorick is the last man on Earth, and it's anyone's guess as to why. He's nothing out of the ordinary—no special powers, no great skills—and yet he and his pet monkey are the only males who survived the quick-moving virus that killed every other male on earth. Staying alive long enough to find an answer will be difficult when the Daughters of the Amazon would like Yorick dead, and an Israeli military group would like him captured for their own purposes.

Readalikes:

Nomansland (Lesley Hauge) for gender-segregated society

Oryx and Crake (Margaret Atwood) for a virus that eliminates most of society

Y: The Last Man (volumes 2-10) (Brian K. Vaughan) for the rest of Yorick's story

Potential Audience:

Published by DC's Vertigo imprint and suggested for mature readers, this title is accessible to upper-high school students but will find a better home in the adult departments of most public libraries.

Chapter 8:

Disaster and Ruin

It's no secret that humans have had a huge impact on the earth, not all of it good: our lifestyles have led to near-catastrophic climate change, and it's only recently that countries are enacting environmental policies to deal with the damage. In the meantime, sea levels are rising, hurricanes are becoming more severe, and Americans are still generating nearly four and a half pounds of trash per person each day.[1] Will it be a shock to anyone when the earth finally gives up supporting human life?

Julie Bertagna bases her novel *Exodus* (and its sequel, *Zenith*) on the idea of climate change and the resultant rise in sea levels. Small islands disappeared first; the only dry cities now left are ones built high above the former continents. In Kate Messner's *Eye of the Storm*, the rise in global temperatures leads to a world of frequent, giant tornadoes across the country, spawning a new industry of weather manipulation.

Paolo Bacigalupi's *Ship Breaker* is set in a world plagued by "city-killer" hurricanes. The residents live off the waste of a previous world, abandoned oil tankers floating in the gulf and items scavenged off the beaches. Such waste is no match for the industriousness of a small robot tasked to clean up the earth in Pixar's 2008 feature *Wall-E*, still collecting trash 700 years after humans have abandoned the planet for life in space.

Even now we can see these possible, horrible futures in store for us if we do not make efforts to correct the damage we've inflicted on the Earth. More dangerous, though, are the threats we can't prepare for, the disasters that will come upon us with little (if any) warning. The tranquility of Mau's island life is shattered by a tsunami in Terry Pratchett's *Nation*, and Mau finds himself leading a new village of refugees.

Threats from the sky are even more terrifying: In the Moon trilogy (*Life As We Knew It*, *The Dead and the Gone*, and *This World We Live In*), Susan Beth Pfeffer weaves together the stories of two families coping with the irrevocably changed environment after an asteroid knocks the moon closer to Earth. The impact sparks a series of volcanic eruptions and tsunamis, flooding some regions and raining ash over others. The world in James Dashner's *The Maze Runner* (followed by *The Scorch Trials* and *The Death Cure*) has been damaged by solar flares, most notably in a hundred-mile swath around the equator. What isn't destroyed by the catastrophic climate change is extinguished by the viruses unleashed from compromised disease-control centers. The unspecified event of Cormac McCarthy's *The Road* could be any of several things, though the most likely scenario is an asteroid impact.

Outside sources of ruination make handy scapegoats, but *Restoring Harmony* by Joelle Anthony takes a different approach: the world has collapsed under socioeconomic strains, a financial crisis that sparked a larger societal collapse. In the absence of a strong financial system, organized crime has risen up to take over such tasks as food distribution and government.

The fourteen titles in this chapter suggest what the world will be like if we don't get ourselves under control, but also what can happen when we have no control over the Earth. Environmental ruin and natural disasters might be the end of us—or a new beginning.

---

[1] http://www.epa.gov/osw/nonhaz/municipal/

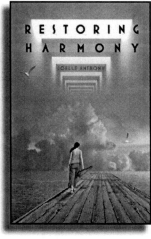

Anthony, Joellé

Restoring Harmony

Putnam, 2010. 320p. $17.99. 978-0-399-25281-5.

Plot Summary:

Molly's family lives on an isolated Canadian island, self-sufficiently farming their land. When a dropped phone call implies that her grandmother has died, Molly is elected to travel down to Oregon to bring her grandfather back. It's not an easy trip: train tracks are out, border crossings have been tightened, and the governmental control over what little fuel is left makes travel slow and expensive. With the help of some kind strangers, Molly eventually navigates to her grandfather's house, where she finds both grandparents alive and unwilling to leave their home, despite their financial challenges and the lack of food.

Using the skills she's developed on her farm, Molly tends a neighbor's garden in exchange for some of its bounty, easing her grandparents' lives and the lives of the neighbor and his children. One of the kind strangers from her trip down still comes around from time to time, and as helpful as he is in so many ways, there's something not-quite-right about his business. It's not the sort of thing Molly ought to get caught up in, nor should she be caught up with him, but she can't help herself for her interest. Each passing day makes it a little harder for Molly to get back home, and still she hasn't convinced her grandparents to leave.

Post-Apocalyptic Elements:

In the world of *Restoring Harmony*, the accepted cause of the economic and social collapse of the United States is the rationing and governmental control over petroleum and the continued reliance on the oil-based economy. From a present perspective, in which gas prices continue to rise, it is easy to imagine the collapse that would come from exhausted fuel stores.

The other, less publicized cause is mentioned only briefly in the book: an outbreak of a cattle virus that killed several thousand people and crippled the fast-food industry. This is a new idea in post-apocalyptic books, or at least one that has not been commonly used, and is frighteningly possible given the recent history of Bovine Spongiform Encephalopathy (BSE, or "Mad Cow" Disease). With one case of BSE identified in the US at the very end of 2003, the Kansas Department of Revenue estimated the total loss of revenue to the US beef industry at $3.2 to $4.7 billion[2]. At just 1 percent of the total $400 billion industry, this would not have a large-scale impact, but a single case in 2003

---

[2] "DJ Livestock Update: Study:US Beef Export Loss $3.2-$4.7 Bln." *FWN Financial News* 28 Apr. 2005. *General OneFile.* Web. 23 Apr. 2011.

is clearly not on the same scale as Anthony's imagined outbreak. The economic impact of just the decreased export market is nothing as compared with the impact on the fast-food industry: in the immediate wake of that single BSE case in 2003, stock prices for McDonald's dropped over 5%; other fast food chains had similar losses[3].

While the novel does not go into great detail about how the cattle disease could bring about economic collapse, it is logical to assume that the decrease in beef production would also decrease the demand for cattle feed (soybean and corn, primarily) and drive those prices down. As the population turns away from eating beef, fast-food chains specializing in hamburgers will close, laying off scores of workers.

Widespread unemployment means that the population owes less money in taxes, and with fewer taxes being collected, the government has less money to support its population and finds itself in a comparatively weak position. The weakening of the government allows organized crime rings to step in and take over, at least in local areas, further impacting economic disparity and law enforcement.

30-Second Booktalk:

Worried about her grandfather living alone far from family, Molly's parents send her to bring him back home to their farm. Molly's inexperience at traveling is made even more nerve-wracking by tightened border security and disrupted railway lines, but a kind stranger helps her complete her journey. He continues to help her family as she settles into Portland, but his help comes from some shady sources Molly shouldn't ask about. Each passing day brings more obstacles to returning home, not the least of which is her grandfather's reluctance to leave.

Readalikes:

Four Seasons (Jane Breskin Zalben) for the love of music

Exodous (Julie Bertagna) for exploration and determination of main character

The City of Ember (Jeanne DuPrau) for the effort to convince loved ones to leave their homes

Ship Breaker (Paolo Bacigalupi) for travel through rough terrain

Potential Audience:

Seventh through tenth graders will appreciate this quiet, character-driven story of what it means to be a family, and a friend, under the harsh conditions of a changed world. Girls in particular will enjoy the romantic subplot, and while some readers will be put off by the lack of action-heavy adventures, there is enough suspense to propel the story.

---

[3] "Report of Cow Disease Hurts Shares in Short Trading Day." *New York Times* 25 Dec. 2003: C5. *General OneFile*. Web. 23 Apr. 2011.

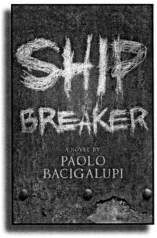

Bacigalupi, Paolo

Ship Breaker

Little Brown and Company, 2010. 326p. $17.99. 978-0-3160-5621-2.
$9.99 pb. 978-0-316-05619-9.
Brilliance Audio. $19.99 CD. 978-1-4418-8348-3.
Google eBooks. $8.99. 978-0-316-08168-9.

Plot Summary:

Along a post-apocalyptic gulf coast, work crews dot the beaches, stripping everything useful off the wrecked ships that have washed up. Heavy crew pulls off metal and other large, bulky parts for recycling; light crew guts the insides of the ships, stripping out miles of copper wire and picking up smaller valuable objects left behind. Nailer works as light crew, and it's on one of his wire-pulling missions that he finds the oil: a nearly-full tank in the belly of the ship, a biggest stroke of luck any of his crew members has ever seen. A fellow crew member's betrayal costs him the oil—and nearly his life. His luck continues to slide when the hurricane hits, a real city-killer of a storm. Days later, as the crews struggle to deal with the wreckage, Nailer's luck finally begins to turn: on the far side of a nearby island, a wrecked clipper ship has washed up. Nailer and his best friend Pim are the only ones who know about it, and in their explorations, they find more silver and food stores than they've ever seen in their lives. This is the luck they've been waiting for, the luck that will pay off all their debts and allow them to buy their way to a better life among the poor.

There's only one complication: while checking all the rooms of the ship, Nailer finds a cabin, and in that cabin is a girl—a fancy-looking girl, pinned under toppled furniture. Over Pim's protestations, Nailer frees her, believing it to be morally right, though not logically, or financially, the best decision he could make. The swank Lucky Girl claims her clipper ship was being pursued by rogues planning to kill her, and if they can escort her back to her wealthy father, they will be well-rewarded. Claiming the wreck as salvage will also provide many rewards, so it's hard to see the worth of a dangerous trek.

Once Nailer's abusive father gets wind of the find, he and his thuggish crew claim the wreck as their own, leaving Nailer and Lucky Girl with little choice: staying is at least as dangerous as going, so they set out toward the city to return Lucky Girl to her father and claim their reward—assuming she was telling the truth. The journey isn't easy (at least as far as the threats on her life are concerned, she told the truth), and being lucky isn't going to be enough to save either of them.

Post-Apocalyptic Elements:

Bacigalupi describes Nailer's world—a world in which Nailer survives on the tattered, neglected remains of our current societal habits—by asking, "What does a world look like, where we used our resources in the most frivolous and stupid ways possible, and what's left to pick over at the end?"[4] In

---

[4] http://teen-readme.com/video/paolo-introduces-ship-breaker; Little Brown Teens

a post-oil United States, on a shoreline plagued by city-killer hurricanes, Nailer and his community scavenge for any useful items they can find. There's not much left: just the rotting corpses of old oil tankers and freighters that have run aground and been left to decay and the occasional item that washes up from the high-tech clipper ships sailing by out beyond their reach—glimpses of an easier, more comfortable world that will never be theirs.

Those who lived along the post-Katrina gulf coast report that the world of *Ship Breaker* brings back memories of that time: scavenging from anything that could be picked up along the shore, attempting to collect enough to sell and survive for another day.[5] This is unsurprising, given Bacigalupi's assurances that his story ideas come not from reading dystopian fiction, but extrapolating from environmental journalism and projecting out twenty, fifty, one hundred years into the future. "[I] turn up the volume on a trendline that already exists and is already playing out," he said in a 2010 interview. "I think of my stories as thought experiments, and to the extent that other people call the results dystopian or post-apocalyptic, I think that reflects how ugly some of our current trends are."[6] Indeed: it isn't difficult to see how Nailer's community would form, especially in the wake of such recent environmental catastrophes as Hurricane Katrina in 2005 or the Deepwater Horizon oil spill of 2010.

Nailer's community survives—even thrives—on the wastefulness of our oil-rich days; on the other hand, they're never more than a single missed salvage quota away from being turned out of the community altogether. That there is such disparity in the world, from Nailer's impoverished town to Lucky Girl's wealthy city, emphasizes issues of environmental impact, sustainability, and class, all of which inform Nailer's decisions and motives throughout the novel.

30-Second Booktalk:

Nailer works stripping copper wire from wrecked ships along the gulf coast, a dangerous job that could kill him any minute. His luck turns after a hurricane, when he finds a wrecked clipper ship full of food, silver—and a girl. Nailer's abusive father and his band of thugs soon discover the wreck, and Nailer has a choice: hand over the girl, the luckiest of Lucky Strikes any of his crew has ever seen, or take her back to her people, where—she *says*—Nailer will be well-rewarded.

Readalikes:

The Knife of Never Letting Go (Patrick Ness) for fleeing one's home to save a newly-found girl

Restoring Harmony (Joellé Anthony) for the economic and social impacts of oil depletion

Drowned Cities (Paolo Bacigalupi, forthcoming) for another story in the same world

A Small Free Kiss in the Dark (Glenda Millard) for traveling and hiding from hunters and killers

Potential Audience:

Ship Breaker won the 2011 Michael Printz Award for Young Adult Fiction and was a 2010 National Book Award Finalist, propelling it to top of many adults' reading lists. High school teens, caring significantly less about awards, will be drawn in by the adventure, the characters, and the richly-developed world Bacigalupi has created.

---

[5] http://bookwormblues.blogspot.com/2010/09/ship-breaker-paolo-bacigalupi.html
[6] http://presentinglenore.blogspot.com/2010/08/author-interview-and-giveaway-paolo.html

Bertagna, Julie

Exodus

Walker and Company, 2008. 352p. $16.95. 978-0-8027-9745-2.
$9.99 pb. 978-0-8027-9826-8.
Adobe Digital Editions ebook. $9.99. 978-0-8027-2381-9.

Zenith

Walker and Company, 2009. 352p. $16.99. 978-0-8027-9803-9.
Adobe Digital Editions (ebook). $16.99. 978-0-8027-2382-6.

- Originally published 2002-2007

Plot Summary:

Mara is fifteen, and has grown up in her island community on Wing. Wing is one of the remaining high spots on Earth, with so much of the planet submerged after the polar ice caps melted, a casualty of rising levels of greenhouse gasses and climate change in the twenty-first century. The water rises just a little more each day, and Mara knows that it won't be long before Wing joins those other drowned villages, islands, and continents.

Mara has been researching alternatives, digging through the Weave on her outdated Cyberwizz computer. In the Weave she meets Fox, the mysterious creature who first tells her about New Mungo, the city built in the sky, but they are disconnected before she can learn more. Mara takes the information to the villagers and convinces most of them to leave Wing in fishing boats, but the older generation refuses to leave their island homes.

Mara guides her people to New Mungo, but on arrival, those who survived the journey are shuffled into a refugee camp at the base of towers supporting the walled city. Mara steals a uniform and sneaks into New Mungo, where she is dazzled by the beauty of it but put off by its superficiality. She searches the computer networks and again encounters Fox, finally learning his true identification as the grandson of New Mungo's creator and enforcer of draconian entrance requirements. She and Fox arrange an escape from the city, in which he will lead the rebellion inside the city walls and Mara will break through them to save the refugees. Many board the supply ships bound for Greenland with Mara at the helm.

Book two, *Zenith*, begins where *Exodus* leaves off: Mara is leading a new group of people to Greenland, the last remaining land mass above sea level, in search of a rumored settlement. Bad luck still plagues them: their ship runs aground in shallow water, leading to their capture and enslavement by a hostile group living near the coast. Mara and a few others break out and hike through the harsh elements to an interior valley beside a glacial lake. Meanwhile, back in the sky city, Fox is leading the revolution against his grandfather, but without Mara's support, he begins to second-guess many of his decisions—including the one about starting the revolution.

Post-Apocalyptic Elements:

From its opening pages, it is obvious that the focus of this series is on environmental issues: the year is 2100, representing a rapid change in the Earth's climate from what we currently experience in the early days of the twenty-first century. While it seems far-fetched to imagine whole islands disappearing under rising ocean levels any time soon, the frightening reality—on which the idea for the book is based[7]—is that this very thing has already happened to the South Pacific islands of Tebua Tarawa and Abanuea[8] in 1999. Sea levels have risen considerably over the last century, and the rate at which they rise seems to be increasing.[9]

Exodus and its sequel *Zenith* take these concerns to a logical end: what kind of world will it be, when the ice caps and glaciers melt and the sea encroaches on land previously thought safe? When the world has only a few habitable places left, the competition for those places will be fierce, and those who can create habitable environments (like the sky city) will be poised to become god-like in their oversight of those cities.

30-Second Booktalk:

The bleak reality of Mara's island community is that the sea is rising, and the people on Wing are running out of high ground. Mara has been digging through the Weave on her outdated computer, though, and has found evidence of a new world built high above the ocean. If her people are to survive, they need to move there. But even if she can convince them to go, there's still the wall to get past.

Readalikes:

Nation (Terry Pratchett) for a teen leading a new community

The White Darkness (Geraldine McCaughrean) for scenes of arctic expedition

First Light (Rebecca Stead) for the seeking of a society under Greenland's surface

The Carbon Diaries (Saci Lloyd) for rapid climate change

Potential Audience:

Middle and high school environmentalists will get a lot out of this series. Readers looking for another post-apocalyptic romance will appreciate the relationship that grows between Mara and Fox, though this is hardly the focus of the plot. The third book, *Aurora*, is still forthcoming, already released overseas.

---

[7] http://www.juliebertagna.com/exodus.html
[8] http://news.bbc.co.uk/2/hi/science/nature/368892.stm
[9] http://www.climate.org/topics/sea-level/index.html

Dashner, James

The Maze Runner

Delacorte, 2009. 384p. $16.99. 978-0-385-73794-4.
$9.99 pb. 978-0-385-73795-1.
Random House Digital. $9.99 ebook. 978-0-385-73794-4.
Listening Library. $44 CD. 978-0-307-58288-1.

The Scorch Trials

Delacorte, 2010. 368p. $17.99. 978-0-385-73875-0.
$9.99 pb. 978-0-385-73876-7.
Random House Digital. $9.99 ebook. 978-0-385-73875-0.
Listening Library. $44 CD. 978-0-307-70659-1.

The Death Cure

Delacorte, 2011. 384p. $17.99. 978-0-385-73877-4.
Random House Digital. $10.99. 978-0-375-89612-5.
Listening Library. $44 CD. 978-0-307-70663-8.

Plot Summary:

Thomas wakes up in a box, remembering nothing but his name. Soon enough, hands are pulling him out, into the Glade, and he knows he's in a very strange place. The other boys have been here for quite some time, and none of them remember a life before, either. Their only hope is to find an exit from the maze, but that's not easy when the walls move every night, and the giant semi-organic, semi-mechanical beasts come rolling out with a thirst for blood.

When a girl shows up—the first girl ever sent through the box—the day after Thomas's arrival, the entire Glader community is thrown into chaos. Teresa turns out to be the key, the catalyst that marks the beginning of the end. Maze walls suddenly stop moving; the Grievers don't wait for nightfall to attack the boys. And somehow, Teresa can talk to Thomas telepathically. There's something nagging at the edge of Thomas's memories, something about Teresa: did they know each other before? Were they somehow involved with the creation of the maze? With nearly the whole Glader community's help, Teresa and the boys crack the code and escape the maze, but that's not the end of their story.

In the second book, the Gladers learn that WICKED, the organization that put them in the maze, was using them to test their reactions to different situations, a years-long psychological and physical experiment. Now that they're free of the maze, WICKED is sending them through another set of trials: a 100-mile walk across the Scorch, the barren strip of land where the sun flares have wiped out nearly all life. The teens are informed that they have the Flare in them, a disease that will slowly attack their brains and make them crazy, and the cure is at the end of the walk. Getting to the Safe Zone means crossing a quarantined city full of Cranks—infected people in varying stages of decline—and surviving the deadly lightning storms on either side of it.

Teresa is no longer traveling with them, and Thomas feels her loss: she's been moved into a group of girls, a Group B who recently escaped from their own version of the maze. Group B has its own leaders and shared history—and they have orders to capture and kill Thomas. Thomas and Teresa still have their telepathic link, and Teresa sends him reassurances begging him to trust her. Between his resurfacing memories and Teresa's increasingly untrustworthy behavior, WICKED is looking more and more conspiratorial.

The final book of the trilogy finally gives the answers we've been waiting for: WICKED chose these teens specifically based on their immunity to the Flare virus, and has been analyzing the teens' reactions to the engineered situations in the hopes that their mapped brain patterns will provide a clue to how their immunity works. Thomas and two friends are shocked to find Brenda and Jorge, the Cranks who'd helped them in the Scorch, working for WICKED—but still offering them help in escaping from the compound. Brenda knows someone in Denver, one of the last remaining safe cities not overrun with the Flare, who can remove WICKED's tracking device from Thomas's brain.

While in Denver, Thomas is contacted by a former Glader who is now working with Right Arm, a resistance movement against WICKED. Thomas knows that WICKED is not to be trusted, but the Right Arm is equally cagey. WICKED is confident that the key to the Flare immunity lies in Thomas's brain, and they'll stop at nothing to get him back—but their confidence does not stop them from finding more Immunes and running another round of the Trials. It's up to Thomas, his friends, and a resistance organization he's not sure he can trust to free the recently-kidnapped Immunes and put an end to WICKED's questionable research.

The trilogy concludes with a report from a trusted Chancellor, discussing the success of the project: while WICKED did not find a cure, the new colony of over one hundred immune men and women will rebuild a society after humanity's near-extinction from the Flare. She defends WICKED's actions, reminding the readers of her report that WICKED's noble goal was the preservation of the human race, by whatever means necessary.

Post-Apocalyptic Elements:

The Maze Runner is, at best, tangentially dystopian in that the boys have had to establish their own society without the aid of adults: they farm, they clean, they maintain order amongst themselves. Calling it a dystopia is a misnomer, though; this is not a society that ever aimed for perfection, but rather one that grew out of necessity. As Thomas's memories begin to surface, there are hints that something terrible has befallen the outside world. The ending sets up the second book, which will involve a journey through a post-apocalyptic landscape.

The Scorch Trials showcases what the world has become: sun flares had already destroyed half the planet before scientists were able to warn anyone. What wasn't decimated by the radical climate change was obliterated by an infection (dubbed the Flare) unleashed from a disease-control center. An attempt was made to quarantine the infected population in a section of the Scorch, but the quarantines are only slowing the spread of the Flare instead of stopping it all together.

Temperatures are finally starting to go back down as the climate self-corrects, and the worldwide political structure is also beginning to self-correct. Countries have united, pooled their technological and other resources to fight the Flare and start WICKED, the World in Catastrophe—Killzone Experiment Department.

The quarantined city is where post-apocalyptic life in the baked-dry belt of land struggles to continue. Residents have banded together to claim abandoned buildings and defend them against other groups. Food comes from the stock left in a handful of former manufacturing plants and warehouses. Cranks—those infected with the Flare—defend their possessions and shelters from any intruders, violently defending their physical and hierarchical spaces.

Finally, *The Death Cure* reveals how the world has come to this. The solar flares were unavoidable, but they compromised the security of many government buildings and agencies, in particular disease-control facilities. The Flare, originally a man-made virus engineered for biological warfare, was released into the general population, and its highly-contagious, airborne nature allowed it to become a pandemic.

The events of *The Maze Runner* and *The Scorch Trials* only touch on the post-apocalyptic nature of Thomas's world, but they are the necessary lead-up to the revelations of *The Death Cure*. Recent global epidemics of SARS, Avian flu, and the H1N1 flu will give context to the panic about this fatal virus, and the efforts that cities will go to in order to prevent the spread of a contagion.

30-Second Booktalk:

The Maze Runner: Thomas remembers nothing but his name when he's pulled into the Glade, a strange place where the only escape means finding an exit from the Maze—not easy when the walls move every night and the mechanical beasts have a thirst for blood. When a girl shows up the day after Thomas's arrival, the Gladers are thrown into chaos: Who is she? And what's with her warning that "everything is going to change"?

The Scorch Trials: Thomas and his friends have all been infected with The Flare, and they have just two weeks to walk one hundred miles across the burned-out Scorch to the cure. Getting there means avoiding the deadly lightning storms. Getting there means crossing through the city, where the infected, insane Cranks are savagely attacking. Getting there means trusting the resurfaced memories that look like conspiracy at every turn.

The Death Cure: Thomas has been through many trials, and he's about to get some answers as to why—but the answers are not the comforting ones Thomas wanted. Instead, he learns that he's immune to the neurological virus, and his brain holds the last bit of information scientists need to solve the puzzle. So it's too bad Thomas's brain is still in Thomas's head, and he plans to keep it that way.

Readalikes:

Sunshine (film) for solar flares resulting in the Earth's destruction

House of Stairs (William Sleator) for experiments with teens trapped in maze-like facilities

Incarceron (Catherine Fisher) for maze-like prisons and search for escape

Percy Jackson series (Rick Riordan) for similar-feeling action/adventure

Enemy (Charlie Higson) for journeys through disease-ridden cities with the diseased attacking

Epitaph Road (David Patneaude) for spread of manufactured disease

The Only Ones (Aaron Starmer) for life in a world without adults

Potential Audience:

Fast-paced action should draw in middle- and high-school boys, though adventure-seeking girls will like this, too. The balance of action and issue will propel readers through the trilogy, whether they're looking for a blockbuster of a book or a novel concerned with environmental destruction and global pandemics.

Book trailers available here: http://www.randomhouse.com/teens/mazerunner/videos.php

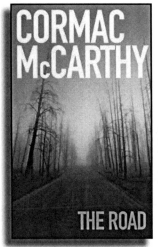

McCarthy, Cormac

The Road

Knopf, 2006. 256p. $24.95. 978-0-307-26543-2.
Vintage, 2007. $15 pb. 978-0-307-38789-9.
Recorded Books, 2006. $29.99 CD. 978-1-4281-1278-0.

- *The Road*, Cormac McCarthy
- Originally published 2006

Plot Summary:

In search of an easier, safer life for his son, an unnamed man sets out with the boy toward the coast. The desolate highway along which they walk is one of the only remaining signs that life once existed.

In flashbacks, readers learn that the boy's mother committed suicide sometime between the unspecified disaster and the story's beginning, leaving the man and the boy to survive on their own. The boy frequently seeks reassurances from his father that they are the "good guys," separate from the "bad guys" who have resorted to violence, theft, or cannibalism to survive. The man struggles to protect the boy from all the realities of the bleak world—the lack of resources, starvation, illness—though he knows that he is dying. His goal is to get his son to a safer, better place, one with warmer weather and more plentiful food.

After months of travel, they do reach the coast, but the new location does little to improve their lot. The man finally succumbs to his illness, leaving the boy sitting with his father's body for three days before he is approached by another man who claims to have been following the boy and his father. The new man, traveling with a woman and their two children, assure the boy that they are also good guys and invite him to join their family.

Post-Apocalyptic Elements:

The cataclysmic event that has rendered humanity all but extinct is never specified, though clues are given through the book. The two most likely scenarios are nuclear war and asteroid impact; both theories have evidence to support and contradict them. The event is never specified, but through flashbacks, readers see enough through the man's eyes to come to one of these two conclusions.

In support of both theories, the man's memory of the night of the event involved a bright light far away, and a recollection of watching cities burn. When the man and boy finally reach the coast, they find the charred remains of vehicles, with equally burned human bodies still within. All of these things could be caused by a nuclear bomb detonation or by a large asteroid slamming into the earth.

Lending credit to the nuclear bomb theory is the fact that the man references that all clocks have stopped at the same time, which could be the result of an electromagnetic pulse generated by the explosion of a nuclear bomb. However, discounting this theory is the lack of concern about radiation fallout, as well as the lack of evidence of mutations or cancers.

In favor of the asteroid impact theory, though, is the ash that continues falling even after years have passed, and the changes to the environment as sunlight has been effectively obliterated. In the man's flashback, he is surprised by the event, suggesting that whatever happened was not predicted by international politics.

The sequence of events following the flash of light the man sees are consistent with asteroid impact, but could also point to the eruption of a super volcano—though these eruptions could easily be triggered by an asteroid hitting the earth. Without more information, it is impossible to say which would have happened first, or if it was any of these scenarios at all.

30-Second Booktalk:

Years after the event that nearly destroyed the world, survival just means putting one foot in front of the other, over and over. You may find some food along the way, or a blanket, if you're lucky. And if you're really lucky, you'll have someone you love with you. This father and son are that kind of lucky. They're surviving. And that's the best they can hope to do.

Readalikes:

The Eleventh Plague (Jeff Hirsch) for father/son road trip across a post-apocalyptic world

Sweet Tooth (Jeff Lemire) for a father's efforts to shield his young son from a changed world

The Road (film) for the movie adaptation of the book

Is the End of the World Near? (Ron Miller) and *Apocalypse: How?* (film) for suggestions on what might have befallen the world of *The Road*

Potential Audience:

While the book is aimed at an adult audience, upper-high school teens will easily follow the plot and language. The emotional resonance of the father's relationship with his son will likely go over their heads, but they will still be interested in the story's outcome.

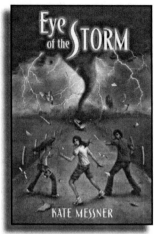

Messner, Kate

Eye of the Storm

Bloomsbury, 2012. 304p. $16.99. 978-0-8027-2313-0.

Plot Summary:

It's been a while since Jaden saw her scientist dad: he spent a few years in Russia researching storm technology, and now that he's back stateside, he lives in his Stormsafe community in Oklahoma—far away from Jaden and her mom in Vermont. This summer, though, will be their chance to reconnect: Jaden will be living with her dad and his new family, while she attends the exclusive Eye on Tomorrow summer science camp run by her dad's company. She and her dad share a passion for meteorological science, particularly the science of storm dissipation—ways to make the frequent tornadoes and huge storms either rise back into the atmosphere or steer away from populated paths.

This interest brings her together with Alex, a local boy also attending the camp, and together Jaden and Alex begin researching some of their own ideas about storm dissipation. It quickly becomes clear that they need more data—specifically, they need Jaden's dad's research. Her dad gives her some abstracts of papers he'd written on earlier, failed experiments, but in snooping through his computer files, Jaden learns that the abstracts he gave her were false. As she and Alex dig more deeply, they find a growing mountain of evidence that those earlier experiments not only weren't failures, but also that they have allowed Jaden's dad to gain such control over the weather that he can send intensified storms to specific locations.

With another storm bearing down on the targeted area, the friends work furiously to turn it away. When they inadvertently turn it toward Jaden's aunt's home outside town, they are out of options: they have no choice but to run their untested dissipation codes and hope that their theories on storm dissipation will work. Their research has served them well: the storm obeys the new commands and is taken back up into the sky, sparing the lives of everyone in its potential path.

Post-Apocalyptic Elements:

Thanks to rising temperatures worldwide and the destabilization of the atmosphere, huge tornadoes have become a part of everyday life. The storms are strong enough that a new scale has been developed to measure them—the New Fujita Scale, after it was clear that the storms had outgrown the Enhanced Fujita Scale currently in use today.

The strength and frequency of these new storms have destroyed many small family farms, which would cripple the food supply if not for DNA-ture, the biobotanicals company Jaden's dad owns and operates. Foods are bioengineered to eliminate seeds, asymmetry, bitterness, and other undesirable qualities, with a goal to revolutionize the food supply and end hunger by allowing more food to be factory-grown and shipped. With this source of factory-grown, durable produce, it doesn't matter that farmland is being destroyed by the frequent tornadoes.

The DNA-ture products also make it easier for Jaden's father to put himself in charge of his own storm-proof dystopia. In building Placid Meadows to be completely impervious to storms, he has made himself something of a god, able to keep bad weather away from his people. In addition, he keeps very tight surveillance over the student researchers, with bugs placed in the library and spot-checks of their DataSlates to find any evidence that students are coming too close to finding the truth about the town.

30-Second Booktalk:

Jaden's dad has been researching storm dissipation, and that's where Jaden's interests lie, too—and so do Alex's, the boy Jaden partners with at the Eye on Tomorrow summer science camp. Unfortunately, their research turns up some troubling data about the work Jaden's dad has been doing, and Jaden will have to decide if her loyalties lie with her father, or with the science that could save thousands of lives.

Readalikes:

The Evolution of Calpurnia Tate (Jacqueline Kelly) for science-minded female main character

Twister (film) for storm-chasing and tornado science

Food Fight: A Graphic Guides Adventure (Liam O'Donnell) for genetic engineering of food

The Other Side of the Island (Allegra Goodman) for weather manipulation

Potential Audience:

This middle-grade novel will appeal most to girls interested in science, who don't see themselves represented often in books. The storm-chasing action will also pull in boys and reluctant readers. The cover art may suggest a younger book to middle-school readers, but the idea of weaponized weather makes this an easy sell.

Pfeffer, Susan Beth

Life As We Knew It

Harcourt, 2006. 352p. $17. 978-0-15-205826-5.
Graphia, 2008. $7.95 pb. 978-0-15-206154-8.
Listening Library, 2006. $45 CD. 978-0-7393-3683-0.
Houghton Mifflin. $3.99 ebook. 978-0-547-41599-4.

The Dead and the Gone

Harcourt, 2008. 336p. $17. 978-0-15-206311-5.
Graphia, 2010. $7.99 pb. 978-0-547-25855-3.
Listening Library, 2010. $45 CD. 978-0-7393-6366-9.
Houghton Mifflin. $7.99 ebook. 978-0-547-42226-8.

This World We Live In

Harcourt, 2010. 256p. $17. 978-0-547-24804-2.
Graphia, 2011. $8.99 pb. 978-0-547-55028-2.
Listening Library, 2010. $39 CD. 978-0-307-58225-6.
Houghton Mifflin. $17 ebook. 978-0-547-48794-6.

- *Life As We Knew It, The Dead and the Gone,* and *This World We Live In,* Susan Beth Pfeffer
- Originally published 2006-2010

Plot Summary:

When an asteroid collides with the moon, knocking it closer to the Earth, the environmental impact is almost immediate: tsunamis and the related flooding, mosquitoes, volcanoes, blizzards and ashy skies. For the survivors, there are flu epidemics, isolation, and dwindling food supplies. Supermarkets are emptied within hours of the impact. Miranda's family is one of the lucky ones: her mom's foresight in loading up supplies means they have not only canned and boxed food but medicines. Other families move south, west, north, anywhere rumored to be better off than Pennsylvania, but Miranda's family stays put and attempts to make the best of the situation. Miranda and her mother cut back on their own food consumption to leave more for Miranda's two brothers, but the family is still perilously close to starvation when rescue appears: Miranda, having walked to town to spare her family the pain of seeing her die at home, finds Town Hall open and distributing food rations, concluding the book on a hopeful note for continued survival.

The Dead and the Gone shows the moon disaster affecting New York City every bit as much as it does Pennsylvania. Alex Morales is seventeen years old and struggling to keep himself and his two little sisters alive in the wake of the flooding and disease that have overtaken the city. Their parents are presumed dead, victims of flooding in Puerto Rico (their father) and New York City's subway tunnels (their mother). Alex, wrestling with his morals, resorts to looting bodies in the street for valuable objects he can barter for food to feed himself and his sisters. He blames himself for every resentment or bitterness his sisters exhibit, taking on full responsibility for their continued survival and happiness. Needing the proper paperwork and plenty of supplies to escape the city, Alex cashes in many favors to salvage what he still can of his family.

A year later, *This World We Live In* opens. Miranda's family has settled into the new routines, fishing and scavenging for food and looting abandoned houses for goods like soap and toilet paper. As best they can, they're holding onto a normal life, but their fragile sense of normalcy is shattered when Miranda's older brother Matt comes home from a fishing trip with a woman, Syl, whom he introduces as his wife. Not long after, more guests arrive: Miranda's dad, her stepmother, their baby, and three strangers traveling with them.

Two of the strangers are Alex Morales and his sister Julie. Alex plans to take Julie to a convent where she'll be safe, while he enters a monastery. It's a noble plan, but one doomed to failure due to Julie's reluctance to enter the convent and Alex's and Miranda's growing feelings for each other—and then by the tornado that whips through what remains of the town, destroying nearly everything they have left and forcing some very difficult decisions.

Post-Apocalyptic Elements:

The environmental effects are still obvious even a year after the initial event. Miranda's brothers need to travel to catch fish or hunt for other game, and still nothing is growing. The climate is still unstable with large storms, extreme temperatures, and even tornadoes cutting across Pennsylvania. Having exhausted the resources of the closest homes, Miranda expands her radius when looting abandoned houses for food and supplies. Government handouts grow scarce, and people need to rely on themselves more instead of seeking help from outside agencies. Where people had been living far apart before the disaster, families—like Miranda's—are now coming together and forming their own micro-communities to survive. Miranda and Alex—and nearly every member of their new family—clearly remember what life was like before the disaster, but by now they've settled into the new routines of the world without the conveniences they'd believed indispensable.

After the moon disaster, families find ways to fit into the larger community: taking care of themselves and neighbors, attempting to maintain friendships, and seeking assistance from local governments offering food to the few residents remaining. While Miranda's narrative shows her feeling very isolated—and in nearly every sense, she is—there is still a community of which her family is a part; Alex's community has shrunk to his siblings and their priest while they struggle to maintain their faith. Alex and his sisters are not just muddling through the disaster; they are surviving and searching for opportunities to create a new life, while holding onto their moral and religious beliefs as best they can. In addition to learning to live in their irreparably-changed environment, the families are learning to live together, to recognize that "family" is no longer only oneself and two or three others, but a larger group with new dynamics. At its heart, this is the story of a family rebuilding a life after a disaster, rather than the story of a disaster shaping a family.

30-Second Booktalk:

Life As We Knew It: An asteroid is bearing down on the moon—and the school is piling on extra assignments as a result. But then the moon gets knocked closer to the Earth. Tsunamis. Flooding. Mosquitoes. Blizzards. Flu epidemics. The months of isolation, with nothing to do and food supplies dwindling. There's literally nothing but canned and boxed goods, and when they run out, that's it. Miranda's family is lucky to have survived, but their long-term prospects depend on every change in the weather.

The Dead and the Gone: An asteroid has smashed into the moon, knocking it closer to earth and causing catastrophic tsunamis, flooding, and more. In New York City, Alex and his two little sisters are waiting for their parents to get home. And waiting. And waiting. Alex has to swallow his ethics and hope God will forgive him as he loots empty apartments and even dead bodies to acquire food and supplies for his family. If he's going to get his siblings out, it's going to take some miracles.

This World We Live In: A year has passed since the moon was knocked closer to the earth by an asteroid, and Miranda's life is settling into a routine: scavenging for food and supplies and trying to make life as normal as they can. Then Miranda's father shows up with his wife, their baby, and three strangers. One stranger, Alex, has been traveling with his sister from New York City, looking for a place to keep her safe. Safety will rely on some very difficult decisions—ones that will shatter the fragile normalcy they've created.

Readalikes:

Nation (Terry Pratchett) for rebuilding after natural disaster

The Diary of a Young Girl (Anne Frank), for isolation and cramped quarters with family members

Homecoming (Cynthia Voigt) for a teen caring for younger siblings in the absence of a parent

Hurricane Song (Paul Volponi) for survival in the wake of natural disasters and uprooted family

Potential Audience:

Life As We Knew It and *The Dead and The Gone* function well as stand-alone books, with the first appealing more to girls and the second to boys. Fans of either of the first two books will likely return for *This World We Live In* to see how the stories interweave and continue. The family drama will likely hook readers accustomed to more realistic fare. Upper-middle and high school students of both genders will appreciate the tension and drama of the Moon trilogy.

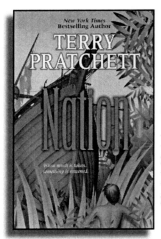

Pratchett, Terry

Nation

Harper Collins, 2008. 384p. $16.99. 978-0-06-143301-6.
$8.99 pb. 978-0-06-143303-0.
Harper Children's Audio, 2008. $29.95. 978-0-06-165821-1.
$8.99 ebook. 978-0-06-197523-3.

Plot Summary:

Mau has just completed his initiation into adulthood, leaving his child-soul behind on a small island off the coast of his home island, when a volcano erupts somewhere far to the south. The resulting tsunami hits just as Mau is paddling back, destroying his island and leaving Mau as the remaining member of his people. With no one to give him his man's soul, and having already given up his boy's soul, Mau has nothing left: he is permanently in-between, neither child nor adult, left in charge of his island's culture by the cruelty of nature.

Mau is not left alone for long: the remains of the *Sweet Judy* soon wash up, and within them is Ermintrude Fanshaw, unwitting heir to the British throne due to the Russian Influenza that has killed all other possible heirs while she has been sailing to join her father. She has now survived a mutiny of her shipmates, a tsunami, and a shipwreck when she meets Mau, but her previous strengths do not prevent her from being scared of the boy who methodically wraps the bodies of his people and sends them to sea. An attempt to shoot him is misinterpreted as goodwill (Ermintrude providing Mau with a spark-maker, instead of firing a gun stuffed with wet gunpowder), and the two establish rudimentary communication. Ermintrude takes the opportunity afforded by the shipwreck to rename herself Daphne, and together they are the start of a new Nation.

Other survivors soon come to their shores, seeking refuge in a Nation that only exists because the survivors cling to it. Mau, still without a man's soul, grows into his new role as a leader for his new people, protecting them from raiders and replacing the God-anchors (the stones that keep the gods from drifting away from the island) displaced by the tsunami. Rebuilding his island is the first step toward rebuilding his culture, but Daphne soon discovers how much more there is of Mau's island culture than anyone ever knew.

Post-Apocalyptic Elements:

Most post-apocalytpic stories begin sometime in our future, but the tsunami that destroys Mau's island happens in an alternate 1860, in a world that is reminiscent of ours while being slightly different. Pratchett references his use of the many-worlds theory as his "literary get-out-of-jail-free card."[10]

---

[10] p369 (hc)

The tsunami has wiped out the majority of people living in the Southern Pelagic Ocean, destroying the entire existent culture. It leaves Mau adrift, physically in his canoe and emotionally between childhood and adulthood, between being cared for and creating and leading a new Nation. Mau does not consider himself to be a leader, or particularly heroic, when he does the sorts of things he recognizes need to be done, such as milking a wild boar to get milk for a refugee's infant. To Mau, the island won't survive without these refugees; to the refugees, Mau is making an incredible sacrifice to keep them safe. Being a leader is not part of his identity; being a contributing member of society *is*, and contributing is all he is trying to accomplish. It is this fundamental desire to be a part of something bigger than oneself that keeps Mau going, that keeps Daphne and all of the refugees going.

Mau's character arc would not be complete without the tsunami that destroyed everything, of course. In addition to his new role as a leader, he also takes on the responsibility of repairing his destroyed culture, to replace the god-anchors and appease the island's Grandfathers. Rebuilding an entire society in the wake of a cataclysmic event such as this means coming to terms with what the island was and being willing to adapt it to the needs of the new Nation of refugees.

30-Second Booktalk:

Mau has just given up his boy's soul and is paddling back to the Nation, where he will be given his man's soul. That's when the wave hits—that all-consuming wave that devours everything in its path, wiping out the entire Nation and killing everyone Mau knew and loved. Mau is alone on the island, but only temporarily—other refugees slowly row up to the Nation's shores. Mau feels responsible for all these new people, and must defend the Nation from the raiders, protect the new refugees, and discover who they can be without the baggage of who they were.

Readalikes:

Lord of the Flies (William Golding) for island survival, and for the subtle references *Nation* makes to events of Golding's novel

Beauty Queens (Libba Bray) for island survival and creating family out of unlikely survivors

Chaos Walking (series) (Patrick Ness) for identity and rebuilding a society out of refugees

Ship Breaker (Paolo Bacigalupi) for shipwrecked refugees following storms

Life As We Knew It (Susan Beth Pfeffer) for rebuilding a society after the majority has been destroyed

Night of the Howling Dogs (Graham Salisbury) for survival in the aftermath of a tsunami

Potential Audience:

Established Pratchett fans, drawn to the sly humor of *Discworld* or his *Tiffany Aching* series, may initially be disappointed in this more serious stand-alone book, but ultimately will be won over by the strength of character and subtle wittiness. The themes of identity and belonging will resonate with high-school students, particularly those struggling with the in-between issues of abandoning childhood while not yet being adults.

WALL-E

Blu-Ray. Color. 98m. Produced and dist. by Walt Disney Studios Home Entertainment, 2011. $39.99. 978-6-3142-1973-4.
$29.99 DVD. 978-0-7888-7693-6.

- Written by Andrew Stanton, Pete Doctor, and Jim Reardon
- Directed by Andrew Stanton
- Originally released 2008

Plot Summary:

When Earth became too toxic to sustain life and its ecosystem too difficult to restore, the Buy-n-Large (BnL) corporation evacuated humans onto fully-outfitted starliners. Left on Earth is a large group of Waste Allocation Load Lifter (Earth Class), or WALL-E, trash compactor robots, intended to work for five years until humans can come back. At the end of that first five-year period, the air is still too toxic for humans to return, so they stay on their starliner communities in space while the robots work down on Earth.

Nearly seven hundred years after everyone has fled, one WALL-E still toils, compacting trash but also saving artifacts from the human time before. In his rounds one day, he finds a small seedling sprouting in a mound of trash. He brings it home and nurtures the tiny plant, the first growth he has seen. Not long after, another spaceship passes over, depositing an Extraterrestrial Vegetation Evaluator (EVE) robot on Earth's surface to search for any sign of life. She does not respond well to WALL-E's initial overtures of friendship, but eventually warms to him. When he shows her the artifacts he has collected, she sees his seedling and automatically stores it, signaling her ship to come retrieve her.

When EVE is taken back to her ship, WALL-E hitches along, unwilling to be left alone on the planet again. What he finds on the ship is a large community of humans whose centuries luxuriating in low gravity have allowed them to become lazy and obese with poor bone density. EVE brings the plant to the ship's captain, who is overjoyed to see that Earth may finally be habitable again. The ship's robotic assistant has other ideas, though, and steals the plant to hide it away. A series of events leads to WALL-E and EVE leading a horde of malfunctioning robots on a siege to prevent the plant's destruction. The captain manages to disable the AUTO function and regain control of his ship. WALL-E and the plant are returned to Earth, and humans follow shortly thereafter, becoming slimmer and healthier with the physical efforts of recolonizing Earth.

Post-Apocalyptic Elements:

WALL-E is not coy about its messages, either about our consumption habits or our tendency toward a lazy, unhealthy lifestyle. For the first half of the movie, WALL-E is alone on Earth, cleaning up the remains of human trash and compacting it. WALL-E sifts through the mountains of trash still remaining, separating objects he'd like to keep for himself (small toys, well-hinged boxes, scraps of clothing) from the rest of the trash (jewelry, car keys, and the like).

The items that WALL-E keeps from his trash rounds highlight how disposable American culture in particular is: cheap plastic toys, broken electronics, clothing. The implication is that the purchasing and disposal was facilitated by the megacorporation Buy-n-Large, which encouraged shoppers to throw away items and replace them with newer equivalents, regardless of whether they could be repaired or recycled. The conspicuous consumption of our current culture is completely worthless by WALL-E's time, as evidenced by his tossing aside a diamond ring in favor of keeping the tiny box with a secure lid.

The film is also heavy-handed in its suggestion that humans are by nature physically and emotionally lazy, evidenced by the humans on the ship becoming giant babies, unable to walk or move freely. Says *WALL-E's* creator Andrew Stanton, "We fall into our habits, our routines and ruts, consciously or unconsciously, to avoid living. To avoid having to do the messy part. To avoid having relationships with other people . . . . That's why we can all get on our cell phones and not have to deal with one another."[11]

In spite of its obvious messages, *WALL-E* remains a charming family movie and cautionary tale at once, giving reminders about caring for our planet and for our relationships with others. Allowing either of these things to fall into disrepair, the film tells us, could have long-term consequences for humanity.

30-Second Booktalk:

WALL-E has been cleaning up Earth for nearly seven hundred years, and he's nowhere near done. In his rounds one day, he finds a tiny sapling growing in a heap of trash. An EVE robot is sent down to search for proof that Earth is habitable again, and when she sees WALL-E's plant, she automatically stores it and signals for her ship to come get her. The ship's captain is thrilled with the tiny plant—but his robotic assistant will stop at nothing to make sure humans don't recolonize Earth.

Readalikes:

Other Pixar films, for similar tones and styles

Fahrenheit 451 (Ray Bradbury) for hoarding of artifacts of an earlier time

The Boy at the End of the World (Greg van Eekhout) for robots left to maintain Earth

The Secret under My Skin (Janet McNaughton) for clean-up of mountains of ancient trash piles

Potential Audience:

G-rated WALL-E is appropriate for virtually any age, though, as with all Pixar movies, older viewers will understand more than younger ones. Children in upper-elementary grades and up will certainly get the environmental messages and may recognize some of the artifacts that WALL-E collects; older viewers will be more likely to understand the effects of prolonged space travel on the human body.

---

[11] http://www.newsarama.com/film/080704-wall-e-stanton-2.html

Part 4: Nonfiction

In the preceding pages, we've seen all kinds of societies go awry, overrun with dictators, hubris, zombies. Many of these can be viewed as cautionary tales, warning us of the dangers of our current policies and trends; others are flights of fancy regarding the sorts of things for which we can't prepare. Some of the stories are based in reality; others have a fantastical element.

The books, movies, and shows previously discussed all have one thing in common: they're all works of fiction, creative imaginings of what might happen to the world in the coming decades or centuries. But how many of these things could actually come to pass? And if the world does come to an abrupt halt, how should the survivors react and regroup? In this final section, we'll look at speculative non-fiction, the books, documentaries, and shows that attempt to answer those very questions.

First, what's likely to happen to us? Ron Miller provides possible answers and scenarios in *Is the End of the World Near?: From Crackpot Predictions to Scientific Scenarios*, in which he debunks some pseudo-scientific beliefs and lends credence to more plausible ideas. Teens looking for a more visual presentation of similar ideas would do well to watch the Discovery Channel documentary *Apocalypse: How*, though this does not separate the realistic threats of supervolcanoes (e.g.) from the science-fiction staples of alien invasions and robotic uprisings. National Geographic's documentary *Collapse* also speculates on what may lead to humanity's destruction, but approaches from a different angle, suggesting that our civilization is more likely to disappear due to our policies governing food, water, and energy than any single global event.

Once the majority of a society is eliminated, what's left for the survivors? The Discovery Channel puts people through that test in their reality show *The Colony*, in which they recruit volunteers for a psychological experiment simulating an apocalyptic event. Both seasons' catalysts are supposed viral outbreaks that have decimated the population; the survivors—the volunteers—are brought together to make their own microsociety for survival. Were the volunteers' reactions to the supposed apocalyptic event realistic? That might best be answered by comparing their stresses to the characters in Josh Neufeld's graphic novel *AD: New Orleans after the Deluge*, which follows four people through

209

preparations for Katrina and the storm's aftermath. Some may argue that Hurricane Katrina was not a true apocalyptic event as most of the country was spared, but for the city's residents with nowhere else to go before or after the storm, it's difficult to view it any other way.

If you are lucky enough to survive an apocalyptic event, it will be as important to keep your sense of humor as it is to know what to do, and to that end, there are two survival guides to help you navigate the changed world. Rob Kutner's *Apocalypse How: Turn the End Times into the Best of Times* provides advice on everything from dressing for the post-apocalyptic world to new sports to play when the world has ended. *The Official Underground 2012 Doomsday Survival Handbook* by W.H. Mumfrey takes a similar tongue-in-cheek approach, though with more information about how the world might end in the first place.

As important as it is to be prepared for the apocalypse, what would become of Earth if humans disappeared? Alan Weisman presents the results of his thought experiment in his book *The World Without Us*, basing his assertions on his observations of deserted cities and his interviews with a variety of scientists. Similar information is presented in the National Geographic documentary *Aftermath: Population Zero*, which shows the disintegration of man-made structures and the earth's own healing process chronologically over 25,000 years.

Chapter 9:

Nonfiction

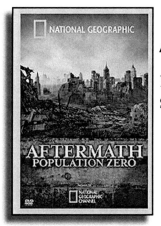

Aftermath: Population Zero

DVD. Color. 90m. Produced and dist. by National Geographic Video, 2008. $19.97. 978-6-3121-1756-8.

- Originally aired 2008

Plot Summary:

If all humans vanished at once, what would happen to the planet? This documentary aims to answer this hypothetical question. Viewers follow the chronology of events from an arbitrary mid-June date (around the documentary's original air date) when the humans disappeared.

In the first day, vehicles run off the road and planes fall from the sky. Blackouts begin as power plants go offline and generators are unable to keep up with the demand. Refrigerated gasses begin to vent, suffocating animals living nearby. Within the first ten days, house pets have broken out of their homes in search of food and zoo animals are no longer bound by electric fences. Domestic cattle herds die of dehydration and domestic chickens are devoured by predators. Most dangerously, spent fuel rods for nuclear power plants boil off their cooling pools and the steam pressure inside the buildings eventually force explosions, raining radiation over the surrounding areas.

As the seasons change, radiation begins to clear from the air, as do other pollutants over cities. With winter approaching, many animals begin migrating south. Cockroaches die in the cold weather, normally relying on the heat of human dwellings to survive the winters. By the following spring, rains have washed away the remaining radioactive particles, new trees and plants scrub more carbon dioxide from the atmosphere, and animal populations swell.

The years pass and the world continues to erase human traces. In the first 60 years, buildings have succumbed to weather and individual dog breeds have been eliminated due to interbreeding. two hundred years after people, London turns back into the swamp it was in Roman times. Fruit-growing regions of California have turned back into desert. Carbon dioxide is all but gone, scrubbed from the atmosphere by the plants and trees that have been allowed to grow wild for centuries. It takes forests nearly 300 more years after this to reach the state they were in 10,000 years prior to humans' extinction.

A new ice age begins after 25,000 years, with glaciers covering most of the northern hemisphere. The only remaining traces of human existence are on the moon, left there from lunar missions.

Post-Apocalyptic Elements:

There is no discussion at all of what may have happened to all the humans; this is more concerned with how long evidence of human civilization will last without humans to maintain it. Some of the implications are cheering: even after nuclear power plants fail, it only takes a year for radioactive particles to be washed from the earth, and endangered wildlife populations will bounce back within a few generations. On the other hand, parts of monuments like the Statue of Liberty and the Eiffel Tower will still stand after a thousand years.

Still, the documentary is useful as a thought experiment and a wake-up call: this is how long it will take the earth to recover from our current habits and policies. Each year that we continue overfishing species, releasing pollutants into the air and water, or overdeveloping the land is another year or more that it will take for the earth to heal the damage. With that in mind, *Aftermath: Population Zero* can serve as a reminder about the need to minimize our footprint while we are still here to do it.

30-Second Booktalk:

If everyone on earth disappeared right now, it would only be minutes before power plants failed and blackouts began. In less than a week, sewage treatment plants would fail. It'll be three months before air quality visibly improves over cities. How long will it take for the populations of endangered species to recover? How much damage have we caused to the earth, and how long will it take the earth to clean up after us?

Readalikes:

Life after People (film) for exploration of similar ideas

The Boy at the End of the World (Greg van Eekhout) for a fictional story of a boy waking into a world without people

The World Without Us (Alan Weisman) for a scientifically-backed explanation of what would happen

Potential Audience:

Environmentalists will appreciate knowing that there is hope for our planet, even if it requires humans to vacate completely. The tone and cinematics of this documentary will fascinate teens and adults in middle school and older.

Apocalypse How

DVD. Color. 87m. Produced and dist. by Discovery Channel, 2010. $14.98. 978-6-3133-6199-1.

- Originally aired 2008

Plot Summary:

Researchers, scientists, and other professionals discuss ways in which the world could end. In a series of twelve potentially world-ending scenarios, experts discuss what the event is, what it would look like, the immediate and long-term impacts, and the science behind it.

Scenarios involving supervolcanoes (of which there are seven worldwide), nuclear weapons, global pandemics, rising sea levels due to melting polar ice, and even asteroid impacts are all relatively likely. However, not all of the doomsday predictions are as promising: the documentary also includes scenarios of alien invasions, robotic uprisings, and self-replicating nanotechnology. The remaining suggestions fall somewhere in the middle: "spaghettification" of black holes traveling in space, black holes created by the Large Hadron Collider, a natural ice age, and the death of the sun.

All potentially world-ending events are presented as equally likely, with no biases for or against any particular catastrophe.

Apocalyptic Elements:

With twelve different scenarios, each covered in under ten minutes, there are many apocalyptic elements to choose from. From plagues to robotic insurrections, scientists across a number of disciplines discuss what would happen in each doomsday event.

There is little discussion of how survivors of each event will likely live, anchoring the scope of this documentary firmly in the apocalyptic world, not the post-apocalyptic.

30-Second Booktalk:

There are seven supervolcanoes under the earth's surface. Asteroids pass through spaces where the earth was only hours before. One ill traveler can kick off a global pandemic. With so many ways the world could end—some more likely than others—it's easy to forget that one apocalypse is all it takes to wipe out humanity forever.

Readalikes:

The Official Underground 2012 Doomsday Survival Handbook (W.H. Mumfrey) for more in-depth discussion of doomsday scenarios

The War of the Worlds (H.G. Wells, or film) for alien invasions

The Road (Cormac McCarthy) for aftermath of one of several potential events

Exodus (Julie Bertagna) for a world under water from melting polar ice

Ashfall (Mike Mullin) for life in the wake of a supervolcano eruption

Potential Audience:

This Emmy-nominated documentary will appeal to doomsday enthusiasts, sci-fi fans, and amateur scientists. The brisk pace and short run time will hold the interest of teens in eighth grade and up.

Collapse

Blu-Ray. Color. 100m. Produced and dist. by National Geographic, 2010. $29.99. 978-6-3137-1567-1.

Plot Summary:

Like many of the documentaries about the apocalypse, *Collapse* is mostly a thought experiment: if archaeologists explored the earth two hundred years from now, what would they find, and what stories would their discoveries tell about us?

In looking at sites like Phoenix and Los Angeles, future archaeologists will find evidence of large populations—too large to be sustained in desert regions—and the irrigation systems we've created to reroute water by hundreds of miles. They'll find large cracks in the ground where aquifers dried up and collapsed. They'll find large containers in houses' backyards, capable of holding a year's supply of water, only to realize that we are currently so unconcerned about water supplies that we used these pools for recreation, not drinking.

As they travel the world, these archaeologists will find more evidence of our wasteful ways: the disintegrating remains of dried-up fuel stations and over two million cars, mitigated by the discoveries of solar panels and wind turbines. Our efforts at switching to renewable energy sources may be "too little too late" for us, adding an energy crisis to the possible water shortage.

These issues alone could be enough to spark a societal collapse, but these are not the only theories the archaeologists are developing: humans are already, in 2010, using almost 90 percent of the available farmland on earth, coaxing more food out of each acre with the use of topsoil-destroying fertilizers. Overgrazing speeds the destruction. Current food production only just supports the earth's current population; as we add another billion (or more) people over the next century, we are heading directly into a food crisis.

Food, water, and energy shortages will all raise the cost of living, which will in turn spark a financial crisis. We have some advantages over previous collapsed societies (namely the Anasazi, Mayans, or ancient Romans), though: widespread education and near-instantaneous worldwide communications will aid countries in finding ways out of the crises in which we find ourselves. On the other hand, the documentary asserts that, "We are the first society that's so interconnected that, if there is a collapse, it will be a global collapse."

Apocalyptic Elements:

In the guise of a futuristic research mission, *Collapse* examines our current trends, policies, and resource usage and compares them against other societies that rose and fell long before ours. In looking at the Anasazi, Mayan, and ancient Roman societies, archaeologists draw comparisons to our current policies regarding water and energy use, food production, and border security.

Currently, we have rerouted water hundreds of miles in order to create sprawling cities and agricultural areas in deserts. California grows a large amount of food for the whole country with the help of an elaborate aqueduct system that transforms the natural desert into a productive growth region, but as prolonged droughts dry the whole region, farmers find themselves uprooting some crops to allow the others to have adequate water. Food prices soar in response to this sudden decrease in supply.

Our energy crisis is another major issue. While we are working on generating renewable energy from solar cells and wind turbines, these devices are not yet matching the efficiency of fossil fuels or nuclear power. The United States is far behind other countries in the fuel efficiency of its vehicles[1]. The looming fuel crisis dovetails with water and food shortages, as food is shipped all over the world.

As our resources dwindle, experts say we could have as little as mere decades left before our society collapses. Our best hopes at avoiding this fate involve restructuring policies governing our water and fuel use and making efforts to correct the damage we've done to the environment. The documentary's frame device of future archaeologists studying our society acts as a cautionary tale, alerting our present-day selves to the problems that will almost surely develop if we continue on our current paths.

30-Second Booktalk:

Two hundred years from now, what will be left of our society? Will archaeologists understand our recreational swimming pools, or applaud our water-storage facilities in the face of looming water shortages? Plenty of other societies collapsed before ours; can we avoid making the same mistakes?

Readalikes:

The Carbon Diaries (Saci Lloyd) for resource shortages

An Inconvenient Truth (film) for documentary about the effects of global warming

Collapse: How Societies Choose to Fail or Succeed (Jared Diamond) for source material

Potential Audience:

Middle and high school students will understand the points made in this documentary and may be intrigued by the potential interpretations of our current society by future researchers.

---

[1] http://www.globalfueleconomy.org/Documents/Updates/Bibendum2011-May2011-IEA-Fuel-Economy-Report.pdf

The Colony: Season 1

DVD. Color. 430m. Produced and dist. by Discovery Channel, 2011. $19.98.
978-6-3137-6469-3.

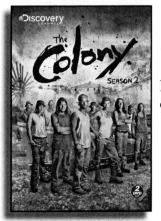

The Colony: Season 2

DVD. Color. 430m. Produced and dist. by Discovery Channel, 2011. $19.98.
978-0-7662-5321-6.

- *The Colony,* Discovery Channel reality show
- Originally aired 2009-2010

Plot Summary:

Through casting calls, volunteers are chosen to be part of the Colony experiment: a simulated post-apocalyptic survival show. The colonists selected are meant to represent a cross-section of society, from teachers to mechanics to doctors to computer engineers.

In the show's first season, the ten colonists were isolated in an abandoned factory building in Los Angeles, California, after a simulated viral outbreak that has eliminated most of L.A.'s population. The volunteers are from a variety of backgrounds and fields, but the majority are from scientific disciplines: computer engineers, rocket scientists, marine biologists, medical professionals. The first challenge they face is their lack of drinking water, which they overcome by building a water filtration system out of sand and charcoal layered in a large plastic storage tank. They also overcome the lack of power (solved by building a generator to charge scavenged car batteries), basic hygiene challenges (solved with a solar-powered shower), and an eventual need to move on from their warehouse (in the truck the colonists rebuilt and reinforced). The colonists work together to defend their compound from attacking marauders and other scavengers and help each other in any ways they can.

Season 2's simulated apocalyptic event is similar: a highly-contagious mutation of the Avian flu. Their colony is in Chalmette, Louisiana, in an area previously damaged by Hurricane Katrina. The second group of volunteers is less science-focused than the previous season's group, this time putting an emphasis on mechanical skills: auto mechanics, construction foremen, industrial architects. Their geographic location provides them plenty of fresh drinking water (particularly from the frequent rainstorms) and opportunities for hunting and fishing, but they still face problems of power generation and security. This group of colonists lacks leadership, and as a result the group fails to achieve the cohesiveness of their Season 1 counterparts. They survive to the end of the season, but only barely; the season's finale implies that the group has been captured by a hostile, neighboring group.

Post-Apocalyptic Elements:

The premise of the show is that an apocalyptic event has taken place: in both seasons, this is a viral outbreak, variant strains of current flu viruses. In the first season, there was little concern over contagiousness (strangers were encountered on a regular basis with no repercussions); the second-season volunteers enforced 12 hours of isolation for any colonist who had contact with outsiders.

Common to both seasons is competition for scarce resources, fending off marauders intent on stealing the colonists' limited supplies and bargaining with travelers who asked for their charity. Colonists gather what they can, and it is up to the security of their colony to defend it.

Producers of both seasons worked closely with experts in a variety of fields, including psychologists, Homeland Security, doctors, and engineering experts, to provide explanations and insight into the colonists' activities. While this in some ways interrupts the narrative flow of the series, it provides background information the average viewer lacks.

30-Second Booktalk:

If you were one of only a few survivors of a global catastrophe, who would you want on your side—and what skills could you contribute to the group? Groups of dissimilar volunteers are about to find that out in the wake of a simulated apocalypse, where the only things they can count on are each other.

Readalikes:

Survivor (television series) for groups of strangers making do with limited resources

A Life As We Knew It (Susan Beth Pfeffer) for scavenging resources after a global catastrophe

The Urban Survivalist Handbook (Shane L. Painter) for survivalist tips

The Official Underground 2012 Doomsday Survival Handbook (W.H. Mumfrey) for a humorous take on necessary survival skills

Potential Audience:

Fans of reality television and survivalism will be drawn to this series. Some content may be inappropriate for younger viewers, but high school students and adults will get a lot out of the experience of watching.

Kutner, Rob

Apocalypse How: Turn the End Times into the Best of Times

Running Press, 2008. 192p. $12.95. 978-0-7624-3233-2.

Plot Summary:

This tongue-in-cheek survival guide breaks the end of the world into easy-to-manage categories: food, location, clothing, social skills, health, recreation, and employment. Stuffed with quizzes ("Apocalyptic Aptitude Test," "Should I Stay or Should I Flee?"), recipes (Giant Cockroach Au Vin, e.g.), and "Before We Blow" checklists to prepare for Armageddon, *Apocalypse How* makes no claim to be a serious survival guide.

A two-page spread at the beginning of the book provides a brief overview of ways the world could end, from realistic suggestions like nuclear war or ecological catastrophe to the unlikely scenarios of alien invasion, robot uprisings, or the evil scheming of a mad genius. This is as much discussion as the book contains on what may bring about the world's collapse.

Post-Apocalyptic Elements:

The levity hides some actual information and tips applicable to even non-apocalyptic life: recognizing that a senior citizen's story about repairing an old Model T conceals knowledge of engines, for example, or the suggestions of stocking survival supplies of dried fruits and non-perishable goods. Teasing out the advice relevant to modern life is not an easy task, as the humor of the book depends on its after-the-apocalypse phrasings, but astute readers may take away some of the more applicable messages. "Try to savor all the accomplishments of our species that you took for granted when they were still functioning,"[2] the concluding paragraphs remind us, which is worthwhile advice even when the world hasn't come to an abrupt halt.

30-Second Booktalk:

It doesn't matter how the world ends—what matters is being ready for it. What's the best outfit to scare off the robot uprising? Are you fit enough to outrun our new ape overlords? How can you pass the time when you're hiding out in your underground, lead-lined bunker, and what sports will still exist after the apocalypse? Just because it's the end of the world doesn't mean your life is over.

---

[2] p179

Readalikes:

The Official Underground 2012 Doomsday Survival Handbook (W.H. Mumfrey) for another satire on survival guides

America (The Book) (Jon Stewart) for more of Kutner's contributions to a satirical non-fiction text

Pocket Guide to the Apocalypse (Jason Boyett) for more humorous end-times predictions

Potential Audience:

The magazine-like layout will appeal to reluctant readers of all ages, though occasional off-color jokes and adult references make this most appropriate for high school teens and older.

Miller, Ron

Is the End of the World Near?:
From Crackpot Predictions to Scientific Scenarios

Lerner Publishing, 2011. 120p. $33.26. 978-0-7613-7396-4.

Plot Summary:

Miller opens with an acknowledgement that humans have been thinking about the end of the world since the beginning of it, and he briefly discusses the end-of-the-world scenarios found in Hinduism, Buddhism, Christianity, Judaism, and Islam. From there he explores some fictional accounts of world-ending scenarios, citing movies from a 1916 Danish film called *The End of the World* to 2011's *Battle: Los Angeles* and famous books from *The War of the Worlds* to *The Stand*. He follows these faith- and fiction-based representations with some information on the rumored 2012 Mayan apocalypse.

Once the reader has some historical and religious context for the potential apocalypse, Miller starts by debunking pseudo-scientific possibilities: a shifting planetary crust [the earth's crust does not actually move as one piece], planetary alignment [gravitational forces will prevent planets from ever aligning perfectly], and reversal of magnetic poles [which has happened several times in earth's history with no ill effects].

With these easily-discounted theories out of the way, Miller is free to cover more realistic possibilities: solar flares, asteroids, supervolcanoes, and gamma-ray bursts from far-off supernovas count among our threats from space, most of which are, at best, thousands of years from destroying the earth. More likely, humans will destroy ourselves, whether through pollution and its related climate change, nuclear war, or pandemics. Finally, he presents the most likely end of earth: long after humanity as we understand it has gone extinct, approximately 1.1 billion years from now, the long, slow process of the heat death of the sun will begin. Miller provides the science of what will happen and how it will affect the planets around it.

The book concludes on a hopeful note, stressing that the unpreventable scenarios are a minimum of thousands of years off and giving suggestions to minimize the damage humans have done to the environment, emphasizing that we have not irreparably harmed our planet.

The end matter includes a glossary, bibliography, and index, as well as suggestions for further reading, viewing, and research.

Apocalyptic Elements:

In one hundred twenty pages, Miller presents a number of ways the world could end, in varying degrees of plausibility. His focus is on the science of the events, more than what would happen in the aftermath, so the discussion of each scenario begins with historical context (has this happened before, and if so, what happened?) and some detail of the circumstances that would allow the scenario to occur. In cases like asteroid impact, Miller includes a section on the likelihood of the event occurring again, and what the impact would be a second time.

Miller does not spend much time detailing what will happen to humanity, but rather focuses on what happens to the earth, summing up the impact on people in a few sentences rather than providing a day-by-day accounting. In cases where the event is primarily human-based (such as with pandemics), the discussion is still based on how a disease would spread rapidly through a population, rather than how it would impact humans at a more personal level.

30-Second Booktalk:

Most major religions have predictions about the end of the world; the Mayans may have provided a date. But many of the proposed end-of-the-world scenarios are unrealistic, or are millions of years off. Ron Miller separates the honest threats from pseudoscientific theory, and somehow both assuages our fears and gives us brand-new ones we'd never considered.

Readalikes:

Apocalypse: How? (film) for a visual presentation of similar material

The Official 2012 Doomsday Survival Guide (W.H. Mumfrey) for a humorous exploration of similar topics

Ashfall (Mike Mullin) for life in the wake of a supervolcano eruption

2012Hoax (www.2012hoax.org) for debunking of many pseudo-scientific beliefs

Potential Audience:

Scientifically-minded middle schoolers will appreciate this fact-based approach, and teens hooked on the current apocalyptic trend in books and movies will be interested in learning what actually is and is not likely. Book and movie references in the text are likely to go over teens' heads, though, generally being older titles or just those lacking in teen appeal.

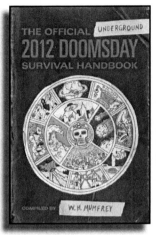

Mumfrey, W.H.

The Official Underground 2012 Doomsday Survival Handbook

How Books, 2011. 220p. $14.99 pb. 978-1-4403-0817-8.
$14.99 ebook. 978-1-4403-1376-9.

Plot Summary:

This tongue-in-cheek guide begins with an overview of the many predicted apocalypses that never happened, from roughly 2800 BC through Y2K, before moving into a discussion of the belief in the Mayan Apocalypse on December 21, 2012. From there, the book segues into several different apocalyptic scenarios and how to survive them. Potential doomsday scenarios range from all-too-likely (supervolcanoes, asteroid impact, nuclear war) to supernatural (alien invasion, zombies). The final section of the book offers tips for surviving many of the scenarios, though many involve significant preparation—advance scouting and outfitting of secluded caves or shelters, for example—or artillery.

An appendix has writing space for apocalypse plans ("People with whom I would like to share my fortified compound," "Things to do one week before doomsday," etc.) and some journal space to begin chronicling the immediate post-apocalypse days. An index completes the book.

Post-Apocalyptic Elements:

For such a short book, this guide provides a decent overview of ten different doomsday scenarios. For the more realistic ones, the author provides some scientific explanation of what would happen in the immediate aftermath—i.e., how heat waves would travel from the epicenter of an asteroid impact; how quickly a plague would spread.

The latter half of the book focuses on the survival skills necessary to these changed environments: things to do to keep oneself safe, people and offers of which to be wary. While some of the tips are clearly included for the humor factor (how to start a new religion, for example), other tips are useful survival skills, apocalypse or not: suggestions of dressing in layers and covering all exposed skin to avoid sun damage, creating hygiene products from natural resources, and remaining aware of time and surroundings to avoid danger could be applicable to everyday life.

30-Second Booktalk:

What do you do when an asteroid hits the earth? Die, most likely—unless you've followed Mumfrey's instructions and have a nearby cave all ready for move-in. How do you survive an alien invasion? You don't—unless you've heeded Mumfrey's advice and ran to an unpopulated area the instant you saw the ships overhead. When the Internet is a memory and food is an occasional luxury, you'll be glad you read this book.

Readalikes:

Apocalypse: How (film) for visual discussion of similar disaster scenarios

War of the Worlds, Waterworld, The Road, The Book of Eli, Planet of the Apes, and *I Am Legend* (films) for movies referenced in the book

The Alien Invasion Survival Handbook (W.H. Mumfrey) for another tongue-in-cheek survival guide from the same author

Potential Audience:

The snarky tone will appeal to high school students, many of whom won't notice the actual information sneaking in. Advocacy of killing or harming other survivors in a post-apocalyptic world may give more conservative readers (and parents) pause, but the tongue-in-cheek presentation may allay fears that these are serious suggestions.

Neufeld, Josh

A.D.: New Orleans after the Deluge

Pantheon Books, 2009. 197p. $16.95 pb. 978-0-375-71488-7.

- Debuted in shorter form at SMITH Magazine in 2007[3]

Plot Summary:

Denise's family has been living in New Orleans for six generations. She is a licensed counselor with a master's degree, living with her mom (a surgical technician at the hospital), her niece, and her niece's daughter. Leo and Michelle grew up in New Orleans; he's a comics-collector who works with mentally challenged kids, and she's a waitress and gymnastics instructor. Darnell stays around New Orleans to experience the storm and help his friend Abbas defend his convenience store against potential looters. Kwame is a high-school student, about to start his senior year. Brobson is a doctor, and he doubts the seriousness of the storm and thus refuses to evacuate.

These seven people have very little in common. *A.D.* follows them from just before Hurricane Katrina hits until a few weeks afterward, chronicling their preparations for the storm and their reactions to its aftermath, then jumps in to check on them all about 18 months later. Some evacuated willingly; others had to be rescued off rooftops. Some had nowhere to go, and none had anything to come back to.

Still, they *do* come back. Staying away is, for most of them, not an option; as Denise says about the time she spends living away from her city in Baton Rouge, "This isn't my life. This is the life of someone I wouldn't even want to shake hands with."[4] All seven people profiled love their city, even after they've lost everything.

Post-Apocalyptic Elements:

With its real-world setting and true stories of the survivors, it can be difficult to make a case for *A.D.* as a post-apocalyptic work: there is no science-fiction here, no genetic experiments or man-made viruses wiping out all of humanity. The impact of Hurricane Katrina was fairly localized; it did not wipe out the entire United States, nor even an entire geographic region.

Still, for the seven hundred people who died in the storm and the thousands of others who lost their homes, Katrina was an apocalypse, an event with catastrophic results. Eighty percent of the city was uninhabitable within days. Government officials steered refugees toward the Superdome

---

[3] http://www.smithmag.net/afterthedeluge/
[4] *A.D.* pg 177

for shelter, but the Superdome had documented problems housing so many people back in 1998, problems that had not been addressed seven years later[5]. Even aside from the stadium's infrastructure problems, the Superdome became a second apocalypse: "It was very dangerous - rioting, looting of vending machines, racial abuse, absolutely terrible sanitary conditions," a traveler told the BBC. "The last couple of days in the dome became completely chaotic and it was too dangerous to even queue for food. There were National Guard soldiers there giving a couple of items out a day - but we ended up giving up," another said.[6]

For the seven people profiled, and the thousands more who were not, Katrina took everything. Starting over in new cities with no job and little money is difficult; starting over in the ravaged city has costs well beyond the financial. As Abbas says about rebuilding his store, "I didn't realize what the hurricane would do to this city. It was a big price to pay. I lost three years. I look back and I say, 'Damn, I'm just where I was three years ago.'"[7]

30-Second Booktalk:

How do you start over after you've lost everything? When Hurricane Katrina hit New Orleans, most people had already evacuated—but many others had no place to go, or had good reason to stick around. Artist and journalist Josh Neufeld profiles seven refugees who lost everything, and for whom starting over means waiting for help that may never arrive.

Readalikes:

Zeitoun (Dave Eggers) for a family's post-Katrina survival

Barefoot Gen (Keiji Nakazawa) for a graphic novel about survival after a localized disaster

Hurricane Song (Paul Volponi) for a fictional account of time spent in the Superdome

Potential Audience:

High school students and adults will appreciate this nuanced look at those who evacuated the city— and those who stayed, either by choice or by necessity. *A.D.* does not address the politics of the situation, allowing each person's story to carry the weight of personal loss rather than governmental failure.

---

[5] http://www.time.com/time/magazine/article/0,9171,1103560-3,00.html

[6] http://news.bbc.co.uk/2/hi/uk_news/4214746.stm

[7] *A.D.* pg 185

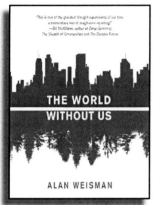

Weisman, Alan

The World Without Us

St. Martin's Press, 2007. $24.95 (HC). 978-0-312-34729-1.
Picador, 2008. $15 (PB). 978-0-312-42790-0.
Macmillan Audio. $39.99 (CD). 978-1-4272-0148-5.
$9.99 ebook. 978-1-4299-1721-6.

Plot Summary:

Rather than an overarching narrative, *The World Without Us* is a basic thought experiment: what would happen if humans vanished from the face of the Earth? In nineteen chapters, Weisman explores what would become of the world we've built up when we're no longer here to maintain it: how buildings will crumble, plastics decompose (or not), and power plants melt down—and how the earth will eventually heal itself from our centuries of damage.

A few of Weisman's assertions may be speculations, but most of his claims are rooted in solid evidence: by analyzing what has become of cities like Chernobyl, Ukraine (abandoned in 1986 following a nuclear disaster) and Varosha, Cyprus (abandoned in 1974 after a military occupation), Weisman can gauge the rate at which man-made structures will decay and nature will take over. He interviews biologists, environmentalists, and other experts, and draws material from his previously-published articles on similar topics.

The bulk of the book focuses on what will become of our buildings and material goods, but what of *us*? Weisman devotes a chapter to that very question, discussing embalming and burial techniques and how they will withstand the passage of time. He also considers how humans could be eliminated, from virulent infections to the Voluntary Human Extinction Movement to the extreme Church of Euthanasia, and suggests that what could ultimately do humans in is the lack of resources to support the projected population.

Post-Apocalyptic Elements:

The very premise of the book is post-apocalyptic in nature: what will happen after humans have been wiped out? The organization of the book is such that it becomes repetitious, as the general details of what happens to unmaintained structures do not vary much from place to place. Some environments will allow the decay to take hold faster than other regions; different species of plants and animals will move in, depending upon what geographic area Weisman is discussing.

What is interesting about this title, as compared with other end-of-the-world scenarios in nonfiction, is that *The World Without Us* makes little suggestion as to what might have happened to create this empty planet. He makes some suggestions at the end, but discounts each theory: a virus with as high as a 99.9% die-off would still leave nearly 700,000 people with natural immunities, far exceeding the number of people needed for a genetically-diverse breeding population. Wars usually lead to population increases, rather than decreases, as both sides repopulate afterwards. Disasters like supervolcanoes or asteroid impact would affect far more living creatures than just humans. With these limitations in mind, it's clear that Weisman conceived of his book as an intellectual exercise rather than any cautionary tale; there are very few, if any, ways that humans could go extinct without taking any other species with us.

30-Second Booktalk:

Humans have done an enormous amount to the earth, both in damage and repair efforts. But how will the planet cope without us? If we vanished tomorrow, how long would it take before all traces of humans disappear completely? Alan Weisman takes the reader along to abandoned cities and interviews biologists, environmentalists, and other scientists to find answers to those very questions. Can everything we've done up to now still be fixed?

Readalikes:

The Boy at the End of the World (Greg van Eekhout) for an exploration of a world long abandoned

Life after People and *Aftermath: Population Zero* (films) for similar subject matter

The Earth after Us: What Legacy Will Humans Leave in the Rocks? (J.A. Zalasiewicz) for other aspects of the effects of humans on the earth

Potential Audience:

Scientifically-minded high school teens will be interested to at least skim this popular-science viewpoint. Eleventh grade and up will have the best chance at parsing the moderately-sophisticated writing style.

Index by Keyword

Index by Author

Index by Title

About the Author

Brandy Danner is the head of teen services in Wilmington, MA. She has been a reviewer for *School Library Journal* and is an active participant in the Massachusetts Youth Services Book Review Group. A member of the planning committee for the Massachusetts Teen Summit conference since 2008, she presented at the conference in 2009 on budget-sensitive teen programing, and again in 2011 on unconventional readers' advisory techniques. She served on YALSA's Technology for Young Adults committee in 2009 and became convener of the related YALSA Interest Group, Teens and Technology, the following year.

Danner's interest in dystopian fiction and apocalyptic scenarios dates back to her own teen years, when she first encountered *Fahrenheit 451*. Her increased awareness of the ways the world could end causes her no small amount of concern. She lives in Cambridge, MA, with her husband and son.

Kcm.

CPSIA information can be obtained at www.ICGtesting.com
Printed in the USA
BVOW051139240213

313997BV00003B/3/P